Word and Light

WORD AND LIGHT

Seeing, Hearing, and Religious Discourse

DAVID CHIDESTER

UNIVERSITY OF ILLINOIS PRESS
Urbana and Chicago

This book is printed on acid-free paper.

Library of Congress Cataloging-in-Publication Data

Chidester, David,
    Word and light : seeing, hearing, and religious discourse / David
Chidester.
        p.   cm.
    Includes bibliographical references and index.
    ISBN 0-252-01863-X (alk. paper)
    1. Languages—Religious aspects.   2. Vision—Religious aspects.
3. Hearing—Religious aspects.   4. Knowledge, Theory of (Religion).
5. Augustine, Saint, Bishop of Hippo—Contributions in theory of
religious discourse.   6. Augustine, Saint, Bishop of Hippo—
Influence. I. Title.
BL65.L2C49 1992
200′.14—dc20   91-18622
                                                                      CIP

For W. Richard Comstock

Contents

Preface

Among other things, ⌐religion⌐ consists of strategies for opening eyes and ears to whatever may be perceived to be sacred. In this book, I examine the significance of eyes and ears in religious discourse. I am interested in clarifying the ways in which seeing and hearing have informed the symbolic discourse of religion. As physiological processes, as culturally constructed processes, and as phenomenological systems that encompass both physiology and culture, seeing and hearing have been implicated in religious symbols, myths, and rituals. Here, I ask: What difference does perception, particularly seeing and hearing, make in the generation and employment of religious discourse?

The importance of seeing and hearing in religious discourse has often been noticed. To cite an example at random: The discussion of perceptual models in Joseph Cahill's recent book on the relations among the history of religions, religious studies, and theology, *Mended Speech*, provides one instance of a general, long-standing interest within cultural analysis in cataloging differences between visual and aural models of cognition. Cahill noted that visual and aural models organize cognition along different lines. Thinking tends to follow the lead of one or the other of the two dominant perceptual models in the human sensorium. As Cahill observed, "Both models of course are necessary in human living and are complementary. The issue here is simply that the stress of one or the other develops quite different intellectual systems."[1] Cahill's assertion harks back to a long history of attempts to classify mental activity in terms of models set by the senses. For example, the notorious nineteenth-century explorer, amateur ethnographer, and popularizer of eugenics, Sir Francis Galton, tried to identify people as "verbalizers" or "visualizers," depending on their charac-

teristic mode of thought—verbalization (thinking in words) or visu-
alization (thinking in images).[2] While both senses may be involved in
cognition, we tend to think either through our eyes or our ears and,
thereby, to become involved in different visual or aural perceptual-
intellectual systems.

Ultimately fruitless conclusions have been drawn regarding the relative importance of the senses as perceptual-intellectual systems. Which
is more important, eyes or ears? Since both sensory coordinates tend
to be drawn upon in the world of perception and thought, conclusions
about the primacy of seeing or hearing merely reveal the perceptual
bias of the analyst. Clemens Benda maintained the primacy of auditory
perception by asserting that "a world without sound is a dead world:
when sound is eliminated from our experience, it becomes clear how
inadequate and ambiguous is the visual experience if not accompanied
by auditory interpretation."[3] However, Stephen Ullmann maintained
the primacy of visual perception by denying precisely this dependence
of vision upon auditory information. In contrast to Benda, Ullmann
asserted that "visual terminology is incomparably richer than its au-
ditorial counterpart, and has also far more similes and images at its
command. Of the two sensory domains at the top end of the scale,
sound stands far more in need of support than light, form, and color."[4]
Rather than requiring support from auditory interpretation, the visual
domain allegedly is a more independent source of information than
hearing. These assertions about the primacy of seeing or hearing in
the human sensorium could be multiplied. Perhaps they only reflect
preferences derived from personal orientations toward the visual or
the auditory domains. In that case, asserting the primacy of seeing or
hearing would reveal a certain tendency to establish one of the senses
as a center of gravity in the sensorium for personal orientation in a
world of perception, thought, and communication. This expression of
preference, however, tells us nothing about seeing and hearing. It only
confirms, as Martin Jay has noted, that "the age-old battle between
the eye and the ear is far from being decided one way or the other."[5]

More ambitious conclusions have been drawn about the perceptual
orientations of entire cultures. For example, Don Ihde suggested that
perception may control concepts within particular cultural environ-
ments. "The most complex ideas within a given culture," Ihde proposed,
"may contain implicit perceptual metaphors which in turn exercise a
certain control over the development of these ideas."[6] On the basis of
such a premise the visual orientation of ancient Greek culture and the
auditory orientation of ancient Hebraic culture became a kind of cliché
of cultural history. This assumption that Hellenic culture was somehow

fundamentally visual in its orientation, while Hebraic culture was fundamentally auditory, was clearly formulated in the nineteenth century by historian Heinrich Graetz:

> To the pagan, the divine appears within nature as something observable to the eye. He becomes conscious of it as something seen. In contrast to the Jew who knows that the divine exists beyond, outside of, and prior to nature. God reveals Himself through a demonstration of His will, through the medium of the ear. The human subject becomes conscious of the divine through hearing and obeying. Paganism sees its god, Judaism hears Him; that is, it hears the commandments of His will.[7]

Graetz suggested that as a result of a characteristically visual orientation the Greeks understood the sacred to be located in the world, immanent and accessible to the sight of the eyes, while the Jews, because they heard the divine word through the medium of the ear, located the sacred at a distance beyond the world. The visual mode, therefore, lends itself to a sensitivity to that which is immanent in the world; the verbal mode lends itself to the experience of a transcendent and invisible authority that speaks over against human beings and commands obedience. Along the same lines, Thorlief Borman developed the difference between Greek and Hebraic thought: "Because the Greeks were organized in a predominantly visual way and the Hebrews were organized in a predominantly auditory way, each people's conception of truth was formed in increasingly different ways."[8] Because hearing was most important to the Jews, Borman concluded that the decisive reality in their world was the word. For the Greeks, however, it was the thing. In both cases, an entire culture organized its conceptual life in terms of a predominant perceptual orientation toward either hearing or seeing.

The relation between perception and thought, however, has rarely been pressed beyond this simple cultural truism. Are there more complex and more subtly nuanced ways in which perception influences and informs religious symbolism? How should we describe and analyze the relations between perception and symbolic forms in the history of religions? To examine the relations between perception and religion, I have ventured a few selected case studies in western religious discourse. In what follows, I have examined the discourse of a Jew (Philo of Alexandria), several Catholics (Arius, Athanasius, and Bonaventure), and a Protestant (Philip Melanchthon). At the center of my investigations is a religious figure claimed by Catholics and Protestants, a truly monumental figure in western religious discourse, Augustine of Hippo. In a sense, the choice of Augustine as centerpiece is somewhat arbitrary. I intend to explore the implications of seeing and hearing for religious discourse, not to contribute to Augustinian scholarship. Yet the choice of Augustine is fortunate for at least two reasons.

First, the fact that the dominant sacred symbols in Augustine's symbolic universe were word and light has provided ample material for my interpretive interests. Were the symbols of word and light related in any meaningful way to hearing and seeing? Were they related to metaphoric perceptual models derived from hearing and seeing? If so, how? Can more general inferences about the relations between perception and symbolic forms be drawn from the example of Augustine?

Second, the choice of Augustine is appropriate because, as a central, dominating presence in the Christian tradition, he allows some of my analysis to be generalized for Christian symbolic discourse. As a historian of religions, I have sought to make Augustine—and, by extension, the Christian tradition—more available to the general history of religions by employing the basic categories of symbol, myth, ritual, and tradition. Therefore, this work is not an essay in theology, nor in the history of theological doctrine, but a work of interpretation in the history of religions. By shifting attention from theological to symbolic discourse, even such a familiar figure as Augustine may appear in new and unexpected ways. This is the mandate of the history of religions: To make the strange familiar and the familiar strange. The choice of Augustine, therefore, is fortunate because if he is allowed to look and sound different then the Christian tradition may also reemerge as unfamiliar territory to be explored by the history of religions. In this book, I explore that familiar territory by paying attention to the strange dynamics of perceptual symbolism in religious discourse.

My interest in this essay is almost exclusively with discourse, its construction and horizons, not with practice, institutions, or politics. Therefore, I make only a limited contribution to any analysis of social or historical process. Yet discourse also has a history. While certainly constrained by physiology, the perceptual models of seeing and hearing can be located in the confluence and conflict of symbols that make up a historical tradition. Rather than that which is handed down, a religious tradition is that which is taken up, the symbols, myths, and rituals appropriated, owned, and operated by a community. Augustine, for example, normalized certain terms and conditions for the deployment of visual and auditory symbols at the end of the fourth century. At the beginning of that century, however, those terms and conditions were up for grabs. Among many other things, the Council of Nicaea illustrated a conflict of word and light (as we will see) that has surfaced periodically in the history of the Christian tradition. For his part, Augustine formulated a particular synthesis of word and light, but thinkers in the later Augustinian tradition often appropriated one or the other as a dominant mode of perceptual orientation. Although conflict over perceptual symbols reveals only one area of conflict, the struggle over the appropriation and legitimated ownership of symbols—a conflict that defines a religious tradition as a common arena of discourse and practice—certainly has continued throughout the Christian tradition.

In this essay, I suggest some possibilities for an interpretation of religious discourse in terms of perceptual metaphors derived from seeing and hearing. In the end, I hope that religious discourse will look and sound different, that the old will become new again. I apologize if that sounds apocalyptic: My real interest here is heuristic. Over the last ten years of lecturing on western religions I have found that the approach taken in this book has interesting pedagogical value. Students seem to like using their eyes and ears. Attention to perceptual metaphors provides new opportunities to notice things. Perhaps that is what a humanistic education is all about—the development of an open, yet disciplined, imagination that empowers us to notice.

Some of this book has already appeared (in different forms) elsewhere. Parts of Chapters 1 and 2 appeared in "Word against Light: Perception and the Conflict of Symbols," *Journal of Religion* 65 (1985): 46-62; a version of Chapter 3 appeared in "Symbolism and the Senses in Saint Augustine," *Religion* 14 (1984): 31-51; a version of Chapter 4 in "The Symmetry of Word and Light: Perceptual Categories in Augustine's *Confessions*," *Augustinian Studies* 17 (1986): 119-33; and a version of Chapter 5 in "The Symbolism of Learning in Saint Augustine," *Harvard Theological Review* 76 (1983): 73-90. Although all has been rethought, revised, and rewritten, I thank the editors and publishers of the above journals for permission to republish some of the material that I have integrated into this book.

Out of all the many debts I owe, I would especially like to acknowledge here my gratitude to W. Richard Comstock, mentor and friend, who provided invaluable encouragement and support when I began this project. If not for him, I would probably still be working in an alcohol clinic in Pasadena. As always, I must pay tribute to the Board of Directors, and to my wife, Careen. Finally, I would like to thank the University of Cape Town for the sabbatical and support that made it possible to finish this book.

In this essay I ask: What difference does perception make in religious discourse? I began work on this exploration of sensory perception and religious discourse about fifteen years ago in a more innocent time, a time in which I thought that the most important sensory modalities for religious symbolism were seeing and hearing. While I still think they are obviously important, I find myself more recently compelled to pay attention to a different range of metaphoric resources than seeing and hearing, a different set of perceptual metaphors frequently drawn upon in the formation of religious discourse within my present working environment. In fact, my research interests have moved in entirely different directions as a result of such things as the accidents of geography, the force of events, and the pressures of working in a highly charged, politicized, and even violent place. I have become less interested in the meaning of symbols than in their power—the power to legitimate, the power to mobilize, the power to focus the concerns of competing interest groups in often violent conflicts. From that perspective, this book might seem somewhat of a luxury item, an indulgent reflection on perceptual symbolism that merely opens the eyes and ears of religious discourse. Perhaps one day I will be able to return to the luxury of meaning, to the leisurely exploration of the poetics of seeing and hearing. For the moment, however, the perceptual metaphors of more immediate (and, I should say, more pressing) concern are tactile—the powerful metaphors of oppression and resistance. While those tactile metaphors dominate my present environment, I offer this book as a recollection of some progress I once made in clarifying the meaningful role of seeing and hearing in the symbolic discourse of religion.

PART ONE

Perception and Religious Discourse

1

Perception

Human awareness is mediated through sensory perception. We do not have to be Aristotelians, insisting that "nothing enters the mind except through the senses," to recognize that sensory perception is of primary importance to cognition and consciousness. The phenomenology of perception of Maurice Merleau-Ponty, for example, provided compelling evidence for the primacy of perception in human experience. According to Merleau-Ponty, "We never cease living in the world of perception, but we bypass it in critical thought—almost forgetting the contribution of perception to our idea of truth."[1] In the excursions into religious discourse that follow, I retrace what is bypassed in conceptual thought and recall what is forgotten in the truth-claims of religious discourse by exploring the ways in which the world of perception may also be the basic horizon for the symbolic universe of religion. My thesis is this: Religious symbolism is grounded in the basic modalities of sensory perception. To adapt (and modify) a familiar aphorism from Paul Ricoeur, perception—particularly the perceptual modes of seeing and hearing—gives rise to symbols, and symbols give rise to thought. Through selected case studies of religious discourse, I hope to trace a logic that retreats along a path from conceptual thought through symbolic patterns of articulation back to their perceptual ground. In this way, perhaps, we can think again about the relations between perception and religious symbolism.

Before testing this thesis, however, it may be useful to reflect briefly on perception. Perception is not merely a level of cognition to be distinguished from conceptual thought, even though many epistemological schemes proposed in the history of western thought have pretended as if it were such a unified, distinct level of cognition. But perception is certainly more diversified and enveloping, more diversified because the various perceptual modes are each differently structured and more enveloping because perception is a fundamental constituent of human embodiment and therefore of human being in the world. In noticing the importance of perception, I do not want to be tied to any epistemological scheme. Rather, I merely suggest that seeing and hearing imply different modalities, different processes and patterns of perception that are necessarily implicated in the deployment of visual and auditory metaphors within religious discourse. Although always overdetermined, religious discourse nevertheless tends to a certain extent to be predetermined by the metaphoric possibilities of the body and the senses. A brief review of the history and phenomenology of perception may indicate some of the potential held by the senses of seeing and hearing for the determination of religious discourse.

SEEING AND HEARING

A phenomenology of perception must be sensitive to the ways in which the senses were understood to operate within specific historical and cultural contexts. Culturally constructed assumptions regarding the operations of the senses, the ways in which they structure information, and the ways in which they orient human consciousness, are particularly important to a historical phenomenology of perception. For example, ancient Greek speculations produced a fairly consistent range of basic assumptions about seeing and hearing. Perception (*aisthesis*) was not merely treated as a level of cognition distinct from mind but rather as a set of distinctive perceptual organs and operations of which seeing and hearing were most important. Scientific analysis of seeing and hearing became a significant ingredient in the perceptual experience of a western culture influenced by Greek science, informing the ways in which seeing and hearing were imagined to operate in perception and cognition. But ancient Greek assumptions may also have been important in the generation of symbolic discourse that employed perceptual metaphors. A religious thinker like Augustine, for example, was conversant with ancient Greek speculations on the workings of the senses. Greek scientific assumptions about seeing and hearing directly influenced his symbolic discourse. When Augustine referred to the "eye of the soul" or the "ear of the heart," at least one aspect of signification was drawn from his understanding of how eyes and ears worked. For that understanding, we must begin with the Greeks.

The scientific explanation of vision was a major concern of those Greek philosophers known as the Atomists. Within that school of thought, visual perception was imagined to result from a direct contact between an object and the organ of vision. That contact was produced by images (*eidola*) or films (*simulacra*) that the Atomists thought were continuously being emitted from visible objects. In the act of seeing, those images or films entered through the pupil of the eye. In this "intromission theory" of vision, images from the object of vision were imagined to enter the eye to be simulated there as in a mirror. The visible object was duplicated in the eye. According to Aetius, "Leucippus, Democritus, and Epicurus say that perception and thought arise when images enter from outside."[2] Or, in the words of Alexander of Aphrodisias, the Atomists "attributed sight to certain images, of the same shape as the object, and impinging on the eye."[3] The pupillar image—thought to be received in the watery substance of the eye, either on the cornea or in the interior humors—signified the presence of a projected image within the eye. Seeing worked because of the continuous emission of images from objects, the contact of those images with the organ of vision, and the presence of those pupillar images within the eye. Although other theorists began their speculations about vision with the organ rather than the object, the Atomists developed certain basic assumptions about the process of seeing that were common to all Greek speculations about vision. Continuity, contact, presence, similarity, immediacy—these were the characteristics of vision in a theory specifying that seeing resulted from the continuous emission of images and the presence of the visual object mirrored in the perceptual organ of the eye.

A second theory of vision, the so-called extramission theory popularized by Plato and adopted by Augustine, explained seeing as the result of visual rays emitted by the eye. Beginning the analysis of vision with the organ rather than the object, the eye was not a mirror but a lamp. The eye was imagined to radiate visual rays that reached out and touched its objects of perception. This theory was first attributed to Alcmaeon of Crotona, who, perhaps under the influence of the Pythagoreans, understood vision to begin with the visual fire in the eye. As evidence of this intraocular fire, Alcmaeon pointed out that a flash of light occurred whenever the eye received a blow.[4] A kind of experimental test, therefore, was available to demonstrate the existence of the intraocular fire. Vision was imagined to be achieved by means of this fire that glowed in the eyes. In the form of a visual ray, the intraocular fire extended from the eye to the object. Contacting the object, the visual ray then doubled back again to the eye, like an arm that is outstretched and then doubled back to the shoulder.[5] According to Alcmaeon's theory of the visual ray, seeing was initiated by the activity of the eye. The eye reached out by means of its inner fire to contact visible objects of perception. Again, continuity and contact were the conditions of vision. In contrast to the Atomists, however, Alcmaeon held that the continuous contact between the eye and its object was initiated by the emanation of a visual ray from the organ of perception.

Empedocles also seems to have taught a version of the visual ray theory. Understanding the lens of the eye to contain what he called primeval fire, Empedocles imagined the eye to be like a lantern with its visual fire at the center. According to Empedocles, vision was analogous to a man walking out on a winter's night carrying a lantern that protects the flame within from the winds but allows its beams to shine out. When Aphrodite created eyes, "primeval fire, enclosed in membranes, gave birth to the round pupil in its delicate garments which are pierced through with wondrous channels. These keep out the water which surrounds the pupil but let through the fire, the finer part."[6] In this way, the surrounding water provided a kind of protection for the inner fire, while also allowing the finer substance of its beams to shine out to contact objects of vision. Although it is not clear precisely how Empedocles reconciled the watery and the fiery elements in vision, it is apparent that an important part of his theory of vision was the emission of visual rays from the eye.

Plato elevated the theory of the visual ray to a level of sophistication and precision, making it a powerful influence upon all subsequent speculations about vision. Plato understood vision to involve three elements: (1) the visual rays of an intraocular fire that emanated from the eye toward external objects; (2) reflections from external objects that were immediately available to the eye; and (3) an external source of light—candle, fire, or sun—that sealed the continuous bond that was established between organ and object in every act of seeing.[7] Plato imagined that the visual rays emitted from the eye were of the same substance as external sources of light, forming a unified, homogeneous bond that extended from the eye to meet the reflections from any visible object. Organ and object were joined in a continuous bond of light (a connection that Francis Cornford called a "sympathetic chain") that made vision possible.[8] All three elements—visual rays, reflections, and external sources of light—merged to form a unified, continuous, and immediate connection between seer and seen in the process of vision.

Rejecting previous theories of vision, Aristotle argued that seeing resulted neither from the intromission of fire, particles, or images into the eye nor from the extramission of visual rays from the eye extending outward to coalesce with objects.[9] For Aristotle, vision resulted from a process of change, a change from potentiality to actuality, within what he referred to as the medium of vision. In its state of potential, Aristotle described the medium of vision as diaphanous or transparent. But its potential was actualized whenever that transparent medium became light. Denying the importance of visual rays, Aristotle nevertheless maintained the notion of a direct continuity between the organ of sight and its objects when the transparent medium of vision was activated by an external source of light. He located that continuity, however, within the medium of vision, "the transparent medium . . . [which] being continuous, acts upon the sense organ."[10] The medium established the necessary connecting link between the visible object and the eye in every act of vision. Stressing the immediacy of that connection, Aristotle noted that the visual medium was not conditioned by time. Temporal considerations were irrelevant to vision. The change of state from transparency to light, which was essential for vision, required no time to effect, but, as Aristotle noted, "may conceivably take place in a thing all at once."[11] However idiosyncratic his formulation, Aristotle also stressed the immediacy of vision.

Finally, we should note that the Stoics also explained the process of vision as a result of visual rays. In the Stoic theory of vision, the optical *pneuma* was imagined to flow from the center of consciousness to the eye, where it stimulated the surrounding air. As it stirred up the air around the eye, the optical spirit merged with an external source of light—again, candle, fire, or sun—to extend outward and establish contact with visible objects. The cooperation of the optical spirit and air in the process of vision inspired Cicero's aphorism: "The air itself sees together with us."[12] Spirit, air, and light were imagined as a visual cone that established contact between the eye and its object of vision. According to Diogenes Laertius, "the apex of the cone . . . is the eye, the base at the object seen. Thus the thing seen is reported to us by the medium of the air stretching out towards it, as if by a stick."[13] Direct contact, as if by a stick, was established between organ and object in every act of seeing. Like Alcmaeon's image of the extended arm, Plato's visual ray, and Aristotle's visual medium, the Stoic notion of a visual cone depicted vision as a continuous bond between seer and seen.

What can be concluded from this all too brief sketch of ancient Greek optical theory? Certainly, the dominant assumption about vision, from all perspectives, was that seeing resulted from a relationship between organ and object based on immediacy or continuity—the immediate presence of images in the mirror of the eye or the continuous bond between organ and object formed by the emanation of rays from the

lamp of the eye. In addition, the extramission theories of the visual
ray suggested that the continuous bond between organ and object was
initiated by the eye. Particularly in Platonic and Stoic theory, theories
of special relevance for Augustine, vision appeared as a process initiated
by the perceiving subject, harmonized with an external source of illumination, which united the subject in continuous, immediate contact
with the object of vision. From ancient Greek speculations on vision,
subsequent thinkers could derive certain basic associations that attended the process of seeing: continuity, connection, presence, similarity,
immediacy, and even the union between seer and seen.

Hearing, however, was an entirely different matter. Ancient Greek
philosophers also analyzed hearing as a separate and distinct mode of
sensory perception. In almost all cases, theorists were particularly interested in identifying vocal sound as the most important type of sound
and the most important object of hearing. Hearing voices, therefore,
became the model for understanding all auditory experience; the verbal
was the prototype for the auditory. While some disagreement about
sight remained, ancient Greek speculations on hearing consistently
explained it as a result of a blow to the air caused by an external object.
Unlike vision, hearing was not a process initiated by the organ of
perception to form a continuous bond with its object. Rather, auditory
perception was always thought to be initiated by an external object.
There was almost unanimous agreement that hearing resulted from a
blow (*plege*) that struck the air, traveled over some distance, and im-
pacted upon the ear. For example, Democritus explained that sound
was produced by means of a shock to the air. As a result of a shock,
the air was broken into pieces, "and thus broken, is rolled along by
and with the fragments of vocal sound."[14] These fragments, or "sonant
particles," eventually entered the ear as a force of condensed air to
strike the organ of hearing. Similarly, Empedocles attributed hearing
to "the cartilage which is suspended within the ear, oscillating as it is
struck."[15] Hearing resulted from the impact of airwaves that struck the
"fleshy bone" inside the ear like striking a gong. According to Empedocles, the eye was a lantern, but the ear was a gong struck from
outside by the impact of airwaves. Examples could be multiplied: Anaxagoras considered vocal sound to be produced by breath "which
collides against the fixed, solid air, and by a recoil from the shock is
borne onwards to the organ of hearing"; Diogenes of Apollonia maintained that hearing took place "when the air within the ear is struck
and moved by sound"; and Diogenes Laertius summarized the Stoic
position when he concluded that "we hear when the air between the
sonant body and the organ of hearing suffers concussion."[16] Since sound

resulted from a blow, a concussion, or a percussion that struck the air, the process of hearing depended upon some action by an external object that was independent of the perceiving subject. In contrast to the visual continuity of seer and seen, hearing established the discontinuous relationship of an external agent acting upon a relatively passive perceiving subject.

The discontinuity between perceiver and object was most clearly revealed in the temporal aspect of the process of hearing. Hearing required time. As we noted, Plato explained vision as a result of the extramission of a visual ray; but he explained hearing as a process dependent upon the transmission of a shock that required time to travel through the air, strike the ear, impact the brain and blood, and eventually end up in the region of the liver.[17] Compared to the immediacy of sight, hearing required a relatively long chain of transmission to effect the perception of sound. Similarly, Aristotle noted the temporal requirement for the transmission of sound. Aristotle distinguished three elements in the process of hearing: (1) a sonant body; (2) a shock to that sonant body produced by some agent; and (3) a change in the medium between the sonant body and the ear. Unlike the change in the medium of vision, which Aristotle suggested occurred instantaneously, the change in the sonant medium required time, involving a graduated transition as the shock was carried through the air to finally strike the ear.[18] Since sound had to travel over a distance, both Plato and Aristotle concluded that the auditory mode was contingent upon time in a way that vision was not. Lacking the immediacy of sight, sound required the incremental transmission of a shock through the air to strike the ear of the perceiving subject.

From ancient Greek speculations on hearing, therefore, subsequent thinkers could derive associations quite different from those that attended the process of seeing. Basically, hearing was associated with a relatively discontinuous relationship between the object of perception and the perceiving subject: An external agent acted upon the air and was only known by the effect that the air-shock eventually had upon the subject. In hearing, the object of perception was not immediately present to the perceiver as it was in vision. There was no presence, no connection, no continuous bond between the subject and the object of perception. Because sound referred back to the agent that produced it, the auditory mode was referential rather than presentational. The scientific consensus about hearing in ancient Greek thought, therefore, made a certain range of associations available to later thinkers—discontinuity, difference, distance, temporality, transmission, reference, and the impact caused by an external agent upon a relatively passive perceiving subject.

After this brief sketch of ancient Greek thought about the senses, two points should be noted. These points may be obvious, but they will be important in our discussion of religious discourse: First, the differences between seeing and hearing were noticed and elaborated. Seeing and hearing were clearly distinguished as distinct perceptual modes that involved human beings in different relationships with the world. Second, it should be no surprise that scientific speculations about the workings of the senses informed metaphoric discourse because those speculations were already worked out in metaphors. What could be more metaphoric than lanterns and gongs? Those metaphors were elaborated as conceptual models through which the different operations of the senses might be explained. Conceptual models for seeing and hearing, however, never departed far from their metaphoric ground. Perhaps the world of perception is already a world of metaphors. Any conception of the senses makes those metaphors explicit as symbolic models for the patterns and processes of perception.

THE PHENOMENOLOGY OF PERCEPTION

A phenomenology of perception should be able to uncover the perceptual basis of awareness and even conceptual thought by identifying the ways in which perception orients human consciousness in the world. Not merely a science of the senses, a phenomenology of perception locates consciousness and cognition in their experiential context, in a network of relations generated and sustained by human embodiment. Since I have in mind a rough, applied phenomenology of perception, a phenomenology of perception that will be suggestive for the analysis of religious discourse, we need not linger long over progress made by the philosophical discipline of phenomenology in analyzing the ways in which the several senses orient human consciousness. Some brief notes, however, might be useful. As reference points for the phenomenology of perception, I refer to the seminal work of Maurice Merleau-Ponty and Hans Jonas. Merleau-Ponty's *Phénoménologie de la perception* (1945) and subsequent work pioneered the field; Hans Jonas, particularly in his *Phenomenon of Life* (1965), attempted to develop a philosophical biology within the phenomenological tradition that would, among other things, account for differences among the perceptual systems. Without doing justice to the subtlety and complexity of their work, I have nevertheless derived some guidelines for the analysis of seeing and hearing as perceptual systems that will be important to remember when we turn our attention to religious discourse.

There are definite contrasts between the ways in which the different sensory modes organize reality. Seeing defines a different orientation to the world than hearing. The most obvious difference between visual and auditory experience has to do with the association of seeing with space and hearing with time. The major structuring principle of visual experience is space; that of auditory experience is time. Vision is diffused in space, words move in time. As a corollary to this, it is important to note the capacity of sight to present simultaneity and the capacity of hearing to present sequence. The coherence of the visual mode may be attributed to the simultaneous spatial presence of the visual field. According to Jonas, "Only the simultaneous presentation of the visual field gives us co-existence as such, i.e., the copresence of things in one being which embraces them all as their common present."[19] The visual mode gives unity to experience by maintaining an extended spatial presence. Although space is the primary structuring factor in visual experience, there is, of course, an element of temporality involved in the process of scanning the visual field. However, in the words of Jonas, "this scanning, though proceeding *in* time, articulates only what was present to the first glance and what stays unchanged while being scanned. The time thus taken in taking-in the view is not experienced as the passing away of contents before new ones in the flux of event, but as a lasting of the same, an identity which is an extension of the instantaneous *now* and therefore unmoved, continued present—so long as no change occurs in the objects themselves."[20] Spatially structured, the perceptual system of vision involves the perceiver in the experience of simultaneity, copresence, and continuity in relation to the visual field.

This kind of spatial simultaneity may be contrasted with the temporal sequence necessarily found in the auditory mode, in which sensory events come into being and pass away in a state of flux. The sequential procession of words moving in time, which served as the definitive model of temporal process for Augustine, reveals, according to Merleau-Ponty, the sequential nature of verbal experience as "an indefinite series of discontinuous acts."[21] Jonas reinforced this notion of the sequential nature of hearing in general by insisting that "it has no other dimension than that of time."[22] The sense of reality in hearing is a dynamic quality, a movement, a trajectory through time. Any reference to space with regard to auditory phenomena is merely the result of transferring spatial metaphors from the visual sphere. Temporally structured, the perceptual system of hearing involves the perceiver in the experience of sequence and discontinuity in relation to the auditory field of perception.

The simultaneity of visual experience also involves what might be called an immediate disclosure of information, whereas the sequential nature of auditory experience involves a mediated experience of the objects that produce sound. Visual information immediately discloses its object, but auditory data disclose some kind of activity in the proximity of the object. According to Jonas, "What sound immediately discloses is not an object but a dynamical event at the locus of the object, and thereby mediately the state the object is in at the moment of occurrence."[23] This mediation is most evident in verbal experience, as Merleau-Ponty noted, where "the meaning of a word is not contained in the word as sound."[24] As a result, visual experience tends toward a presentational disclosure of information, while auditory experience tends toward a referential transmission of information. Visual experience implies an immediate, continuous presentation of information, but auditory information requires a referential sequence. The referential sequence of the auditory mode is a series of discontinuous acts in which the immediate object of hearing, the sounds themselves, indicate certain actions producing those sounds, and only in the third place, an agent that is independent of the sounds it is causing. There is, therefore, a certain continuity in visual experience that is absent in verbal or auditory experience. Again, seeing requires continuity, but hearing involves discontinuity in the relations established between the perceiver and the world of perception.

A final distinction between seeing and hearing lies in their inherently different dispositions toward action. The initiative for perception tends to begin with the subject in vision yet with the object in hearing. In hearing, the perceiver, according to Jonas, "cannot let his ears wander, as his eyes do, over a field of possible percepts, already present as material for his attention, and focus them on the object chosen, but has simply to wait for a sound to strike them."[25] This fact leads to a greater degree of contingency in auditory experience, a greater dependency on the actions of the external environment. Objects in the environment are by nature visible. They reflect light and are, therefore, immediately accessible to visual perception. But objects are not, in the same way, constantly available to auditory perception. They do not emit sounds simply by virtue of their being objects in the same way that they reflect light. Therefore, the perceiver cannot choose to hear something but must wait until something happens in the environment to cause sound. It is on this basis that hearing and seeing imply different relationships with the environment. Hearing is dependent on actions, events, and occurrences in the outer world, a world in the process of becoming, while seeing has a constant and continuous access to the world's state of being.

From these two perceptual orientations we might even derive active and contemplative dispositions toward the world. Hearing evokes action, while seeing allows for a more neutral contemplation of the environment. Vision involves the discernment of patterns, configurations, spatial relationships—in other words, the recognition of order. Seeing permits a relatively neutral disengagement that contrasts with the dynamic interaction inherent in auditory experience. Sound informs the perceiver of an event, not merely the existence of things in a certain configuration. Something is happening in the environment, some change in the surroundings, which is conveyed in acoustical experience. The hearer is compelled to respond to this independent change in the environment. Reacting to the impact of sound, the hearer's course of action may be determined by the acoustic information. Not free to contemplate in a self-determined way, the hearer is called to action. One of the more intriguing paradoxes revealed by the phenomenology of perception is this: Although the visual domain tends toward continuity in its fundamental structure, in the immediacy, simultaneity, and copresence of the visual field, the visual system allows for a more or less detached contemplation; and although the auditory domain involves discontinuity in its fundamental structure, in the sequential, referential, and mediated character of hearing, the auditory system requires a more or less engaged, dynamic, and active involvement in the world of perception.

These generalizations about seeing and hearing derived from the phenomenology of perception are certainly too schematic. But if the world of perception is not William James's "big, blooming, buzzing confusion," then it is due to the consistent relations with the world organized by the senses. Contemplation and action, order and agency, space and time, simultaneity and sequence, continuity and discontinuity—these oppositions merely suggest the fundamentally different ways in which seeing and hearing organize consciousness within the world of perception. At this point, I merely want to suggest that a phenomenology of perception reveals not only that "we never cease living in the world of perception" but that the world of perception is organized in fundamentally different ways by the sensory modes of seeing and hearing. It remains to be seen whether or not that difference makes a difference in religious discourse.

Differences between seeing and hearing have been noticed, however, in the aesthetic experience of literary discourse. There may be visual and auditory dimensions inherent in literary forms. Literary theorists have suggested different ways of understanding the differences between the visual and auditory dimensions of literature. For example, Northrop Frye indicated the difference between the spatial coordinate of the eye and the temporal coordinate of the ear in the aesthetic perception of imaginative literature. While some principle of recurrence may be fundamental to all works of literature, Frye suggested that recurrence "is usually spoken of as rhythm when it moves along in time, and as pattern when it is spread out in space."[26] Works of literature demonstrate a temporal dimension by moving in time like music and a spatial dimension by spreading out images in patterns like painting. Frye made the connection with ears and eyes explicit when he identified the temporality of literature with hearing and its spatiality with sight. In every work of literature, narrative movement is the domain of the ear, while patterns of meaning are the domain of the eye. According to Frye, "the word narrative or *mythos* conveys the sense of movement caught by the ear, and the word meaning or *dianoia* conveys, or at least preserves, the sense of simultaneity caught by the eye."[27] Therefore, phenomenological distinctions—between eye and ear, space and time, simultaneity and sequence—are discovered in the aesthetic experience of literature. Hearing governs the temporal sequence of narrative, but seeing intervenes in any vision or insight or simultaneous apprehension of patterns of meaning.

The distinction between visual continuity and auditory, aural, or verbal discontinuity has often appeared in literary theory. For example, in his *Essay on the Origins of Language*, Rousseau distinguished between visual and verbal communication by observing that "one speaks more effectively to the eye than to the ear."[28] Visual communication is more immediate, direct, and continuous than verbal communication. "Although the language of gesture and spoken language are equally natural," Rousseau suggested, "still the first is easier and depends less upon conventions. For more things affect our eyes than our ears. Also, visual forms are more varied than sounds, and more expressive, saying more in less time."[29] Relatively independent of time, visual communication may be more immediate, establishing a continuous flow of information, while verbal communication depends upon referential conventions that require a series of relatively discontinuous temporal acts to process information. Certainly, Jacques Derrida's insistence upon difference and absence in verbal communication can be understood in one sense as incorporating Rousseau's distinction between visual and verbal communication. As opposed to the more immediate presence of the visual, verbal communication—whether written or spoken—is an absence, its discontinuity inherent in its inability to immediately present its referents. According to Derrida: "The written sign is absent from the body but the absence is already announced within the invisible and ethereal element of the spoken word, powerless to imitate the contact and movement of bodies."[30] Therefore, visual communication is based on immediate and continuous presence, but verbal communication establishes a fundamental discontinuity, a difference that may be reducible to the different perceptual requirements and conditions involved in the sense of hearing.

Finally, the literary theorist who has probably paid most attention to differences between seeing and hearing has been Walter Ong. On several occasions, Ong stressed a distinction between visual contemplation and auditory action as two orientations toward literature. Philip Sidney referred to a poem as a "speaking picture," but critical approaches to the interpretation of poetry have tended to emphasize either the picture or the speaking. The former approach to literature is concerned with "objective correlations" which consist in the contemplation of structures, forms, and patterns in a work of literary art. In the visual mode, literary theorists treat literature as if it were the production and contemplation of order. By recognizing the auditory qualities of literature, however, attention may be directed to action. The aural power of the spoken word, echoing even in the written text, reveals the "radically acoustic quality of the dialogue between man and man in which all verbal expression has its being."[31] Consistently, Ong rejected the visual mode of literary criticism, as if it were only the contemplation of lifeless, skeletal systems, in favor of the more active, involving, and captivating aural correlatives of literature. Counteracting what he regarded as the visualist bias in modern literary criticism, Ong advocated attention to literature's aural and active dynamics. Without trying to resolve the question of whether it is better to interpret literature through the visual or aural mode—a question most probably fruitless since both perceptual coordinates are necessarily involved—it is useful to note the distinction between the visual contemplation of order and the aural engagement with agency and action. These associations will be important when we turn to the analysis of literary and symbolic discourse in Augustine: Vision is associated with space, continuity, and the contemplation of order, while the verbal, aural, or auditory mode is associated with time, discontinuity, and the dynamic engagement with action.

Again, all we must notice at this point is that seeing and hearing are different, different in perception, in communication, and in the ways they orient human consciousness in the world. The phenomenology of perception is concerned (among other things) with identifying those differences. As Erwin Strauss noted: "Seeing and hearing differ not only with respect to the physical stimuli, functional organs and kinds of objects sensed, but much more essentially in regard to the specific manner in which the self is linked to the world."[32] In the phenomenology of perception, therefore, the difference between seeing and hearing makes a difference in the fundamental orientation of human beings in their world. Perhaps the difference between seeing and hearing also makes a difference to the understanding of whatever human beings may perceive as sacred in their world.

SYNESTHESIA

The visual and aural modes may represent different ways of orienting human consciousness in the world, but those differences are also grounded in a fundamental unity of the senses. Sensory perception embodies diversity in unity, and unity in diversity. First, perception involves the body as a relatively unified whole in its environment. The unity of the senses, as Heinz Werner noted, "is based on the fact that the psycho-physical organism reacts as a whole."[33] Second, perception involves common dimensions of measurement—such as intensity, brightness, or softness—that overlap sensory domains. Third, perception acquires composite information about objects, such as Aristotle's common sensible attributes of motion, rest, number, form, magnitude, and unity. And that information depends upon the coordinated workings of the several senses. Fourth, perception depends upon common neural patterns and processes in the relations between stimuli, neural responses, and sensations that suggest a psycho-physical unity in perception. While the differences of the several senses remain important, those differences are coordinated in a basic unity of the senses that can be noticed in their ordinary perceptual operations.

The most radical demonstration of the unity of the senses, however, is found in examples of extraordinary convergences and interpenetrations of the senses known as synesthesia. In perception, language, and literature, synesthesia demonstrates a remarkable unity of the senses. As Lawrence Marks noted, "That curious sensory phenomenon known as synesthesia, where, for instance, sound takes on visual qualities, has a counterpart in language: A synesthetic factor—the metaphorical combination of words describing sensations of different modalities—infiltrates both the language of the common man and the language of the poet."[34] In perception, synesthesia involves either the association of one mode with another—for example, the association of colors with sounds—or the more radical transmodal perceptual experience in which a person may see sounds or hear colors. Synesthesia, or symbolic synesthesia, has been important within the Christian symbolic universe in which the aural symbolism of word has not only been associated with the visual symbolism of light, but word and light have in fact been identified. As we will see, religious discourse has often been structured around a symmetry and interpenetration of the visual and the verbal, aural, or auditory coordinates. For the moment, however, it might be useful to look briefly at the phenomenon of synesthesia in perception, language, and literature.

In perceptual psychology, two major approaches to the analysis of synesthesia have been pursued—one presupposing the independence of the senses, the other beginning with the premise of the unity of the senses. Assuming the independence of the various perceptual modes, P. von Schiller explained synesthesia as the result of corresponding physiological excitations that transfer across sensory sectors. In synesthesia, "excitations brought about by disturbing stimuli in the acoustic or tactical sector, affect—chemically or electrically—the optic sector, thereby causing a modification of the optical impressions."[35] From this perspective, synesthesia results from a kind of chemical or electrical seepage across sensory sectors, as corresponding stimuli are transferred across independent sensory domains. Criticizing Schiller, Erwin Strauss argued that synesthesia revealed the unitary root of all perception. Seeing and hearing, for example, may be distinct but not separate; they are differentiations of a unified perceptual apparatus. Synesthesia demonstrates the fundamental unity of perception. "The question is thus no longer directed to the possibility of uniting," Strauss concluded, "but rather to the circumstances which in a particular case occasion this, and not another, bringing together."[36] Nevertheless, even if synesthesia shows the natural unity of the senses, it remains a rather extraordinary type of perceptual experience. Rarely do people seem to experience the sort of sensory convergence or intermodal transfer found in synesthesia. Therefore, whether it is explained as a cross-circuit transfer across independent sensory modes or as a dramatic example of a more basic unity of the senses, synesthesia remains an extraordinary sensory experience in which perceptual modes come together in unexpected combinations, create new sensory configurations, or interpenetrate in unusual transsensory perceptions of lights that are heard or sounds that are seen.

The frequent appearance of synesthesia in ordinary language has often been noticed. Metaphoric convergence of sensory modes occurs in conventional figures of speech such as "loud colors," "dark sounds,"

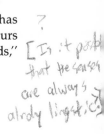

"sweet smells," or "sour notes." Intersense analogies seem to be an important element in ordinary language production and usage. But intersense analogies also captured the imaginations of a diverse range of European and American philosophers, scientists, and artists. In his *Essay Concerning Human Understanding,* John Locke noted that a blind person should be able to understand the color scarlet by analogy to the sound of a trumpet.[37] Isaac Newton speculated on analogies between sound and color, concluding that the spaces occupied by the seven colors of the spectrum were analogous to the relative intervals between notes in the octave.[38] Attempting a practical application of Locke's and Newton's observations, Father Louis Bertrand Castel experimented with a color organ that was designed to create a synesthetic correspondence between music and color. Castel announced that "the deaf in this way will be able to see the music of the ears, the blind will hear the music of the eyes, and we who have both eyes and ears will enjoy music and colors better by enjoying them both at the same time."[39] Finally, literary artists, particularly Romantic poets and authors from Blake to Baudelaire, effectively explored the convergence and interpenetration of sensory modes to create a rich texture and dynamic tension in their literary work.[40]

On rare occasions, attention to intersense analogies, transfers, and interpenetrations has been proposed as a useful topic for cultural analysis. The anthropologist E. B. Tylor, in his *Researches in the Early History of Mankind* (1865), suggested that the curious analogies between the senses that appear in language and literature might reveal something basic about the human mind. "Language shows clearly," Tylor noted, "that men in general have a strong feeling of such analogies among the impressions of the different senses. Expressions such as 'schreiend roth,' and the use of 'loud,' as applied to colours and patterns, are superficial examples of analogies which have their roots deep in the human mind."[41] Having remarked that intersense analogies should reveal something important, Tylor was unclear about what that something might be. Two possible avenues for the investigation of synesthesia, however, were suggested by William James and Claude Lévi-Strauss.

William James proposed that intermodal sensory transfers held the potential for scrambling ordinary expectations about the world. Evelyn Underhill recorded that "William James once suggested as a useful exercise for young idealists, a consideration of the changes which would be worked in our ordinary world if the various branches of our receiving instruments exchanged duties, if, for instance, we heard all colours and saw all sounds."[42] Whatever effect this exercise might have on young idealists, James suggested that intermodal transfers among the senses would shatter ordinary, normalizing expectations about the world. Hearing colors and seeing sounds demonstrate radically new modes of perception and awareness that break the ordinary structural relations between the senses and their perceptual environment. Therefore, synesthesia demonstrates a type of antistructure, a radical breakthrough of the ordinary structural relations between self and world obtaining within an ordinary phenomenology of perception.

Claude Lévi-Strauss, however, proposed that intersense analogies and interpenetrations also have observable regularities that may be investigated. Not merely an antistructural disruption of the senses, synesthesia combines the senses within a limited range of structural possibilities. Lévi-Strauss observed that "space has its own values, just as sounds and perfumes have colours, and feelings weight. The search for such correspondences is not a poetic game or a practical joke (as one critic has had the audacity to say it is, in connection with Rimbaud's 'sonnet des voyelles'; which is now a classic text for linguists who know the basis not of the color of phonemes — which is a variable depending on the individual — but the relationship between them, which admits of only a limited scale of possibilities)." Intersensory correspondences, therefore, may have their own logic. The logic of synesthesia would not reside in particular associations but in the limited structural possibilities involved in the combination of sensory modes. In those possibilities of combination, a grammar, syntax, and pragmatics may be disclosed in synesthesia. As Lévi-Strauss concluded, "[synesthesia] offers absolutely virgin territory for research where significant discoveries are still to be made."[43]

Merging the suggestions of James and Lévi-Strauss, I find that synesthesia — particularly the symbolic synesthesia employed in imaginative, literary, and religious discourse — signifies both antistructure and the unexpected combination of the structural associations that may be built into the different senses. First, synesthesia is antistructure. In defying ordinary, normalizing expectations about the world of perception, synesthesia breaks through structured limitations that organize experience. Intersensory metaphors provide an important antistructural resource in what has been called literary synesthesia by opening up new possibilities of signification. Those possibilities are always more than the limitations of the structured, ordinary world of perception, perceptual experiences beyond ordinary perception. Employing metaphors that combine light and sound, or cross-sensory modes to describe colors that are heard or sounds that are seen, literary synesthesia enters the antistructural world of paradox. The paradoxical collision of sensory modes creates an unusual language event. As a self-involving utterance, the phrases "I see sounds" or "I hear colors" announce a paradoxical relationship to the world of perception. Perhaps these utterances also announce a paradoxical relationship to the world of language, evoking something both expressible in language but inexpressible in ordinary sensibility. Noting the paradoxical quality of synesthesia, as a way of expressing something inexpressible, does not take us very far. As Ninian Smart once noted, "If paradoxes were all intended merely to point to the inexpressible, they could be any sort (like 'Ultimate Reality is both a tomato and a banana')."[44] Because synesthesia is grounded in the senses, it presents a particular kind of perceptual paradox. Concrete like sense experience, synesthesia is nevertheless something more: (1) more immediate, charged, and compelling; (2) more transcendent, extraordinary, and supernatural; and (3) more unified, complete, total, and all-encompassing. The multiple layers of paradox in literary or symbolic synesthesia can be demonstrated by some brief examples.

Synesthesia is like ordinary sensory experience but more immediate, charged, and compelling. As a literary device, synesthesia provides metaphors that intensify the language. Synesthetic metaphors grab attention; they carry more dynamic impact than single sensory metaphors. For example, Coleridge argued that poetry derived its power from an intermodal sensory transfer, "the excitement of vision by sound and the exponents of sound."[45] Coleridge employed synesthetic imagery as well in the text of his "Aeolian Harp," describing "a light in sound and a sound like power in light."[46] Whatever that intermodal transfer might signify, if anything, synesthetic metaphors intensify perceptual experience, merging the senses in unexpected combinations to create a highly charged symbolic effect. Perhaps the most prominent literary exponent of synesthesia, Baudelaire, deployed this imagery to fashion an immediate, highly charged interpenetration of light and sound. Colors and tones collide with each other in an electrified atmosphere: "Immediately great blue shadows rhythmically pursue in front of them the throng of orange and fragile rose tones, which are like the distant enfeebled echo of light. The great symphony of yesterday, that succession of melodies, where infinity generates variety, that complex hymn goes by the name of color. In color there is harmony, melody, counterpoint."[47] As both sense and non-sense, synesthetic metaphors break the ordinary structures of perception to generate an intense symbolic energy.

Beyond sense and non-sense, however, literary synesthesia points to signals of transcendence, rising above and going beyond the ordinary world of perception. Literary synesthesia may be employed in poetic depictions of other worlds, or heavenly realms, their transcendence signaled by the confluence of light and sound. For example, Balzac symbolized the transcendence of heaven in terms of synesthesia: "In heaven all things are homogeneous. Light engendered melody, melody engendered light, and colors were light combined with melody, and movement was number endowed with the Word."[48] Similarly, Swinburne employed the imagery of literary synesthesia — "light heard as music, music seen as light" — to achieve a certain effect of transcendence in which the poet:

> Finds the radiant utterance perfect, sees the word
> Spoken, hears the light that speaks it. Far and near
> All the world is heaven; and man and flower and bird
> Here are one at heart with all things seen and heard.[49]

Examples could certainly be multiplied. By defying ordinary expectations of how the senses work, literary synesthesia indicates a transcendent sensory perception that is above and beyond sense. Crossing sensory modes, synesthesia suggests the possibility of seeing beyond seeing and hearing beyond hearing. The apparent contradiction of the confluence of the senses provides what Ninian Smart has called a "unificatory paradox." In unifying separate aspects of experience, "the very idea of the contradiction is to point people beyond human concepts."[50] As an antistructural, unificatory paradox, therefore, literary synesthesia provides a perceptual vocabulary that is sensory but at the same time points beyond sense to an experience that is more transcendent.

Finally, literary synesthesia indicates a more unified sensibility. For example, Shelley orchestrated the senses in a musical harmony in which "every motion, odour, beam, and tone with that deep music is in unison."[51] And Yeats indicated the unified emotive effect of synesthesia by suggesting that "when sound and colour and form are in a musical relation, a beautiful relation to one another, they become as it were one sound, one colour, one form, and evoke an emotion that is made out of their distinct evocations and yet is one emotion."[52] Synesthesia, therefore, signals a more unified, complete, total, all-encompassing, and harmonious experience than experiences provided by ordinary perception. In the antistructural unity of synesthesia, the structurally differentiated senses are dissolved into a single, unified perceptual experience.

To say that synesthetic metaphors signal antistructural qualities of energy, transcendence, and union seems more like a recipe for mysticism than imaginative literature. And so it is. The language of mysticism provides a convenient transition from literary synesthesia to the symbolic synesthesia that occasionally surfaces in religious discourse. Commentators on mysticism have often been struck by the mystic's recourse to synesthesia. For example, Evelyn Underhill noted that mystics reported "a rare moment of consciousness in which the senses are fused into a single ineffable act of perception, and colour and sound are known as aspects of one thing."[53] Mystical reports may combine the senses in a single, unified experience: Juliana of Norwich announced that "we shall all be endlessly hidden in God, truly seeing and wholly feeling, and hearing him spiritually and delectably smelling him and sweetly tasting him."[54] Whatever the experiential content, Juliana used language that signaled an intense, transcendent, and unified experience of the sacred through the unity of the senses. But more radical, transmodal sensory experience may also appear in reports of mystical experience. In the literature of the Desert Fathers, the words of Pachomius were described as "a flash of light coming from his mouth"; the mystic St. Martin declared, "I heard flowers that sounded, and saw notes that shone"; the mystic Ruysbroeck signaled an intense, transcendent, and unified experience by declaring that "the Word is no other than See."[55] These examples simply hint at the metaphoric deployment of synesthesia in mystical literature.

Perhaps the perceptual breakthrough of synesthesia signifies the antistructural social position of mystics to the extent that their detachment from entanglements in a social world may be duplicated in their imaginative transcendence of the ordinary structures of perception. Certainly, radical spiritualities seem to employ the metaphors of synesthesia most intensively. As we just noted, the monastic communities of the North African deserts known as the Desert Fathers frequently employed synesthetic metaphors in their discourse. As the monks listened to the Abbot Pachomius, they reportedly had a dramatic synesthetic experience: "All the brethren were like men drunk with wine, and . . . saw the words coming forth from his mouth like birds of gold, silver and precious stones, which flew over the brethren in secret and went into the ears of many of those who listened well."[56] A number of versions of an encounter between Macarius and two strangers were recorded in the literature of the Desert Fathers in which one of the guests recited the Psalms "and at every verse a flame came forth from his mouth and went up to heaven."[57] Withdrawn from attachments to their social world, the monks of the desert seemed conversant with the antistructural perceptual metaphors of synesthesia.

Supporting a possible linkage between social antistructure and synesthetic metaphors, the alternative Hellenistic, Jewish, and Christian movements known as Gnosticism commonly deployed synesthetic metaphors in composing a literature of radical spirituality. In the Gnostic literature of Nag Hammadi, a concern for what is beyond sense— "what no angel eye has [seen] and no archon-ear had heard"—was worked out symbolically in the convergence and interpenetration of the senses.[58] For example, the *Gospel of Truth* described an encounter with Jesus in terms of a convergence of all the senses: "For when they had seen him and had heard him, he granted them to taste him and smell him and to touch the beloved Son."[59] Frequently, however, Gnostic literature referred to a more radical interpenetration of seeing and hearing by many allusions to the "voice of light." In creation, "light spoke through [the Father's] mouth, and his voice gave birth to life"; that voice was multiplied in "the seven powers of the great light of the seven voices"; and the Son of God appeared in the "beautiful garment of light which is the voice of the immeasurable mind."[60] Many more examples could be cited. Taken out of context, these examples of synesthesia merely suggest that intersensory transfer was part of the vocabulary of Gnostic spirituality. Did symbolic synesthesia reinforce the antistructural position of Gnostics in relation to their religious traditions and social worlds? Perhaps. But the antistructural impetus of symbolic synesthesia was itself structured by traditions that had religious and social histories.

First, the Christian tradition provided a sacred history that was structured in terms of symbolic synesthesia, by crucial eruptions of the sacred that were symbolized as synesthetic events. The most important manifestations of the sacred in the tradition were symbolically structured by the convergence or interpenetration of visual and auditory modes. Christian salvation history was a pattern of synesthetic events: (1) Creation, in which the Word said, "Let there be light"; (2) the giving of the Law, in which Moses experienced the voice from the midst of the fire; (3) the advent of Grace, in which the savior figure of Christian myth was symbolized as Word of God, light of the world; and (4) the outpouring of the Spirit, in which the disciples of Jesus experienced tongues of fire at Pentecost. This must seem a strange way of describing the Christian mythic horizon, but it was a story structured by events in which visual and aural metaphors converged, combined, and interpenetrated in the form of symbolic synesthesia. This was the mainstream of the tradition, the basic contours of its symbolic universe. Anyone participating in that universe had to move in some way or another within the basic metaphoric configuration of word and light. Synesthetic metaphors may be antistructural; but within a particular tradition they participate in the prevailing symbolic structure of myth. In Christian myth, that symbolic structure was provided by the perceptual symbolism of word and light, particularly by the crucial synesthetic events—a creative voice speaking light, a commanding voice from fire, a saving word that was the light of the world, and a Pentecostal fire speaking in strange tongues—events that marked the most important manifestations of the sacred in the tradition.

Second, symbolic synesthesia was structured by the relatively consistent associations that attended the senses of sight and hearing. The symbolic associations of sight and hearing resulted from their different physiological processes; but they also depended upon how those senses were understood to operate within a particular culture. Combining physiology and culture, sight and hearing emerged as perceptual systems associated with the consistent range of structural oppositions that we have noticed: space and time, continuity and discontinuity, simultaneity and sequence, presence and distance, contemplation and action, and so on. In the act of combining sight and hearing, symbolic synesthesia signals a coincidence of these structural oppositions, a symbolic strategy, for example, that can embody continuity and discontinuity in a single perceptual configuration. The voice of light or the light that is heard fuses the structural oppositions that are physiologically, culturally, and phenomenologically associated with the separate senses of seeing and hearing. In this way, symbolic synesthesia is not only an antistructural breakthrough in language but also a structured combination of the binary oppositions associated with the different senses.

To restate my thesis: I explore the implications of three basic premises for an analysis of religious discourse. First, religious symbolism is grounded in sensory perception. In other words, religious symbolism is embodied in the primacy of perception. Alfred North Whitehead once remarked that "the animal body is the great central ground underlying all symbolic reference."[61] That observation is even more crucial in the analysis of religious symbolism. Part of the power of religious symbolism, as in the case of such symbols as word and light, lies in the vitality of sensory experience. It is an inadequate rendering of such symbols merely to assign them a theological or doctrinal content. Symbols participate in a more intense and visceral range of physical associations. The index to the power of these bodily, physical, or sensory associations is found in the aesthetic category of "imagery," the vital embodied life of language. Careful attention to textual imagery can reveal the ways in which religious language is either consciously or implicitly grounded in sensory experience.

Second, different sensory processes give rise to different symbolic associations. When these associations assume a relatively consistent pattern they can be usefully considered as symbolic models. The symbolic model arising from visual processes is dramatically different from the symbolic model emerging from verbal, aural, or auditory processes. In western religious discourse, the crucial difference between the visual model and the verbal model may be the association of the former with continuity and the latter with discontinuity; but all the other structural associations that we have considered may also come into play in the construction of symbolic models based on perception.

Third, at significant moments, these different patterns of sensory imagery—these different symbolic models based on seeing and hearing—meet, converge, and interpenetrate in the phenomenon of symbolic synesthesia. Not only does this dramatic convergence and interpenetration in religious discourse signal a more intense, transcendent, and unified experience of the sacred, but, to the extent that hearing lights or seeing voices represents a convergence of the visual and verbal models, symbolic synesthesia signals a structural coincidence of opposites in which continuity and discontinuity (for example) may be simultaneously affirmed. Of course, this is not to say that seeing is the opposite of hearing. It is merely to recognize that the convergence of visual continuity and verbal discontinuity is a *coincidentia oppositorum,* a fusion of structural oppositions in symbolic discourse.

Lévi-Strauss noted that all human thought strives "to apprehend in a total fashion the two aspects of reality . . . continuous and discontinuous."[62] In collapsing the visual and aural models, symbolic synesthesia achieves a simultaneous apprehension of the continuous and discontinuous associations that define the symbolic power of imagery derived from visual and auditory sensory processes. Continuity and discontinuity are held in vital and creative tension. When this tension appears in religious discourse, the human realm may be affirmed as simultaneously continuous and discontinuous with the sacred by means of this very tension present in metaphors of symbolic synesthesia. To situate religious discourse at the center of this tension is to make it available to the history of religions in new and perhaps strange ways. New contours of religious universes of discourse may be disclosed. As we noted, the fundamental tension between continuity and discontinuity resonates with (and reflects) the central Christian paradoxical affirmation that Christ is simultaneously divine and human—Word of God, light of the world. Word and light affirm simultaneously the different and the same. Appreciation of this creative, contradictory tension is enhanced by attention to the relation between symbolism and sensory perception.

Christians have occupied a religious universe in which the mythic horizon was structured around certain crucial synesthetic events—a creation in which the Word of God said, "Let there be light," a revelation of law in which the voice of God spoke from the midst of a fire, and an incarnation of God symbolized in synesthetic terms as "Word of God, light of the world." Deployments of perceptual metaphors, particularly word and light, have been structured by that mythic horizon. As we will see in the next chapter, however, the Jewish religious thinker Philo of Alexandria was also engaged in working out the implications of seeing and hearing for a symbolic universe. Attention to perceptual symbolism reveals the ways in which a symbolic vocabulary can be informed by a very specific and carefully articulated understanding of the senses and how they operate in perception. Visual and verbal symbolic models have emerged as structural oppositions but also as symbolic resources that can be fused in symbolic synesthesia. In those instances of synesthetic fusion, religious discourse has embodied the tension between continuity and discontinuity in the relation between human beings and the sacred; but, more important, it has demonstrated the ability to move through that tension, not merely in the familiar terms of doctrine or theological exposition, but by means of a dynamic symbolism of the senses.

2

Religious Discourse

If it is true that we never cease living in the world of perception and that perceptual categories contribute to our conceptualization of truth, then the visual and auditory associations we have outlined provide important resources for symbolic discourse that links perception and conceptual truth-claims. To what extent does sensory perception inform religious discourse? As visual and auditory patterns are appropriated in the formation of religious symbol systems—in the deployment of imagery within texts and traditions of religious discourse—relatively consistent symbolic associations may be discovered to emerge. It may be useful to define the differentiated and elaborated metaphoric resources of the eye and ear as symbolic models. A visual model may be contrasted with a verbal, aural, or auditory model based on the consistent range of symbolic associations derived from seeing and hearing. For the sake of economy, we will use the term verbal model for the metaphors and associations derived from the sense of hearing, not only because vocal sound was regarded by Greek scientists (and, later, by western theologians) as the prototype for understanding the production, transmission, and reception of all sound, but also because aural or auditory experience was consistently related to the symbolism of the word (or Word) in the symbolic discourse I want to investigate. Visual and verbal models, therefore, will refer to the differentiated and elaborated symbolic associations that attend seeing and hearing in religious discourse.

Based on what we have noted so far, we might expect a visual model to tend (for example) toward associations of continuity, while a verbal model would tend to involve associations of discontinuity. To illustrate these associations, I would like to examine two examples of religious discourse: the work of Philo of Alexandria and the controversy between Arius and Athanasius that culminated in the Council of Nicaea. These two examples demonstrate the potential of perceptual models—both in the coincidence of the visual and verbal, as well as in the conflict between the visual and the verbal—to symbolize the relationship between human beings and the sacred.

In some discursive situations, the associations that attend visual and verbal symbolic models may be harmonized, reconciled, or held in a symmetrical balance; they may even be fused in the kind of symbolic strategy we have labeled symbolic synesthesia. As symbolic models, seeing and hearing may be grounded in a fundamental unity of perceptual categories in symbolizing relations between humans and the sacred. The coincidence of seeing and hearing as symbolic models may be found in the discourse of Philo of Alexandria. Philo carefully distinguished between seeing and hearing: Each operated differently, governed a different domain of human activity, and ultimately symbolized a different relationship between human beings and God. But at the crucial moment when the Law was given to Moses, the visual and verbal coincided in a synesthetic symbolic event in which Moses and the people of Israel saw the voice of God on Sinai. Careful attention to visual and verbal models in the work of Philo may disclose the significance of seeing the voice on Sinai in his symbolic universe.

In other discursive situations, however, the tension between verbal and visual models may not be resolved in a coincidence of opposites. Whether in a doctrinal debate within a single exegetical tradition or a confrontation between two divergent traditions, the structural oppositions inherent in the visual and verbal models may come into conflict. One side of a conflict may appropriate symbolic imagery derived from hearing, while the other may appropriate symbolic imagery derived from sight. The conflict over fundamental perceptual orientations may inform a conflict of symbols, a conflict in which resources from one perceptual model may be deployed against another. Such a conflict between visual and verbal symbolic models appears at the heart of the fourth-century Trinitarian controversy. Arius's preference for working out symbolic relationships in terms of metaphors derived from the verbal model contended against Athanasius's abiding preoccupation with the implications of visual imagery. In this respect, the Arian controversy was a conflict of word against light. The controversy may have been a contest over the legitimate ownership of Trinitarian symbols, but claims to ownership were certified by recourse to dramatically different symbolic models derived from sensory perception. It may be useful briefly to recall this contest in order to develop a better understanding of how ideological conflicts can be embodied in the appropriation and deployment of contrasting perceptual models.

BODY SYMBOLISM

Before turning to the coincidence and conflict of perceptual models, however, it is important to recognize that these symbolic models derived from seeing and hearing are part of a genre of symbolic discourse that might be called the symbolism of the body. The phenomenology and anthropology of the body have received considerable attention recently. From Husserl to Merleau-Ponty (and perhaps including the work of Michel Foucault) a phenomenology of the body has suggested that embodiment is both fixed and fluid, fixed in its basic, unavoidable givenness, but fluid as a mobile field of organized energy and consciousness.[1] Concurrently, an anthropology of the body—traced back to the seminal work of Robert Hertz on the bipolar body symbolism of right and left and Marcel Mauss on techniques of the body—has suggested that the body is the primary reservoir of symbolic signification.[2] Mary Douglas noted how the body operates as a symbol of social relations, that "the symbols based on the human body are used to express different social experiences."[3] Although Mary Douglas has usefully examined the socially inscribed body, I limit my explorations to the perceptually inscribed body that is embodied in religious discourse. The body in either case appears as the basic ground for symbolic reference. Is this attention to the body warranted? Does the body form a unified field of symbolic reference and signification? Is body symbolism a distinct genre of symbolic discourse that can be examined, outlined, and schematized for purposes of analysis?

Two objections to the systematic analysis of body symbolism have been raised—one objecting to the isolation of the body as a separate reservoir of symbolic reference, the other objecting to the systematic analysis that tends to be imposed upon the always overdetermined living resources of the body. At the risk of oversimplifying, one objection claims that physical symbols are not physical; the other claims they are not symbols. The first objection was raised by Rodney Needham in a paper entitled "Physiological Symbols." Needham argued that so-called body symbols were only accidentally related to the body and bodily processes. Examining representative physiological symbols— right and left, the half-man, the color associations of white-black-red, percussion, and elementary designs—Needham found that arguments for the physiological origin of these symbols were unconvincing. We are not justified in considering these symbols as examples of a common genus, body symbols, because they owe their origin to some prior pattern of logical classification that takes precedence over physiology. Like other symbols, these so-called body symbols are "archetypes of human imagination," rather than the results of organic or physiological processes of the body. Needham concluded:

> It looks as though some other factors were at work, namely whatever it is that impels men to employ symbolism in the first place; for example to make the right stand for probity, red for indeterminacy, percussion for transition. Clearly, the physiology of symbolism is not going to do much toward isolating the factor that may be responsible. It seemed initially to offer a promising recourse, by reference to the human organism and its universal capacities and attributes, but under inspection that promise is dissipated.[4]

In contrast to Needham's argument that the body does not present a universal ground of symbolic reference, anthropologist Michael Jackson spoke for an opposing position in an essay on "Knowledge of the Body." Jackson argued that "the 'anthropology of the body' has been vitiated by a tendency to interpret embodied experience in terms of cognitive and linguistic models of meaning."[5] Rather than maintaining (as Needham) that conceptualization is prior to body symbolism, Jackson insisted that the lived experience of the body, what he called "somatic praxis," has precedence over any conceptualization. Resisting what he described as the "intellectualist tendency to regard body praxis as secondary to verbal praxis," Jackson argued for what may be a more phenomenological appreciation of the lived experience of the body. Schematic analysis of body symbolism tends to reduce the living human body to the status of a sign, an object of purely cognitive and linguistic operations. But the meaning and power of the body lies in lived experience that (citing the words of Pierre Bourdieu) "is incomparably more ambiguous and overdetermined than the most overdetermined uses of ordinary language."[6]

The analysis of body symbolism, therefore, runs these two risks: the risk of reducing symbolic systems to the body or the risk of reducing the body to symbolic systems. In this book, I navigate a middle course by examining what might be regarded as a dialectical relationship between the body and symbolic discourse. To put this dialectic simply: First, the perceptual symbolism I want to investigate is to a certain extent predetermined by physiology. The eyes and ears are given in perceptual experience, and they predetermine certain differentially structured relations within the human perceptual environment. But those relations are already symbolized by the time they are conceptualized in any cultural attempt to make sense out of the senses. Second, therefore, perceptual symbolism may be predetermined by the potential (and limits) of the senses, but the precise character of that symbolism is determined by culturally constructed associations that attend the several senses. Particularly in the event that seeing and hearing become structural oppositions in symbolic discourse—representing the opposition between continuity and discontinuity, for example—we find situations in which the potential of the body has been organized and determined by human imagination, rather than merely predetermined by the perceptual resources of the body. Therefore, perceptual symbolism may form a continuous feedback loop that alternates back and forth between the perceptual resources of the body and the symbolizing operations of discourse. Perceptual symbolism is predetermined by the body, determined (as Needham noted) by whatever it is that impels human beings to symbolize oppositions (and, as we will see, resolutions), but third, and finally, perceptual symbolism is unavoidably overdetermined by the surplus of signification in discourse and the irreducibility of the body to symbolism, discourse, or thought in lived experience. Symbolism is more than the body, but the body is also more overdetermined in its meaning and significance for human experience than the most complex symbolic systems. Perception may give rise to symbols, predetermining their conditions of possibility, but symbols are constantly being forced back to the body by its unavoidably overdetermined meaning and power in human life. In summary: The perceptual symbolism I examine is predetermined by the body, determined by symbolic discourse and practices within a specific cultural context, but inevitably overdetermined by the elusive, irreducible nature of the human body.

Perception is implicated in symbolic discourse through metaphors and models. As Carlyle observed, metaphors are the raw material of discourse, the "Body of Thought." In other words, thought is embodied in "Metaphors, recognized as such, or no longer recognized; still fluid and florid, or now solid-grown and colourless."[7] Part of the vitality of religious discourse lies in metaphors drawn from the senses, perhaps no longer recognized in theological or doctrinal thought, but brought back to life by attention to perceptual symbolism. The consistent development and deployment of perceptual metaphors within a field of discourse may usefully be considered as symbolic models. As an extended metaphor, a symbolic model in religious discourse may organize and pattern conceptual relations—such as the relations between self and world or between human beings and the sacred—in terms of consistent symbolic associations built into the model.[8] By visual and verbal models, therefore, I mean metaphoric patterns based on imagery derived from sense perception and developed with some consistency to structure conceptual relationships. In the discourse we will examine, the relationship between human and divine is structured by perceptual models drawn from seeing and hearing, visual and verbal models. Those symbolic models may be structurally opposed, or merged in some higher resolution, but visual and verbal perceptual models represent the "body of thought" in religious discourse, even when they are employed to symbolize that which is beyond the body and beyond thought.

PHILO: SEEING THE VOICE ON SINAI

Philo's *De vita Mosis* is a work regarded by most Philonic scholars as part of a sequence of exegetical exercises designed to defend the Pentateuch as perfect law in harmony with the cosmos, as well as in harmony with the most sophisticated speculations of Greek cosmology, science, and ethics. In his exegesis, Philo presented the regulations and prohibitions of the decalogue, and their systematic specification in the 613 special laws, as rational extensions of the perfect *nomos*.[9] In the *De vita Mosis*, Philo depicted Moses as the perfect lawgiver; yet, almost in passing, Philo observed that the law was not actually given through Moses but through an extraordinary theophany on Sinai in which the divine voice was visible. The divine commands were "promulgated by God, not through his prophet but by a voice which, strange paradox, was visible and aroused the eyes rather than the ears of the bystanders" (Mos.II.213). Philo developed this perceptual transference between ears and eyes at Sinai in more detail in his *De decalogo*, where he described how, in the revelation of the law, "from the midst of the fire that streamed from heaven there sounded forth to their utter amazement a voice, for the flame became articulate speech in the language familiar to the audience, and so clearly and distinctly were the words formed by it that they seemed to see rather than to hear them" (Decal.46). The voice from the fire of heaven transferred across sensory modes. Likewise, the reception of that voice involved a transmodal perception: the voice was seen rather than heard. Unlike ordinary words, the speech of the divine voice was seen. As Philo noted, "the voice of men is audible, but the voice of God is truly visible" (Decal.47).

Critical scholarship on Philo's curious interpretation of the theophany on Sinai has been minimal. While recognizing that Philo's interpretation takes literally the Septuagint rendering of Exodus 20:18— "And all the people saw the voice"—Harry Wolfson argued that Philo merely wanted to emphasize that the divine voice was an "articulate" voice by describing it as a "visible" voice. Wolfson presented a rather confused description of Philo's revelation on Sinai, interchanging the terms "visible voice," "articulate voice," and "invisible sound" without any appreciation for the consistent visual and auditory associations implicated in Philo's terminology.[10] Erwin Goodenough offered a clearer explanation. In keeping with his emphasis on the emanation of the divine light-stream and initiation into the mysteries underlying Philo's thought, Goodenough asserted that "the great voice from Sinai . . . was 'seen' by them, since the voice was the outflowing of the Light-Stream of the Logos."[11] Supporting this assertion, Goodenough referred to the Stoic conceptual scheme that distinguished between the unspoken *logos* (*logos endiathetos*), which was singular, constant, and transcendent, and the spoken *logos* (*logos prophorikos*), which was dualistic because it combined unspoken thought with spoken sound. When Philo maintained that the divine voice was seen, Goodenough concluded, he simply meant that the unspoken *logos* was beheld in the Sinai revelation.

Considerable controversy remains regarding the precise nature of the divine *logos* in Philo's thought. Goodenough's simple distinction between a divine *logos* (unspoken and singular) and a human *logos* (spoken and dualistic) has not been shared by all commentators. Philo's understanding of the divine *logos* may not have allowed such a clear distinction between the unspoken and the spoken. Rather, a continuum may be observed in Philo's discussions of *logos* between a *logos endiathetos*, which was the unspoken source of rational speech within the *nous hegemonikos*, and the *logos prophorikos*, which was the stream flowing from the mind to the tongue, teeth, and mouth to issue forth in audible speech.[12] In this sense, *logos* was associated in all its forms with speech. Philo's understanding of the divine *logos*, the word of God, was in line with the general tendency to hypostasize breath, voice, speech, and word in the religions of the ancient Near East. As David Winston has reminded us, "The hypostasization of word proceeds via its character of breath and wind. Thus it is conceived as something concrete, nearly material, which, having left the mouth of the deity, acquires an independent existence."[13] By grounding the divine *logos* in the speech act, we can appreciate the truly extraordinary character of Philo's rendering of the revelation on Sinai as a voice that was seen.

Philo symbolized the revelation of the law as a synesthetic event in which the people saw the voice on Sinai. To appreciate this crucial instance of symbolic synesthesia it will be necessary to take seriously the visual and auditory associations that operated in Philo's symbolic universe. We have already outlined the Greek philosophical and sci-entific speculations on seeing and hearing that were available to Philo. But we can also analyze the consistent assumptions regarding seeing and hearing employed by Philo in his own work. Philo carefully and consistently distinguished the different operations of seeing and hearing in the human sensorium. But he also developed consistent visual and verbal symbolic models—models that systematically elaborated met-aphors derived from the senses of seeing and hearing—to symbolize the relations between God and human beings. Only after examining Philo's assumptions about seeing and hearing, along with the visual and verbal models derived from those assumptions, can we appreciate the significance of the synesthetic transfer across sensory modes in Philo's symbolism of seeing the voice on Sinai.

Philo separated the three senses of taste, smell, and touch, which he considered animal and servile, from the senses of sight and hearing. "The other two," Philo noted, "have a link with philosophy and hold the leading place—hearing and sight" (Abr.149-50). The distinctive place held by hearing and seeing in the human sensorium was a consistent theme in Philo's thought, as "knowledge, the opposite of ignorance, may be called the eyes and ears of the soul" (Ebr.158); "the mind is the eye's eye and the hearing's hearing" (Congr.143); and "for those who love to learn the benefit of knowledge is gained from seeing much and hearing much" (Post.137). In these cases, Philo suggested a symmetrical relationship between seeing and hearing in human con-sciousness. Seeing and hearing elevated the soul in knowledge, but their degradation represented the soul's descent into ignorance. Ig-norance destroyed the soul's "powers of seeing and hearing" (Ebr.157). In ignorance, hearing and seeing became channels for lust (Agr.34), desire (Deus.15), and the deceptive stories of the myth-makers that "beguile the two leading senses, sight and hearing" (Spec.I.29). Philo noted that it was common to speak of the feet as the foundation that upheld a human person, but "in reality that is done by the faculties of sight and hearing." When seeing and hearing are possessed in their fullness, a person stands upright and erect; but deprived of those senses, a person "gives way and is utterly prostrated" (Ebr.156).

Although the eyes and ears—both as physical senses and as met-aphors for the powers of the soul—often operated in a symmetrical balance in his thought, Philo nevertheless insisted on a clear distinction between seeing and hearing. Deep structural differences were drawn between the two most important senses. Following Greek science, Philo noted that the sense of hearing was "a sluggish sense inactive until aroused by the impact of air" (Decal.35). Using blatantly sexist language to represent the passivity of hearing, Philo maintained that the ears were "more sluggish and womanish [sic] than eyes" (Abr.150). Therefore, Philo represented the ear as a passive organ dependent on the activity of an external impact of air. In contrast, the eyes were self-directed. In keeping with the Greek scientific theory of the visual ray, Philo noted that the eye ventured forth to meet, contact, and form a continuous bond with its objects of perception. According to Philo, "the eyes have the courage to reach out to the visible objects and do not wait to be acted on by them, but anticipate the meeting and seek to act upon them instead" (Abr.150). Therefore, Philo relegated the sluggish sense of hearing to second place and gave special precedence to the sense of sight.

While both seeing and hearing were integral functions of the soul—both identified with knowledge and philosophy—Philo attributed preeminence to sight, "for God has made it the Queen of the other senses and set it above them all, establishing it as it were on a citadel, has associated it most closely with the soul" (Abr.150). Philo accumulated evidence for the close relationship between sight and the soul: The eyes were active in their operations like the soul; the eyes changed with the phases of the soul; the eyes were conversant with light, "the best of existing things," like the soul; and, finally, the visual potential of the eyes was ultimately fulfilled in the soul's highest achievement—philosophical contemplation (Abr.151). The sense of hearing, however, was seriously limited as a vehicle for knowledge. "As a means of giving a sure apprehension of truth," Philo noted, "hearing is proved to lag far behind sight and is brimful of vanity" (Conf.141). Even when hearing was excited by the impact of air to its fullest range of activity, "it halts within the air that surrounds the earth" (Abr.160). Hearing was confined within the earth's atmosphere, "but the eyes leave the earth and in an instant reach heaven and the boundaries of the universe" (Abr.160).

Therefore, we must modify our initial impression that Philo held sight and hearing in a symmetrical relationship as the two most important senses. Although he often held them together as metaphors for the powers of the soul, Philo developed a hierarchy of value that placed seeing above hearing. That hierarchy not only appeared in Philo's analysis of perception, but also in the way he symbolized the acquisition of knowledge in philosophy. In his theory of the learning process, Philo associated hearing with progress toward knowledge, but sight with the perfection of knowledge. Philo represented the process of learning as a transition from hearing to a direct vision of the ideal contents of wisdom. According to Philo, wisdom "made us spectators rather than hearers of knowledge, and substituted in our minds sight, the swiftest of the senses, for the slower sense of hearing." Having achieved the insight of wisdom, "it is idle any longer to exercise the ear with words" (Sac.78).

On several occasions, Philo identified the transition from hearing to seeing in the acquisition of wisdom with Jacob assuming the name of Israel. Jacob was interpreted as a typological symbol for the sense of hearing, while Israel symbolized seeing (Conf.72). Therefore, the name Jacob represented the progress toward knowledge that Philo associated with the sense of hearing; Israel represented the perfection of knowledge associated with sight. In Philo's allegorical exegesis, "Jacob is a name for learning and progress, gifts which depend upon hearing; Israel for perfection, for the name expresses the vision of God" (Ebr.82). Therefore, Philo suggested that Jacob's change of name to Israel signified the exchange of hearing for eyesight, the transition from progress to perfection, as the "current coin of learning and teaching from which Jacob took his title is reminted into the seeing of Israel" (Mig.39). In a similar discussion, Philo demonstrated the connection between his understanding of sensory perception and the acquisition of philosophical wisdom. When Jacob's name was changed to Israel, Philo explained, God planted eyes in his understanding that enabled him "to see clearly what before he had grasped by hearing, for sight is more trustworthy than the ears" (Ebr.82). As senses, sight was better than hearing; as metaphoric models for human understanding, hearing was superseded by the direct vision of wisdom. For Philo, therefore, the senses were more than perceptual systems: They were symbolic models that organized different relations between the senses, the mind, and God along lines established by the metaphoric resources associated with eyes and ears.

Many passages in the Philonic corpus outlined symbolic associations between sensory perception, mind, and God based on visual and verbal models. One of the most intriguing passages appeared in Philo's interpretation of the golden calf (Post.165-69). Because the golden calf was made out of earrings, Philo decided that it signified the inferiority of the sense of hearing to sight. Philo contrasted the idolatry of the golden calf, associated with the sense of hearing, with the epiphany on Mount Sinai that demonstrated the superiority of the sense of sight and the visual model in God's exhortation, "See, see that I AM." This passage may serve as a revealing example of Philo's deployment of sensory models to symbolize supersensory relations between human beings and God. We will return to it in a moment. But first it is necessary to review the consistent associations of the visual and verbal models in Philo's symbolic universe.

Philo's commitment to the superiority of sight was reflected throughout his work. Particularly in his extended analysis of creation, the *De opificio mundi*, he was preoccupied with the visual model, explaining the entire process of creation in terms of light, sight, and the eye. Philo explained creation in terms of visual correspondence: God fashioned the visible world in direct correspondence to an intelligible pattern. Philo compared the creator to an architect, "keeping his eye upon his pattern and making the visible or tangible objects correspond in each case to the incorporeal ideas" (Op.18). The visual model, therefore, was associated with correspondence, similarity, and a pattern of continuity. Elsewhere, Philo explained the continuity inherent in the visual model as a result of the way sight established a continuous bond between subject and object, as "nature created light to be a link between the two, a link which unites and connects the color and the eye" (Sac.36). As a visual model, this same pattern of continuity was transferred by analogy from the eye to the mind. "Of all things light is best," Philo noted, "indispensable means of sight, the best of the senses; for what the intellect is in the soul, this the eye is in the body" (Op.53). Visual continuity, therefore, operated in both the intellect and the eye, "for each of them sees, one the things of the mind, the other the things of the sense" (Op.53). Philo's tendency to associate the visual model with continuity was further extended to the way he symbolized the relationship between human beings and God. The visual model symbolized a continuity between human and divine. The eye symbolized continuity between the material and spiritual realms because when God created eyes, Philo maintained, He placed them high up in the head, "that [humans] might gaze on heaven, for man, as the old saying is, is a plant not earthly but heavenly" (Plant.17). Human beings were like the heavens because they could see the heavens; seeing, therefore, established symbolic relations between human and divine based on similarity and continuity.

Philo's deployment of symbolic imagery derived from the verbal model, however, was very different because it established relations of difference and discontinuity. Philo devalued the verbal model as a way of symbolizing the relations between God and the world just as he relegated the sense of hearing to a secondary status. Perhaps for this reason Philo omitted any reference to the word or voice of God in his most sustained commentary on the Genesis account of creation in his *De opificio mundi*. Considering the importance of the verbal model in Rabbinic and Christian interpretations of the beginning of Genesis, it may be curious that Philo chose to leave it out of his most extensive analysis of God's creation of the world. Philo was certainly familiar with the traditional role of the divine word or voice in creation (e.g., Sac.8), but he analyzed creation as an exclusively visual event—the divine architect looking at a perfect pattern and fashioning the world to correspond to its design. Philo's apparent disregard for the verbal coordinate in the symbolism of creation may have been related to his general attitude toward speech and hearing in human perception, cognition, and knowledge. Hearing was a sense "on which no reliance can be placed" (Abr.60); therefore, the word, voice, or speech of God may not have seemed to Philo as a reliable foundation for the creation of the world.

Nevertheless, Philo did develop a consistent symbolism regarding the word of God. The verbal model, however, generated two types of discontinuity that Philo associated with the word, voice, or speech of God. First, the word of God was radically different than human speech and hearing. The verbal model organized a discontinuous relationship between human and divine that insisted on the radical transcendence of the divine word. The word of God was separate, distinct, different, "a lover of the wild and solitary, never mixing with the medley of things that have come into being only to perish" (Her.234). Human speech and hearing depended on two factors that Philo called the dyad of breath and air. But God spoke in an entirely different way, "for His Word is not a sonant impact of voice upon air, or mixed with anything else at all, but it is unbodied and unclothed and in no way different from unity" (Deus.83). The solitary, unitary monads of God's speech, Philo claimed, "transcend our capacity of speech and hearing, being too great and august to be adjusted to the tongue and ear of any mortal" (Op.4-5). Therefore, the verbal coordinate established a discontinuous relationship in the radical difference between divine speech and human hearing. Consistent with the Greek scientific understanding of sound, however, the discontinuity between speaking agent and perceiver was already built into the auditory mode of perception. In this regard, Philo merely adapted that inherent discontinuity into a symbolic model for the relation between God and human beings that isolated the radical difference of divinity.

Second, Philo associated the verbal model with discontinuity in his descriptions of the divine "severing word" (*logos tomeus*). By means of his word, God separated, divided, and apportioned everything in the universe (Her.235). Unlike visual connections, correspondences, and similarities, the verbal model was associated with differences. Philo imagined that God was "severing through the severer of all things, that is his Word, the whole succession of things material and immaterial whose natures appear to us to be knitted together and united" (Her.130). Drawing on the visual model, Philo noted that things might appear united, but through God's severing word things were divided. Visual continuities contrasted with the discontinuities produced by the divine word. In the process of establishing discontinuities, Philo insisted, "that severing Word whetted to an edge of utmost sharpness never ceases to divide" (Her.130). In these two respects, therefore, Philo associated the verbal model with discontinuity, the separation between human and divine and the divisions among things in the world. Both forms of discontinuity were symbolized by extending the verbal model — employing metaphors derived from vocal, aural, or auditory processes — to the activity of God.

Now to return to Philo's analysis of the golden calf: Philo made the curious assertion that the worship of idols referred directly to the sense of hearing. Although we might expect the idolatrous worship of graven images to be associated with the sense of sight, drawing attention from an invisible God to some visual representation, Philo insisted that idolatry was based on the sense of hearing:

> Bulls and rams and goats, which Egypt honours, and all other objects of worship of perishable material as well, are held to be gods on hearsay only, not being really such, all falsely so-called. For those who deem life a show got up for foolish dotards make counterfeit impressions in the yet tender souls of the young, employing their ears as their ministers, and filling them with the nonsense of myths. (Post.165)

Certainly this association of idolatry with the sense of hearing must seem forced. Philo worked hard in this exegesis to maintain the structured relations between visual and verbal models that persisted throughout his work. His textual support for the connection between idolatry and hearing was the fact that the golden calf was made from earrings. Rabbinic interpretations of the golden calf explained that it was made from the earrings of the men because the women refused to give theirs up. The rabbis were more interested in the virtue displayed by the women and often took this opportunity to praise them.[14] They did not connect the earrings with the sense of hearing. In addition, however, due to a fortuitous variant, Philo was happy to follow the Septuagint in attributing the golden earrings that were melted down to make the idol to the women.

> The calf, you observe, is not made out of all the things with which women deck themselves, but only their earrings (Ex 32:2), for the lawgiver is teaching us that no manufactured god is a God for sight and in reality,

but for the ear to hear of, and vogue and custom to proclaim, and that too a woman's ear, not a man's, for to entertain such trash is the work of an effeminate and sinewless soul. (Post.166)

In his analysis, Philo clearly relegated the sense of hearing to a status lower than the sense of sight, not only as two different modes of sensory perception, but also as symbolic models for representing the workings of the mind and the apprehension of God. False apprehension, such as the idolatry of the golden calf, can be known only through the ears; but "the Being that in reality is can be perceived and known not only through the ears, but with the eyes of understanding" (Post.167). At this point in his exegesis, Philo turned from the golden calf to the theophany on Sinai to illustrate the superiority of the visual over the verbal model. God announced, " 'See, see that I AM,' showing that He that actually is is apprehended by clear intuition rather than demonstrated by arguments carried out in words" (Post.167). The visual model provided a direct means of apprehending the existence of God, while the verbal model, either through the inadequacy of the sense of hearing or the futility of arguments conducted in words, was incapable of achieving direct access to the divine reality. Visual continuity and verbal discontinuity in these symbolic models defined different relations between human and divine based on associations that were ultimately derived by Philo from sensory perception.

In relation to perceptual models, Philo isolated two types of religious experience, the contemplative and the prophetic. The clear intuition of "He that actually is" was Philo's version of the contemplative ascent, the ultimate extension of the continuity inherent in the visual model to the relationship between human and divine. Philo observed that "there is an intimate connection between seeing and contemplation" (Mig.165). Writing about the Therapeutae, he found it appropriate that "a people always taught from the first to use their sight, should desire the vision of the Existent and the Sun above the Sun of our senses" (Vita.11). Vision represented immediate access to that divine light, a continuity based on the symbolic model of sight. That visual model represented the basis for contemplation, wisdom, and philosophy, which "owe their origin to no other faculties but the princess of the senses, sight" (Abr.164). Like Plato in the *Timaeus*, Philo maintained that philosophy originated when the eyes gazed upward to behold the light of the heavens. According to Philo, "light has proved itself the source of many other boons to mankind, but preeminently of philosophy, the greatest boon of all. For man's faculty of vision, led upwards by light, discerned the nature of the bodies and their harmonious movement" (Op.53-54). But philosophical contemplation did not merely stop at observing the regularities of the celestial bodies; the eyes of the soul assumed wings "to attain not only to the furthest region of the upper air, but to overpass the very bounds of the entire universe and speed away toward the Uncreate" (Plant.22). The visual model, therefore, established a continuity that extended all the way up to the direct, immediate contemplation of God.

Given the superiority of sight over hearing, given the visual model of ascent in contemplation, and given the ultimate goal of contemplation as the vision of God, we are now in a position to ask: How far does this visual model of continuity between human and divine extend? The answer, of course, will be pretty far, but not all the way. At some point, the continuity of the visual model confronted the inaccessible transcendence of God. Returning to Philo's analysis of the golden calf, we find that he qualified the visual metaphor, "See, see that I AM," by noting that "in the passage just quoted He does not say, 'see Me,' for it is impossible that the God who is should be perceived at all by created beings" (Post.168). Philo rendered the phrase, "See that I AM," as if it referred to the understanding that God exists, rather than a direct vision of the inaccessible essence of God. Such a direct vision into the essence of God was denied to Moses (Ex 33:23; Post.169). Even in what was perhaps Philo's most ecstatic description of the visionary ascent of contemplation, the visual model of continuity confronted a limit. In contemplative ascent, the mind "seems to be on its way to the Great King Himself; but amid its longing to see Him, pure and untempered rays of concentrated light stream forth like a torrent, so that by its gleams the eye of the understanding is dazzled" (Op.70-72). Therefore, Philo's visual model defined a certain degree of continuity between human and divine. But that continuity was limited in Philo's symbolic universe when the immanence of the visual model confronted an unbridgeable transcendence.

The unbridgeable was bridged, however, in Philo's understanding of prophetic experience. Not only contemplative ascent, prophetic experience involved the descent of divine influences upon the prophet from God, the impact of the voice of God upon the relatively passive prophet. The vectors of movement were different in prophetic experience. Ascent merged with descent. Visual access merged with the verbal model of the prophet as one who is spoken to by God and speaks on behalf of God. The prophet was engaged in a verbal model of relationship with God. Philo described the prophet as a spokesman for the holy word, echoing a transcendent voice: "Now with every good man it is the holy word which assures his gift of prophecy. For a prophet (being a spokesman) has no utterance of his own, but all

his utterance comes from elsewhere, the echo of another's voice"
(Her.259). Suggesting a verbal model for the relation between human
and divine, Philo identified the prophet as the echo of a distant voice —
different, transcendent, entirely other than his own.

Abraham provided the prototype of prophetic experience for Philo.
By paying close attention to the perceptual metaphors he employed to
analyze Abraham we can gain a greater appreciation of Philo's understanding of prophetic experience as a fusion of the visual and verbal
models. Particularly concentrating on two passages from Genesis —
"about sunset there fell on him an ecstasy" and "it was said to Abraham" — Philo's exegesis of Genesis 12:1-6 outlined his understanding
of prophetic experience. Abraham's ecstasy at sunset signified the setting of the light of the mind in order that it might be replaced by the
divine light, just as the human utterances of the prophet were replaced
by the divine voice. Philo recalled the familiar analogy between the
sun and the mind by noting that " 'sun' is his name under a figure for
our mind, for what the reasoning faculty is in us, the sun is in the
world, since both are light bringers" (Her.263). Philo then proceeded
to develop an interpretation of prophetic ecstasy that represented it as
the setting of the sun of the mind and the dawning of divine light.

> So while the radiance of the mind is still all around us, when it pours
> as it were a noon-day beam into the whole soul, we are self-contained,
> not possessed. . . . For where the light of God shines, the human light
> sets; when the divine light sets, the human dawns and rises. This is
> what regularly befalls the fellowship of the prophets. (Her.263)

What God spoke to Abraham, therefore, was divine light that possessed
and supplanted the luminosity of Abraham's own mind. That Philo
represented prophetic experience in both verbal and visual terms may
prove to be highly significant. As Philo explained, God instructed
Abraham to "look up into heaven." That upward gaze followed the
pattern of contemplative ascent. But as Abraham looked up God exhorted him to see the divine word, "to look steadfastly for the manna,
which is the word of God" (Her.78). Elsewhere, Philo repeated this
fusion of visual and verbal models in his identification of manna as
the divine word that causes a brilliant light to shine (Det.118). Therefore, Philo symbolized Abraham's prophetic experience as an ecstatic
convergence of divine voice and light. In other words, Philo symbolized
the ecstasy of the prophet, in the merging of voice and light, as a
synesthetic event. Philo represented prophetic experience as a fusion
of verbal and visual models that resulted in symbolic synesthesia.

Philo was well aware that synesthesia did not normally occur in perception. In one text, he noted that "the eye cannot hear, nor the ears see" (Conf.194). Nevertheless, Philo symbolized the prophetic experience of the sacred in terms of a synesthetic fusion of voice and light. God spoke light to the prophets and the prophets saw the word of God, the manna from heaven, as a brilliant light. What was the significance of this symbolic synesthesia? I would suggest that synesthesia enabled Philo to symbolize the experiential breakthrough of the prophet as a coincidence of opposites, as a simultaneous affirmation of the contrasting associations Philo attributed to the visual and verbal models. If the visual model implied immanent continuity and the verbal model signified transcendent discontinuity, then their convergence in prophetic experience defined a relationship between human and divine that was simultaneously continuous and discontinuous. Certainly, a paradox, but a paradox that signaled an experience represented by Philo as concrete and definite like sensory perception, but more intense, extraordinary, and all-encompassing than perception or cognition, an experience of a God who was simultaneously immanent and transcendent. God could not be seen or heard; but Philo symbolized the prophet's experience as a fusion of sensory modes—seeing the divine voice, hearing the divine light—that signaled an experiential breakthrough by stretching perceptual metaphors to their breaking point. In fusing visual and verbal models, Philo represented the relationship between God and the prophet—continuous, yet discontinuous—in terms of symbolic synesthesia.

In Philo's analysis, the clearest example of a synesthetic eruption of the sacred into human experience occurred at the giving of the law on Sinai. As we noted, Philo described the theophany on Sinai as a synesthetic event in which the divine commands were "promulgated by God not through His prophet but by a voice which, strange paradox, was visible and aroused the eyes rather than the ears of the bystanders" (Mos.II.213). Now what can we make of this paradox in which "the voice of man is audible, but the voice of God truly visible" (Decal.47)? The basic themes we have been exploring converge in Philo's interpretation of the vision of the voice on Sinai. Philo's biblical prooftexts, "All the people saw the voice" (Ex 20:18) and "Ye have seen that I have spoken to you out of Heaven" (Ex 20:22), suggested to Philo that the voice of God appeared on Sinai "shining with intense brilliance" (Mig.47). Visual and verbal models coincided as the people's contemplative vision ascended and the voice of God descended to meet in the middle.

As Philo understood it, the contemplative vision might be limited, but its limit was bridged by the miraculous descent of the visible divine voice. In another text, Philo analyzed the synesthetic epiphany on Sinai as the ultimate fulfillment of contemplation: "For what life is better than a contemplative life, or more appropriate to a rational being? For this reason, whereas the voice of mortal beings is judged by hearing, the sacred oracles intimate that the words of God are seen as light is seen" (Mig.47). The sense of hearing may be appropriate for mortal voices, but not for hearing the voice of God. Clearly, Philo referred to "hearing" not merely as a sensory mode, but as a symbolic model for organizing the relationship between human and divine. Again, we find Philo developing a symbolic relationship of discontinuity in the verbal model, the discontinuity between the divine speaker and the human hearer. The verbal model symbolized distance, difference, and the radical transcendence of the divine speaker over against the inadequate human sense of hearing. In the verbal model, the inferiority of the sense of hearing was directly proportional to the transcendence of its divine object, the word of God. That word or voice of God was symbolized within the verbal model as beyond the scope of human capacities. The voice of God could not be heard, but it could by strange paradox be seen. This paradox captured Philo's contention that God was simultaneously beyond human experience, yet somehow accessible to it in the ecstasy of prophecy or the theophany of revelation. In his analysis of those dramatic manifestations of the sacred, Philo deployed the strategy of symbolic synesthesia. The visual and verbal concomitants of seeing the voice on Sinai encompassed (to borrow again the terms of Lévi-Strauss) "in a total fashion the two aspects of reality... continuous and discontinuous." A simultaneous apprehension of identity and difference was embodied in the fusion of verbal and visual models in Philo's analysis of the synesthetic manifestation of the sacred.

To summarize: Philo developed a consistent analysis of the senses of seeing and hearing and elaborated that analysis in the form of consistent visual and verbal symbolic models that organized his understanding of the relation between God and human beings. As we have seen, the visual model organized the relation between human and divine in terms of continuity. The verbal model, however, tended to symbolize discontinuity, particularly in the unassimilable difference between divine speech and human hearing. Commenting on a passage from Deuteronomy — "Ye heard a voice of words, and saw no similitude but only a voice" (Dt 4:2) — Philo reinforced the difference between human and divine that was built into the verbal model. Philo understood this passage to be "making a very subtle distinction, for the voice dividing itself into nouns and verbs and the parts of speech in general he naturally spoke of as 'audible' for it comes to the test of hearing; but the voice or sound that was not of verbs and nouns but of God, seen by the eye of the soul, he rightly represents as visible" (Mig.48). Again, Philo was dealing with sight and hearing, visible and audible, not as modes of sensory perception but as perceptual models that symbolized the relationship between human and divine. The verbal model required discontinuity between these two spheres, while the visual model, with its appeal to the eye of the soul, allowed for a certain degree of continuity as the "words spoken by God are interpreted by the power of sight in the soul" (Mig.48). Since the word of God was radically different from the words of nouns, verbs, and other parts of speech, the sense of hearing adequate for human speech was inadequate, even as a symbolic verbal model assimilated into the human soul, for apprehending the voice of God. Continuity between human and divine depended upon the visual model. The eye of the soul was capable of apprehending the voice of God. But the fusion of visual and verbal, the figurative language of symbolic synesthesia, allowed continuity while still maintaining the discontinuity, difference, and distance of God from human beings.

We can conclude with a citation from Philo that seems to summarize his position on hearing, seeing, and synesthesia: "The truth is that our sound-producer is not similar to the Divine organ of voice; for ours mingles with air and betakes itself to the place akin to it, the ears; but the Divine is an organ of pure and unalloyed speech, too subtle for the hearing to catch it, but visible to the soul which is single in virtue of its keenness of sight" (Mig.49). Here we find a review of the major dynamics of Philo's symbolic discourse of perception: First, the radical transcendence of divine speech over against human speech and hearing was consistent with Philo's development of the verbal model. In this regard, God was affirmed as wholly other, the divine as radically transcendent in relation to the human. Second, the adequacy of sight, "in virtue of its keenness," to define a visual continuity between human and divine was integral to Philo's development of the visual model. Finally, the phenomenon of symbolic synesthesia fused verbal discontinuity and visual continuity to represent the paradox in which God was simultaneously beyond human experience, yet somehow also accessible. Philo symbolized that paradox by fusing the verbal and visual models in his analysis of the theophany in which (by strange paradox, by coincidence of opposites) the voice was seen on Sinai.

NICAEA: WORD AGAINST LIGHT

Like most of his work, Philo's perceptual symbolism had little impact on subsequent Jewish thought. But his verbal and visual models might

have affected the development of Christian symbolic discourse. Philo
was one avenue through which Greek—and particularly Platonic—
assumptions about seeing and hearing were transmitted to Christian
theologians. In the development of those perceptual models, the Greek
phos was obviously and necessarily incorporated in a visual model.
Unequivocally associated with vision, the awareness of light was easily
assimilated within a visual model of perceptual symbolism. The Greek
logos, however, was a little more problematic. Beginning with the pre-
Socratics, the term was applied both to speech, whether spoken or
written, and to the exercise of reason. Stoics provided a technical
vocabulary for separating the two basic meanings of *logos* by distinguishing between the *logos endiathetos* (*ratio*) resident in the human
breast and the *logos prophorikos* (*oratio*) expressed in speech. But other
implications of *logos*, such as the "cutting" *logos* (*logos tomeus*) and the
"seed-bearing" *logos* (*logos spermatikos*), were also worked out in Stoic
and Middle Platonic thought.

Tensions among the various meanings of *logos* were certainly evident
in the development of Christian thought, as witnessed by the many
meanings of the term detailed in Origen's commentary on the prologue
of the Gospel of John. But behind the Christian appropriation of *logos*—
and the deployment of that term in the development of Trinitarian
symbolism—was the hypostasization of word, speech, and voice in
the religions of the ancient Near East that we have already noted. In
the biblical tradition, the various meanings of "Word of God"—including the exercise of sacred power, divine communication with human
beings, the text of the Bible, and, in Christian thought, the second
person of the Trinity—did not support the notion of *logos* as the reason
of God, so much as the identification of *logos* as the voice of God. The
Arians carried out this association of *logos* with the voice of God so
literally that, as John Henry Blunt noted, "they wished to establish
that the Son was only the *logos prophorikos*, by which they assigned
to Him a beginning, inasmuch as the thought must precede the sound
which gives it utterance."[15] For the purpose of an analysis of perceptual
symbolism in the Arian controversy, therefore, it is possible to situate
the symbol of word easily within a verbal, aural, or auditory symbolic
model. As we will see, the Arian appropriation of the verbal model
conflicted directly with the appropriation and deployment of the visual
model by the Athanasian party in the Trinitarian controversy of the
early fourth century.

Speaking to his disciples, Jesus said, "He who sees me sees Him
who sent me. I have come as a light into the world" (Jn 12:45). The
visual immediacy of Jesus' presence in the world defined a symbolic

continuity between human and divine. The phrase, "He who has seen me has seen the Father" (Jn 14:7, 9; 17:21), suggested the qualities of immediacy, simultaneity, similarity, and presence that characterized the visual model. Participating in that visual model, the symbol of light tended to establish relations based on symbolic continuity. Still speaking with his disciples, however, Jesus followed this visual imagery of presence by turning to the verbal model. Jesus declared, "He who rejects me and does not receive my sayings has a judge; the word that I have spoken will be his judge on the last day. For I have not spoken on my own authority; the Father who sent me has himself given me commandment what to say and what to speak" (Jn 12:48-49). In the visual model, the Father was presented by Jesus: "He who has seen me has seen the Father." In the verbal model, however, the Father was represented by Jesus, as the words of Jesus referred back to the utterance, commandment, and authority of the Father. This verbal referentiality, therefore, defined a symbolic discontinuity. The Father God was not immediately present in the verbal mode as he seems to have been in the visual. The visual presence contrasted with a verbal absence. On the level of symbolic discourse, the Trinitarian controversy of the fourth century was contained in this tension between visual continuity and verbal discontinuity as different perceptual models for organizing the relation between Father and Son in the Trinity.

As the first to introduce the word *trinitas* and the first to speak of the divine economy as *una substantia, tres personae*, Tertullian was tremendously influential in the development of Trinitarian and Christological imagery. In his *Apologia*, Tertullian explained the incarnation of the Word as the projection of light from light. The second person of the Trinity proceeded from the first in the same way that a ray of light extends from the sun: "When a ray is projected from the sun, it is a portion of the whole, but the sun will be in the ray, because it is the sun's ray, nor is it a division of substance, but an extension. Spirit from Spirit, God from God—as light is lit from light."[16] Tertullian, who originated much of the crucial symbolic and theological language of Western Christianity, developed this important metaphor of the light and its radiance. The ray of light was a portion of the sun, yet at the same time the sun was fully present in the ray of light. There was a coessential continuity between the light of God and the radiant Son. This visual imagery necessarily symbolized the eternal generation of the Son as a continuous process of divine radiance. In the East, Origen also employed the language of radiance in describing the Savior as the effulgence of the Father's glory. By the beginning of the third century, the powerful metaphoric model of God as light and Christ as radiance had achieved a certain prominence among both Greek and Latin fathers.[17]

In the mid-third century, however, an entirely different Christological strategy was introduced by Paul of Samosata. The bishop of Antioch denied the continuity of essence between Father and Son. According to the Syriac text, "He conceived otherwise the conjunction with wisdom, making it according to friendship and not according to substance."[18] Christ had no primordial unity of essence with God, but a relationship of love and will that eventually resulted in a communion with God. Irrespective of the theological subtleties of this dynamic monarchian position, its important symbolic ramifications were derived from the verbal discontinuity Paul of Samosata maintained between human and divine. The divine Word and Christ had distinct, separate, and independent existences. According to Paul, "The Word conjoined to him who came from David, i.e., Jesus Christ who was begotten from the Holy Ghost. And him the Virgin bore, through the Holy Ghost. But the Word was begotten of God, apart from the Virgin and apart from any other but God. Thus it was that the Word took an independent existence."[19] The separate existence of the Word—separate, independent, different, discontinuous with Christ—represented a pattern of verbal discontinuity between human and divine. The Word was not coextensive with Jesus, but referred back to God because, in the words of Paul of Samosata, "the Word is from above, Jesus Christ is man from hence."[20] In the verbal symbolic model, therefore, the divine and human realms were defined as separate and distinct domains.

The visual model of the continuity between light and its radiance and the verbal model of the discontinuity between the divine Word and the human Jesus collided in the Trinitarian controversies of the early fourth century. According to the *Historia Ecclesiastica* of the church historian Socrates, the controversy broke out when Alexander, Bishop of Alexandria, delivered "too ambitious a discourse about the Holy Trinity."[21] Alexander's dissertation on the coterminous essence of the Trinity outraged one of the local presbyters, Arius, who, solely "from love of controversy" (according to the official history), countered with the opposing view that the Father was not coeternal with the Son. Arius's familiar argument ran: "If the Father begot the Son, He that was begotten has a beginning of existence; and from this it is evident, that there was when the Son was not."[22] Arius was clearly working out the logical extension of the metaphor of sonship. If the Son was begotten, there must have been a time when he was not. But it is also possible that Arius's position, like that of Paul of Samosata, represented a precritical appropriation of the verbal model of discontinuity.

The clearest passage in Arius's writings that testified to his appropriation of the verbal model was his statement in the *Thalia* that "God is ineffable to his Son."[23] The Word of God was symbolized as so transcendent that it ultimately could not be spoken or heard, not even by the Son. The divine Word was clearly beyond human words, so the divine Father was beyond the human Son. The distinction between God and the Son was symbolically structured in terms of verbal discontinuity. God was not only ineffable to the Son, but He also defied investigation and comprehension. To quote again from Arius's *Thalia:* "He is to Himself what He is, that is, unspeakable. So that nothing which is called comprehensible does the Son know how to speak about; for it is impossible for Him to investigate the Father, who is by Himself."[24] The model of verbal discontinuity suggested the incomprehensibility and inaccessibility of the Father. That which could not be spoken was beyond comprehension and investigation. Therefore, the Son was separate from the Father in the verbal model. Unlike the visual presence suggested by the radiance of light, Arius asserted that the existence of the Son referred back to the will of the Father. We might even say that the existence of the Son was not presentational, but referential. The Son represented the will of the Father who sent him because, according to Arius, "the Son does not know His own essence: for, being Son, He really existed at the will of the Father."[25]

Athanasius seems to have fully recognized this problem of symbolic appropriation. Reflecting back on the controversy in his *De synodis* (c. 359), Athanasius recalled it as basically a dispute about metaphoric terminology in a common tradition. Athanasius commented on the problem he had perceived in the metaphoric imagery of the Son as the Father's word. He pointed out that when the verbal model was employed, a discontinuity between speaker and that which is spoken was inevitably suggested: "For not even man's word is part of him, nor proceeds from him according to passion, much less God's Word, whom the Father declared to be his own Son."[26] Athanasius was concerned "lest anyone, if he merely heard the expression, 'Word,' should suppose him impersonal [*anhypostasis*], like the word of men."[27] Recognizing this problem, the bishops at Nicaea appropriated and deployed the visual model of divine radiance. In anathematizing the doctrines of Paul and Arius, they asserted that the Father's essence was the true origin of the Son "and not of a different nature, as we are, and separate from the Father, but that as being from him, he exists as Son indivisible, as radiance with respect to light."[28] The Son was not separate from the Father, as in the verbal model, but was indivisible, coessential, and continuous as symbolized by the visual model of light from light.

The response to Arius's claim that there was a time when the Son was not consisted primarily in invoking the visual model of the radiance of the Father, which, as Jaroslav Pelikan noted, Athanasius "never tired of repeating."[29] In his *De sententia Dionysii*, Athanasius elaborated the visual imagery of the coessential continuity between Father and Son. "Being the radiance of eternal light, [the Son] is surely eternal himself; for if the light exists always, it is evident that the radiance, too, exists always. . . . God is eternal light, neither beginning nor ending. Therefore the radiance lies before him and is with him eternally, having no beginning and being eternally begotten."[30] The themes of eternal generation, consubstantiality, and continuity were all contained within a common visual frame of reference in the metaphor of divine radiance. Continuity was emphatically asserted in the *Orationes contra Arianos* when Athanasius insisted that "of course the light and the radiance are one, and the one is made evident in the other, as the radiance is in the sun, in such a way that anyone who sees the one sees the other as well."[31] This appropriation of the visual model of continuity directly reflected the presentational immediacy found in Jesus' statement that "He who sees me sees the Father."

It is certainly evident that the metaphors "Word of God" and "Light from Light" structured different relationships between human and divine as they were appropriated and deployed in the Trinitarian theologies of Arius and Athanasius. In this process of symbolic appropriation, Word of God became the center of gravity for an Arian symbolism of discontinuity between Father and Son. For Athanasius, however, the symbolic center of gravity was clearly the continuity between Father and Son represented by the visual model of light and its radiance. This tension between verbal and visual models was embodied in the creedal statements that emerged from the controversy. The letter of Eusebius of Caesarea to his church recorded the transactions of the Council of Nicaea. The Council began with the traditional creedal formula they had received in which belief in the Father and the Son was affirmed. Eusebius recorded the familiar words of this creed: "We believe in One God, Father Almighty, the Maker of all things visible and invisible. And in One Lord Jesus Christ, the Word of God, God from God, Light from Light."[32] These symbolic attributes of Jesus, both Word and Light, were included in the creed and accepted as beyond contradiction.

At this point, however, Constantine intervened, according to the account of Eusebius, to suggest the addition of a single word, consubstantial (*homoousios*), into the creed. According to Eusebius, the emperor felt it was necessary to emphasize that the Son was of the same essence as the Father. And, of course, this affirmation implied the anathema of all contrary positions, such as that of Arius, which insisted that the Father and Son were of different substances. The creed was therefore revised to include the notorious *homoousios*. However, in what is both a curious and, for our understanding of the deployment of verbal and visual imagery, a crucial move on the part of the Nicaean bishops, the inclusion of "consubstantial" was accompanied by the exclusion of "the Word of God." The phrase "from the substance of the Father" was substituted for the phrase "Word of God." The revised creed then read: "We believe in one God, the Father, Almighty, Maker of all things visible and invisible. And in One Lord Jesus Christ, the Son of God, begotten of the Father, Only-begotten, that is, from the substance of the Father, God from God, Light from Light."[33] Absolutely no reference to the "Word of God" remained in this revised creed. It is difficult to say whether the elimination of the "Word of God" was a conscious statement in favor of the imagery of light and its radiance or if this was a profound example of a more fundamental precritical appropriation of visual continuity to combat the Arian emphasis on verbal discontinuity. The result, however, was indisputably in favor of the visual continuity between Father and Son defined by "Light from Light." This conflict between verbal and visual imagery was further underscored by Arius's own *Confession of Faith*, in which there was no mention of divine Light and the divine Word featured prominently. Omitting any reference to light and its radiance, Arius declared: "We believe in One God, the Father Almighty; and in the Lord Jesus Christ his only begotten Son, who was begotten of him before all ages, God the Word through whom all things were made."[34] Rather than capitulating to the Nicaean consensus, Arius continued the conflict of Word against Light by remaining within the verbal model of symbolic appropriation and deployment and excluding any reference to the visual model of light in his creed.

Opposing parties in any controversy agree to disagree. There is a common ground, a common universe of discourse in which both contestants meet. The Arian controversy was primarily contested on the grounds of common terminology within a common tradition. The dispute centered on the appropriation and deployment of Christian terminology. Prior to technical terminology, however, was the metaphoric imagery in which it was constructed. The symbols of word and light were given in the oral and written tradition of the church. The opposing parties, however, each adopted different strategies of appropriation. The Arians appropriated the model of verbal discontinuity that had been championed by Paul of Samosata. The Nicaeans appropriated the model of visual continuity, of radiance from light, which had been developed by Tertullian and Origen. These associations were present in the phenomenology of perceptual modes, they were developed historically in the theological tradition, and they were demonstrated in the dominant conceptual terminology of the Arian controversy. The structure of the dispute was informed by the options available for symbolizing the relationship between Father and Son. Although the images of root, fountain, wisdom, power, life, and, of course, sonship were also invoked, the most significant symbolic options were presented by the verbal and visual models of word and light. Rather than embracing both, the contestants appropriated one or the other of those models in order to claim legitimate ownership of a symbolic universe in which both word and light operated. Not coincidence, but conflict between word and light permeated the symbolic discourse of the Arian controversy.

The contest between Arius and Athanasius, therefore, provides a valuable case study in the appropriation of perceptual models, a vivid example of what happens when the appropriation of different perceptual models, and the deployment of perceptual imagery generated by those models, results in a dramatic conflict of symbolic orientation. The conflict may suggest the power and even the primacy of perception itself in the formation of religious discourse. A religious symbol, such as "Son of God" in this case, cannot be conveniently reduced to purely doctrinal or theological content. Symbols participate in more dynamic, visceral, and overdetermined associations, particularly when they are implicated in the precritical symbolic entailments of the body and perception. In the Arian controversy, symbolic associations were predetermined, determined, and overdetermined by the imagery—particularly, perceptual imagery—in which the relation between human beings and the sacred could be articulated. The conflict between visual and verbal models of symbolic articulation at Nicaea reveals how the appropriation, deployment, and conflict of symbols can operate within a single universe of religious discourse.

PART TWO

Augustine and the Augustinian Tradition

3

Symbol

Contrary to etymology, a religious tradition is not that which is handed down, but that which is taken up, the discourse and practices appropriated and operated within a living community. In this way, traditions are always being invented and reinvented. Augustine of Hippo took up the visual and verbal models outlined in the previous chapter—both their potential for conflict, as well as coincidence—in his deployments of the symbols of word and light. Normalizing the terms and conditions for their use, Augustine worked out a symmetrical balance between the visual and the verbal models in his symbolic universe. Nevertheless, Augustine also carefully and consistently distinguished the visual from the verbal as separate perceptual categories. In perception, memory, and ordinary language usage, Augustine noted the separate and distinct operations of seeing and hearing. At crucial moments, however, the visual and verbal fused in the symbolism of synesthesia.

One type of symbolic synesthesia was based on the convergence of sensory metaphors—the merging of seeing, hearing, smelling, tasting, and touching—in a unified experience of the sacred. But a second and more radical type of synesthesia involved a crossmodal transfer from seeing to hearing or hearing to seeing that represented a dramatic breakthrough in discourse and experience of the sacred. As we have noted, the synesthetic convergence of the visual and auditory was prominent in the structure of Christian myth, in the most important manifestations of the sacred within the tradition. Augustine took up the discourse of synesthesia and deployed it at crucial points in his own symbolic universe. Since the sacred was simultaneously verbal and visual, both word and light, Augustine suggested that discourse, practice, and experience in relation to the sacred might embody a synesthetic quality. As we will see, Augustine deployed the discursive strategy of symbolic synesthesia in his descriptions of the religious experience of the human heart in which hearing was seeing and seeing was hearing; in the structure of his autobiographical narrative and conversion in the *Confessions;* and in his definition of Christian sacramental ritual (including the ritual practice of learning) as "visible words." In all these cases, visual and verbal models were distinguished only to be fused in the strategy of symbolic synesthesia as Augustine worked out a perceptual symbolism of the sacred.

We should not make the mistake, however, of assuming that Augustine occupied a single, consistent, uniform symbolic universe during the entire course of his career. It is common to distinguish between early and later periods. R. A. Markus, for example, noted that in his early work, the Cassiciacum dialogues composed in philosophical retirement after his conversion, Augustine was primarily concerned with spatial symbolism: Augustine distinguished between "higher" and "lower" levels of reality, associating the spiritual with the higher and the carnal with the lower. In his later work, as bishop of the small Christian community of Hippo in North Africa, Augustine's concerns were predominantly temporal in his distinction between "old" and "new" that associated the carnal with the old and the spiritual with the new, regenerated individual or the new city of God unfolding in human history.[1] For our interests, however, we might note that Augustine's spatial concerns in his earlier work were to a certain extent predetermined by his central preoccupation with the problematic of illumination, while the temporal concerns of the later period were related to the verbal, aural, or auditory symbolism of the ineluctable, mysterious call of election in his understanding of predestination. At either extreme of his career, therefore, we find Augustine working out the implications of the visual model of illumination or the verbal model of the divine call of election in predestination. While recognizing these extremes, we may nevertheless notice a consistent range of visual and verbal associations—and a symmetrical balance of those associations— that occupied the midpoint of Augustine's career and the center of his symbolic universe. At its center, Augustine's symbolic universe was organized by the balance and fusion of word and light.

Later Augustinian tradition also developed the symbolic entailments of the visual and verbal models. In the monastery of Quito a sixteenth-century wall painting entitled "Augustine ascends to heaven" depicts a flying Augustine moving through the heavenly spheres toward the divine light. The whole scene is bathed in a unifying supernal glow as the form of Augustine merges into the divine illumination. In the Augustinian monastery of Neustift another scene is depicted, Augustine's dramatic conversion experience in the garden of Milan—"The revelation, *tolle lege*"—in which Augustine is prostrated in supplication and surrender before the divine and mysterious words from an unknown source that descend upon him and strike him to the ground with the supreme force of their authority. Rather than rising in the light, Augustine is struck down by the impact of the word.[2] Visual and verbal—these symbolic, metaphoric resources were appropriated by Augustine, normalized in their implications for religious discourse, practice, and experience, and subsequently reappropriated throughout the later Augustinian tradition. Not only a theological tradition, the Augustinian tradition was a history that consisted in appropriations and deployments of the symbolic configurations of word and light that had assumed a particular normative pattern in the work of Augustine.

PERCEPTION, MEMORY, LANGUAGE

The tenth book of Augustine's *Confessions* closed the narrative of his conversion and baptism, not with the triumphant victory song of the Christian hero but with an intensely personal introspective journey through the life of the senses, the memory, and the heart. Augustine outlined the temptations of the senses, the dimensions of the human memory, and the still-unfulfilled longings of the heart in a kind of meditative self-diagnosis. In the words of Peter Brown, it was the "self-portrait of a convalescent."[3] Augustine may have been healed through the sacraments of the church and the hand of God upon his heart, yet he remained subject to temptation, uncertainty, and desire in a lifelong process of gradual recovery. Augustine explained that this journey of self-discovery was motivated by his intense love of God. He represented his dramatic experience of a divine presence in his life as a light shining upon him and a word striking him, illuminating him with knowledge and impelling him to love. Augustine discerned a connection between self-knowledge and his new knowledge of God, "because what I know of myself," he observed, "I know by means of your light shining upon me." The light of illumination combined with a sense of devotion that Augustine described as resulting from the activity of the divine word: "You struck my heart with your word and I love you" (X.6).[4] Invoking the divine light and the divine word, Augustine began his investigations in the tenth book of his *Confessions* into what he might discover about himself in relation to his new awareness of God.

Augustine first examined his senses. He understood the power of sensory perception to be ordered by God in such a way that each sense had its distinctive and separate function. "The Lord created this power in me," Augustine noted, "commanding the eye not to hear and the ear not to see, but giving me the eye to see by and the ear to hear by" (X.7). On the level of sensory perception, hearing and seeing, as well as the other senses, were found to have diverse and clearly distinguishable functions, each governing a different domain of sensory experience. Together they contributed to the identity and awareness of a single soul, but nevertheless each sense had been assigned its own place in the human sensorium.

Augustine next examined his memory. Deciding that he must go beyond the level of sensory perception, which humans shared with "horses and mules," Augustine entered the "fields and spacious palaces of memory, where lie the treasures of innumerable images of all kinds of things with which our senses have been in contact" (X.8). Like perception, memory preserved the content of each of the five senses in separate categories according to the sense organ through which they had entered the memory. "Here are kept distinct and in their proper classification," Augustine discovered, "all sensations which come to us, each by its own route" (X.8). The data of the senses were preserved in separate compartments in the vast storehouse of memory. Light, colors, and shapes of bodies that had entered through the eyes did not flow into all the different kinds of sounds that had entered through the ears. Sight, hearing, smell, taste, and touch remained separated in the great harbor of memory, as the perceptual experiences admitted through each of these different channels were stored and ready for recall.

Not only were the senses separate in perception and memory, but ordinary language usage also maintained a definite order in talking about sensory experience. "We do not say," Augustine reminded us, " 'Hear how it flashes,' or 'Smell how bright it is,' or 'Taste how it shines,' or 'Feel how it glows' " (X.35). This interpenetration of sensory categories would violate the ordered structure of perception and the basic perceptual logic of ordinary language. Augustine did point out that terms from vision may be conventionally used to describe the process of knowing in general, but, in ordinary language, to say that we see voices or hear colors would be nonsense.

In his analysis of perception, memory, and language in Book Ten of the *Confessions*, therefore, Augustine ruled out the possibility of the transsensory phenomenon we have been calling synesthesia. Synesthesia did not occur in sensory perception because God had ordered the eyes so they did not hear and the ears so they did not see; it did not occur in memory because perceptual contents were preserved in separate categories determined by the sense through which they were admitted; and it did not occur in ordinary language because speakers maintained strict distinctions among the senses so that the appropriate objects of perception corresponded to each sense organ. Therefore, Augustine concluded that perception, memory, and ordinary language did not allow for the synesthetic transfer across sensory modes.

In symbolizing his experience of the sacred, however, Augustine's language broke into the radical perceptual transfer of symbolic synesthesia. Having established that the senses were separate in perception, memory, and ordinary language, Augustine demonstrated that they merged at certain points in religious discourse. In special instances of religious discourse—in the curious imagery of lights that are heard or divine words that are seen—the senses interpenetrated in the imagery of symbolic synesthesia. When Augustine summarized the introspective journey taken in Book Ten of the *Confessions,* he noted that his path led toward truth, but, paradoxically, the truth that he sought had been walking beside him all along. Truth was a transcendent goal; yet at the same time it was already present. Augustine symbolized this paradoxical notion of truth—distant, yet present—in the imagery of intermodal sensory transfer. Truth was a light that is heard: "You are the permanent and abiding light which I consulted in all these things, asking whether they are, what they are, and what they are worth. And I heard you teaching me and commanding me" (X.40). Throughout Augustine's writings, truth wore a mysterious aura. In the *De trinitate,* for example, Augustine encouraged his readers to remain in the twinkling of light they might experience when they heard the word *truth* spoken, rather than allow any finite limitations to be placed on that truth.[5] At the beginning of Book Ten of the *Confessions,* Augustine observed with the Gospel of John that "the man of truth comes to the light" (X.1). When Augustine came to the light he heard its teachings and commandments. The light of truth was already present, yet at the same time it was a voice that spoke, taught, and commanded from a transcendent position over against the seeker after truth. The light spoke, the voice illumined, as Augustine symbolized this sacred truth in synesthetic terms.

This language of a light that is heard might seem to be merely a casual category mistake in Augustine's meditations on truth. Perhaps it was nothing more than a careless mixed metaphor. But this instance of the convergence and interpenetration of seeing and hearing was part of a larger context of perceptual imagery in Augustine's discourse. Often Augustine had recourse to a type of symbolic synesthesia in which two or more sensory modes converged in a single perceptual experience. In his *De libero arbitrio,* for example, Augustine undertook an exploration of the senses that was similar in many respects to Book Ten of the *Confessions,* particularly in its goal, the experience of a sacred truth.[6] Again, Augustine began by asserting that each sense organ had its proper object of perception (II.3.23). Each organ of sense, then, referred its distinctive perceptual data to an "inner sense" (II.3.24). This "common sense" was responsible for an immediate evaluation of sensory data. "By means of the inner sense," Augustine observed, "corporeal objects are perceived through the senses of the body, and the senses of the body are perceived by the inner sense" (II.4.41). This faculty, which was shared alike by animals and humans, weighed and balanced the information provided by the sense organs and responded to that input in terms of either attraction or avoidance.

What distinguished the perceptual experience of humans from that of animals, however, was the human capacity for reason. Only at the level of reason, by which all things were distinguished and defined, was the separate and distinct order of the senses discerned. According to Augustine, "Whatever we know, we grasp and hold it by reason. Moreover, we know that we cannot perceive colors with our hearing or voices with our eyes, to say nothing of the other senses" (II.3.29-30). Reason distinguished and defined the separate orders of sensory perception. Humans were different than animals in at least this one respect: They had the rational ability to identify the separate senses and to distinguish their separate functions. When we are aware of this rational order, "we know it neither by the eyes, nor by the ears, nor by the inner sense which beasts do not lack. We must not believe that beasts know that light is not perceived by the ears nor a voice by the eyes, for we perceive this only by rational thought and reflection within the soul" (II.3.29-30). At levels of perception beneath reason, Augustine suggested, the several senses were not distinguished from each other. Animals had eyes, ears, and common sense, but no awareness that they did not hear with their eyes or see with their ears. Only reason identified the separate and distinct operations of the senses.

But did Augustine think that there was something above reason? Augustine was determined in *De libero arbitrio* to demonstrate the existence of God by answering this question: "Therefore, whether there is something superior or not, it will be proven that God exists, when, as I promised, I show with God's aid that there is something superior to reason" (II.6.57). For Augustine, this "something" was again an experience of a sacred truth. That which was higher than eyes, ears, common sense, and reason was truth itself. Truth was beyond the outer senses, beyond the inner sense, and beyond the reason that distinguished between the senses. However, Augustine deployed the imagery of sensory experience, a convergence of all the senses, in his praise of this sacred truth:

> Do we doubt that we are happy in the embrace of truth? . . . Shall we deny that we are happy when we are given the food and drink of truth? . . . Do we hesitate to say we are happy when we breathe the truth? . . . Do we ask for any other happy life, when, so to speak, the silent eloquence of truth glides noiselessly into our minds? . . . Are we afraid to place the happy life in the light of truth? (II.13.138-40)

Beyond the corporeal senses, beyond reason that distinguished and separated the senses, this sacred truth was represented by Augustine in a metaphoric convergence of all the senses. Augustine declared that it was truth itself that was embraced, eaten, smelled, heard, and seen in the happy life of the highest good. Again, this may all be a careless mixture of metaphors, figures of speech, all "so to speak," and, therefore, not to be taken too seriously. However, it may help to recall that Augustine thus combined the senses in his *Confessions* to represent his love of God: "I do love a kind of light, melody, fragrance, food, embracement when I love my God" (X.6). Both divine love and sacred truth were symbolized as a unified experience by means of the metaphoric convergence of all the senses. That metaphoric convergence might have been a figure of speech, but it was also a symbolic strategy for representing an intense, transcendent, and unified experience of the sacred.

Augustine wove imagery from all the senses into his symbolic description of truth. But he maintained that "the objects that we touch, taste and smell are less like truth than the things we see and hear" (II.14.147). The objects of seeing and hearing provided more valid analogies for truth because they could be perceived in common, they could be perceived in their entirety, and they could be perceived as much by one person as another (II.14.147). Augustine noted that such was not the case with the other senses. In taste and smell perceivers alter the objects of perception by consuming them; therefore, food and fragrance are relatively mutable and unstable elements from which to draw analogies for unchanging truth. In the sense of touch perceivers cannot experience the object of perception in its entirety, but only in part; and two persons cannot share the same tactile experience simultaneously. For these reasons, Augustine dismissed taste, smell, and touch as fully adequate models for the experience of sacred truth. The analogy of truth with the processes of seeing and hearing, however, was fundamental to Augustine's representation of truth's universality, wholeness, and perfection. "The objects which we perceive in common by means of the eyes and ears — colors and sounds, for example, which you and I can see and hear at the same time — these objects do not belong to the nature of the eyes or ears, but are common for both of us to perceive" (II.12.131). Although Augustine deployed all the senses to symbolize that sacred truth above reason, he regarded sight and hearing as the closest models for the experience of truth. Ultimately, Augustine decided that the truth beyond reason that demonstrated the existence of God was better symbolized by the models of seeing and hearing and perhaps best symbolized by their fusion in symbolic synesthesia.

At other times, Augustine's meditations upon truth took the form of a more radical type of synesthesia in which sensory modes not only converged but actually transferred across modes. In his commentary on the Gospel of John (*Tractatus in Ioannem evangelium*), for example, Augustine symbolized the highest, most sacred truth in terms of a synesthetic fusion of hearing and seeing.[7] Again, Augustine asserted that we "who see in one way, and hear in another way" have diverse senses with distinctive functions. In human beings the senses were kept separate and distinct. But was that the case for the Son of God? "If the Son hears and sees," Augustine asked, "are we yet to search for eyes and ears in him in separate places?" (XVIII.10). Augustine could have replied to his own question by saying that the Son of God did not have eyes and ears, that the Son was somehow beyond seeing and hearing. But he did not. Characteristically, Augustine attempted to symbolize a sacred truth that was beyond sensory experience and beyond ordinary language by means of symbolic imagery that violated both. Augustine was certain that the Son of God transcended the finite limitations of sensory experience. Nevertheless, he described the Son of God in terms of sensory processes, but only in terms of a sensory configuration that broke through the limitations of ordinary experience and ordinary language.

Augustine found this sensory configuration in the highly charged, extraordinary, and unifying imagery of synesthesia. Augustine asked: "Cannot His ear do what His eye does; and cannot His eye do what His ear can? Or is He not all sight, all hearing?" His answer was a dramatic deployment of synesthesia as a rich source of imagery for symbolizing the Son of God: "That seeing of His, and that hearing of His, is in a way far other than it is with us. Both to see and to hear exist together in the Word: seeing and hearing are not diverse things in Him; but hearing is sight, and sight is hearing" (XVIII.9). It is difficult to tell how Augustine's formula—hearing is sight, sight is hearing—would have been received at Nicaea. He certainly departed from the exclusive appropriation of either the visual or the verbal model that had characterized the Arian-Athanasian controversy over the symbolization of the Son of God. In Augustine's formula, the Son of God was both hearing and seeing. These perceptual models were not only interpenetrating functions but also central ingredients in the very being of the Son of God. According to Augustine, "To hear is to Him the same thing as 'to be,' and to see is to Him the same thing as 'to be' " (XVIII.10). Augustine symbolized the essential being of the Son of God as a synesthetic fusion of sight and hearing.

Not only was the being of the Son of God defined by the symbolic synesthesia of hearing and seeing but His essence was simultaneously auditory and visual: word and light. Any human experience of the Son of God had to include a synesthetic element in order to correlate with this identification of hearing and seeing, word and light in the divine being. According to Augustine, this synesthetic correlation occurred in the human heart. The importance of the heart in Augustine's thought, as the central locus of interaction between human and divine, is obvious in the *Confessions*, as his heart was stirred, awakened, even "massaged and set" by the hand of God. In iconography Augustine is often depicted holding a heart pierced by an arrow. In the discussion of the heart in his commentary on the Gospel of John, Augustine identified it as the place in which the senses converged in direct correspondence to the fusion of visual and auditory categories in the Son of God. "In the flesh, you hear in one place, see in another," Augustine said, "in your heart, where you see, there you hear" (XVIII.10). This experience of synesthesia in the human heart corresponded directly to the interpenetration of seeing and hearing that defined the essential being of the Son of God. Augustine symbolized the possibility of communion between the heart and the Son of God by insisting that both shared this remarkable characteristic: In both, seeing was hearing and hearing was seeing. In his analysis of the human heart and the Son of God, Augustine's religious discourse incorporated the radical interpenetration of sensory modes, the strategy of symbolic synesthesia.

VISUAL AND VERBAL MODELS

The convergence and interpenetration of the visual mode and the verbal, aural, or auditory mode was not merely an antistructural breakthrough in discourse, but also a merger of the structural oppositions that Augustine associated with sight and hearing. To appreciate the

significance of the fusion of sight and hearing in symbolic synesthesia
it is necessary to examine Augustine's detailed analysis of the workings
of eyes and ears and their elaboration into consistent perceptual models.
As we noticed in the work of Philo, Augustine deployed those perceptual models as symbolic models for organizing different relationships
between human beings and the sacred. Augustine analyzed the operations of the eyes and ears, assimilated those senses into his understanding of the human mind, and then developed sight and hearing
into symbolic models for the relations between human beings and a
divine reality that was word and light. In other words, Augustine
derived metaphors from the eyes and ears that he deployed in symbolizing the continuity and discontinuity between the mind and God.
In this section, I would like to outline the way in which Augustine
developed distinctive visual and verbal symbolic models.

As we saw in *De libero arbitrio,* Augustine found that the eye and
ear provided suitable models for human cognition that transcended
the level of sensory perception and gained access to a sacred truth that
was symbolized by visual and aural models. It seems to be the case
that there was a greater sensitivity in the ancient world to the symbolic
significance of sensory metaphors and models. For example, the sensory
model that defined the mind as the "eye of the soul" showed greater
sensitivity to perception than later models that represented the mind
as a clock, a machine, a telephone switchboard, or a computer. But I
am not interested in merely clarifying Augustine's modeling of the
mind. I am primarily concerned with the way in which Augustine
deployed visual and verbal models to symbolize the relations between
human and divine. In the Christian tradition, those relations have been
structured in a variety of ways. Discussing metaphors and models in
religious discourse, Ian Barbour noted four traditional models for the
relationship between human and divine. God's relation to the world
has been variously symbolized as that of a king to his kingdom, a
clockmaker to a clock, a person to another person, and an agent to his
actions.[8] Each symbolic model implied a different kind of interaction
between God and the world. I suggest that Augustine's most important
symbolic models for defining the relationship between God and the
world were located in the configurations of sensory perception. Augustine organized the relations between human and divine in terms of
models related to the perceptual processes of seeing and hearing, both
their separate operations and their possible combinations. The way
Augustine understood the processes of seeing and hearing contributed
to the formation of visual and verbal models. Even the symbols of
word and light participated in these larger patterns of visual and verbal

metaphoric imagery that were derived from sensory perception. Within Augustine's perceptual models, word and light defined different modes of relationship between human beings and the sacred.

Augustine's *De trinitate* contains his most fully developed analysis of the relations between sensory processes and the sacred. There he spelled out the visual and verbal models that defined different relationships between human and divine. In Book Two, Augustine proposed to refer to the testimony of the eyes, because they surpassed the rest of the senses. The operation of the eyes provided an adequate analogy—"nearer to the sight of the mind"—for the mind's access to truth (XI.1.1). An examination of vision revealed a three-fold operation: (1) "the object itself which we see," (2) "vision, or the act of seeing," and (3) "the attention of the mind." These three elements came into conjunction in the visual process. The object of vision—a stone, a flame, or any other thing seen by the eye—existed independently of the act of seeing. But this act of seeing defined what Augustine described as a union between the eye and the object. The second element in the visual process, therefore, was not merely the perceiver's sense organ; it was the act in which an object was present to sensory perception. This union between organ and object in the act of vision was described by Augustine in terms of similarity and continuity. The visible object "produces the form, which is, as it were, its own likeness, which comes to be in the sense, when we perceive anything by seeing" (XI.2.3). Augustine employed similes to represent this likeness of the object in the eye: It was like the image of a ring imprinted in wax, or like the trace of an object in water which is impressed in it for as long as the object remains in the water. By this imagery, Augustine understood an intimate formal union in vision, a union in which the objective form of an external body was indistinguishable from the form produced in sense. Augustine emphasized union between object and perceived form in vision: "We do not distinguish, through the same sense, the form produced by it in the sense of him who sees, since the union of the two is so close that there is no room for distinguishing them" (XI.2.3). In order to maintain this visual union a third element was necessary: the attention of mind. Attention was "that which keeps the sense of the eye in the object seen, so long as it is seen" (XI.2.2). The visual process consisted not only in the perceived object and the perceiving sense, but also in an act of will, in the attention of the mind that "keeps the sense in the thing which we see and connects both" (XI.2.2). For Augustine, therefore, vision was a trinity, a *vestigium trinitatis*, of identifiable, yet integral constituent elements. On the level of external vision, the visual model clearly embodied imagery of similitude, likeness, connection, and union between seer and seen. Like Father, Son, and Spirit, "the body that is seen, and vision itself, and the attention of the mind which joins both together," constituted a Trinitarian pattern of integrated operation and cooperation in the visual model.

The trinity of external vision set the pattern for Augustine's understanding of internal vision. Augustine's general psychology was comprised of the basic components of memory, inner vision, and will. A similar formal union occurred between the eye of the mind and the contents of memory. "In place of the vision which was outward when the sense was informed through the sensible body," Augustine held, "there comes a similar vision within, while the eye of the mind is informed from that which memory retains" (XI.3.6). The vision of thought was an intimate conjunction between the inner eye and recollections retained in memory. There was such a close union in this conjunction that it was difficult to distinguish between inner vision and memory. They were distinct, but inseparable. "The conjunction of both," Augustine noted, "that is, of that which memory retains, and of that which is thence expressed so as to inform the eye of him who recollects, makes them appear as if they were one, because they are exceedingly like" (XI.3.6). Finally, the attention of the will performed a similar function in inner vision as it performed in outer vision: Attention was the connecting link that joined objects of memory and the vision of thought. The eye of the mind—like the eye of the body—was connected to its objects by the continuous attention and intention of the will.

Therefore, Augustine outlined the visual model as a carefully patterned analogy between the eye and the mind. The objective body in space was analogous to the recollected object in memory. The eye of the body, illumined by corporeal light and informed by the sense object in the act of vision, was analogous to the eye of the mind that was illumined by a certain incorporeal light and informed by the objects of memory in every act of thought. Finally, both seeing and this visual model of thought depended upon an analogous unifying act of will. In the visual model, the will established a continuous and unified relationship between subject and object. Augustine explained:

> What the intention of the will is towards a body seen and the vision to be combined with it, in order that a certain unity of three things may therein take place, although their nature is diverse, that the same intention of the will is towards combining the image of the body which is in memory, and the vision of the thinker . . . in order that here too a certain unity may take place of three things, not now distinguished by a diversity of nature, but of one and the same substance. (XI.4.7)

The consubstantial nature of vision, in the union of subject and object, was common to the eye and the mind. On both levels Augustine noted a conjunction of seer and seen based on the integration of three constituent elements in a unified relationship.

When Augustine proceeded to a third level of the visual model, the relation between human consciousness and the sacred, he observed that the three components not only persisted, but, as God became the object of contemplative vision, the human seer became the image of God. "Not only a trinity may be found," Augustine declared, "but also an image of God, in that alone which belongs to the contemplation of eternal things" (XII.4.4). The Trinitarian pattern consisted in the sense-object, vision, and attention on the physical level, while it consisted in memory, inner vision, and will on the psychological level. As the human mind was directed toward eternal reality, however, the object of vision became God, the act of vision became contemplation, and the unifying force that held them together was the love of God. This trinity was not merely a vestige of the divine pattern, but according to Augustine it was the very image of God. Augustine transposed the union between seer and seen that he observed in ordinary vision to the contemplative vision of God. In contemplation, the human soul was identified with the divine. "When as a whole it contemplates the truth," Augustine insisted, "it is the image of God" (XII.7.10). Contemplative vision, as a union between seer and seen, was a common theme in Augustine's early writings. In the *Soliloquiae*, for example, Augustine observed that a visual assimilation of seer with seen occurred in the contemplative "gaze of the soul" toward the divine. "Such looking," he said, "is followed by the vision of God himself." In ordinary vision, Augustine understood a union between the sense object and the organ of sight. In this contemplative or intellectual vision, therefore, he noted an analogous union of seer and seen: "In this intellectual vision is that which is in the soul a conjunction of seer and seen: as seeing with the eyes results from the conjunction of the sense of sight and the sensible object" (I.6.13). Returning to the *De trinitate*, Augustine saw the supreme transformation of human being as a transformation in seeing. Based on the scriptural authority of 1 John 3:2, Augustine concluded that humans become divine at the point that they see the divine: "We know that, when He shall appear, we shall be like Him; for we shall see Him as He is" (XII.14.22). The visual model—on the physical, psychological, and contemplative levels—defined a continuous and even unifying relationship between subject and object. At its highest level, the visual model promised a conjunction between seer and seen that would reveal a continuity, likeness, and perhaps union with God.

The verbal model, on the other hand, was an entirely different matter. Augustine noted that words that vibrated the air and were lost in the sequential flow of time bore no likeness to the reality they tried to represent. Words had no ability to present, but only to represent. The power of signification in words was not presentational, but referential. Words mediated between the knower and the known but had no ability to present immediately the one to the other. The word might be known to the ear, Augustine noted, but the thing to which it referred could only be known by the eye. For example: "When the bisyllabic word *mundus* is uttered, then something that is certainly corporeal, for it is a sound, has become known through the body, that is, through the ear. But that which it means has become known through the body, that is, through the eyes of the flesh. For so far as the world is known to us at all, it is known through sight" (XIII.1.4). The verbal model cannot be ignored in our discussion of Augustine's theory of knowledge because (as we will see in Chapter 5) it was an integral part of his analysis of the process of learning. Clearly, the verbal model generated a range of differences, disjunctions, and discontinuities that were in tension with the visual model. A complete analysis of Augustine's theory of knowledge must appreciate both the visual and the verbal models in which it was formulated. The word of human speech and hearing was an outward sign that referred by way of representation to some content of knowledge. But that content itself could only be accessed by sight. By merely indicating the absent object, this referentiality of human speech and hearing contrasted with the presentational immediacy of vision.

Throughout his career, and most forcefully in the *De trinitate*, Augustine was quick to reject the words heard by the ears that could only refer to what was more intimately known by the eyes. In a formula that he had developed in more detail in his *De magistro*, Augustine declared that "the word that sounds outwardly is the sign of the word that gives light inwardly" (XV.11.20). Certainly, Augustine found that the intellectual process of the mind was more adequately described in terms of the light of the eyes than the sounds of the ears. Likewise, in seeking to understand the divine and eternal word of God, Augustine found it fundamentally different than human words. "Whoever desires to arrive at any likeness, be it of what sort it may, of the Word of God," Augustine observed, "must not regard the word of ours that sounds in the ears, either when it is uttered in an articulate sound or when it is silently thought" (XV.11.20). Neither was a likeness to the word of

God to be found in the words of prophecy, "spoken to this or that prophet," nor in the words of faith "that cometh by hearing," nor in the words of scripture. The divine word was not adequately represented in terms of any of these verbal forms. Nevertheless, a kind of eternal, transcendent speaking operated in the eternal "Word of God." As Augustine noted, it was the word of creation of which the scriptures said, "All things were made by Him." It was the incarnate word, of which the scriptures said, "The Word became flesh." And it was the word of wisdom, of which the scriptures said, "The Word of God on high is the fountain of wisdom." This transcendent word—eternal, creative, incarnate, and illuminating—could not be understood in terms of external, human words that were heard by the ears. "We must pass by this," Augustine advised, "in order to arrive at that word of man, by likeness of which, be it of what sort it may, the Word of God may be somehow seen as in an enigma" (XV.11.20). That human word which provided a model for understanding the divine word was the inner word, "the word that gives light inwardly." The inner word, "which is neither utterable in sound, nor capable of being thought under the likeness of sound," approximated as nearly as possible the divine word.

The words of human voice, speech, and hearing were inadequate to the divine word; but that discontinuity was already built into Augustine's understanding of the difference between seeing and hearing: One presented reality, while the other merely referred to an absent reality. To present the reality of the divine word, Augustine had to resort to the visual model. The inner word assumed a visual quality. Augustine noted a greater similarity between our inner word, "which has neither sound nor thought of sound," and the word of God, than between our outer, spoken words, which reverberated in the air and passed away in time, and the divine word. The analogy between the human inner word and the divine word was based on the fact that this inner word was comprised "of that thing in seeing which we speak inwardly" (XV.14.23).

Despite this approximate similarity, however, a fundamental discontinuity remained. The word remained the symbol of discontinuity. Augustine declared: "How great is the unlikeness between our word and the Divine Word" (XV.14.23). He observed an immeasurable gap between human beings and God that was embodied in the discontinuity between human words and the word of God. "Our knowledge is unlike the knowledge of God," Augustine remarked, "so our word also, which is from our knowledge, is unlike that Word of God which is born of the essence of the Father" (XV.15.22). Augustine explained this difference by means of three distinctions: First, human words were false when humans were deceived or when they lied. The word of God, however, was truth itself. It could not lie. It was "sight of sight, knowledge of knowledge" (XV.11.20). Second, human words were not eternal. Only God spoke a word that was coeternal with himself. Again, the divine word embodied a characteristic associated with the visual category, simultaneous copresence. In Book Eleven of the *Confessions*, Augustine observed that "the present time of things present is sight" (XI.20). In *De trinitate*, he explained the eternal presence of the word of God in terms of sight: God knows neither past nor future, but "sees all things simultaneously" (XV.14.23). Third, human words were formed, but the divine word was form, the image of God. "Who could not see," Augustine asked, "how great would be the unlikeness between it and the Word of God, which is so in the form of God" (XV.15.25).

Dependent upon the formative agency of God, the internal human word was different than the divine word because it was formed. In fact, Augustine suggested, this was the ultimate point of difference between human and divine. Even in the most intimate union between humans and God there remained a fundamental difference. In union with God, the human word may become true. "At that time," Augustine promised, "our word will not indeed be false, because we shall neither lie nor be deceived." The human word may no longer be subject to temporal limitations. Therefore, human knowledge would be like the knowledge of God to the extent that "we shall see all our knowledge at once, at one glance." But a fundamental discontinuity remained: Because the human word had been formed by the agency of the divine word, even in the most intimate identification between human and divine, Augustine explained, "our word is never to be equalled to the Divine Word, not even when we shall be like God" (XV.16.25). The likeness suggested by the visual model confronted an unassimilable difference. Not even when the visual model suggested an integral union between seer and seen would the symbolism of the verbal model relinquish the inevitable discontinuity between human and divine. Augustine concluded: "Wherefore, since we have found this enigma (i.e., the inner word) so great an unlikeness to God and the Word of God, wherein yet there was found before some likeness, this, too, must be admitted, that even when we shall be like Him, when 'we shall see Him as He is' . . . not even then shall we be equal to Him in nature" (XV.16.26).

In Augustine's symbolic universe, light was identity, word was difference. Light was continuity, word was discontinuity. These associations, as well as others we have noted, resulted from Augustine's detailed elaboration of the perceptual models in which the symbols of word and light participated. The different symbolic associations that attended word and light were informed by the contrasting characters of the verbal and visual models. In turn, those models were in consonance with the qualitatively different functions that Augustine attributed to eye and ear. In this way, Augustine's symbolization of word and light, divine voice and illumination, was grounded in sensory perception and the differentiated visual and verbal symbolic models that Augustine derived from his analysis of the sensory processes of sight and hearing. As we found in the religious discourse of Philo, the visual and verbal models provided Augustine with a symbolic vocabulary for affirming both continuity and discontinuity in the relation between human beings and the sacred. In addition, like Philo, Augustine frequently fused those structural oppositions in the discursive imagery of symbolic synesthesia.

SEEING, HEARING, SYNESTHESIA

Augustine was certainly conversant with the standard Greek scientific speculations regarding the senses of seeing and hearing. He understood sight in terms of the theory of the visual ray, a perceptual process initiated by the eye that extended its stick-like projections to immediately contact visible objects of perception.[9] By contrast, he understood that hearing was initiated by the external agency of some object that struck the air and caused the air to register that shock on the ear. Origen had noted that this was the consensus on hearing in the standard "text-books on sound" in the ancient world; Augustine adopted it into his understanding of the sense of hearing.[10] Therefore, Augustine had available the differentiated range of associations in Greek science for the perceptual processes of seeing and hearing and he drew upon and elaborated those associations in his religious discourse. As we have seen, Augustine's understanding of the relation between human and divine was organized in terms of symbolic associations derived from hearing and seeing, sound and sight, word and light.

In addition, Augustine was conversant with Origen's doctrine of the interior senses. As Origen explained: "The organs of the soul are designated by the same words as the corporeal organs and have analogous functions."[11] Reference to interior senses became a metaphoric convention in Greek Christian discourse. Macarius proposed that "this is a thing that everyone ought to know—that we have eyes within, deeper than these eyes; and a hearing deeper than this hearing."[12] Examples of this rhetorical convention could certainly be multiplied. As we have seen in his *Confessions*, Augustine also had recourse to the metaphors of the interior senses that perceived the "light, melody, fragrance, food, and embracement" that symbolized an intense, extraordinary, and unified apprehension of God. This convergence of all the senses in the interior apprehension of God was also a literary convention. For example, Origen held that the interior senses merged into what he called the "generic divine sense." Origen symbolized that generic divine sense as if it were comprised of the inner correlates of all the human senses and as if all the interior senses were modes of one generic sense. Origen explained:

> There are many forms of this sense: a sight which can see things superior to corporeal beings, the cherubim or seraphim being obvious instances, and a hearing which can receive impressions of sounds that have no objective existence in the air, and a taste which feeds on living bread that has come down from heaven and gives life to the world (Jn 6:33). So also there is a sense of smell which smells spiritual things, as Paul speaks of "a sweet savour of Christ unto God" (2 Cor 2:15), and a sense of touch in accordance with which John says that he has handled with his hands "of the Word of Life." (1 Jn 1:1)[13]

Origen's explanation of the interior, generic divine sense was certainly stylized and self-consciously literary. Nevertheless, Origen made a point about the interior senses that would also be important to Augustine: The five interior senses merged into a unified, generic, divine sense. That unified interior sensibility was symbolized by a synesthetic convergence of all the sensory modes.

Perhaps the quickest way from sense to non-sense was provided by the metaphoric resources of synesthesia. Symbolic synesthesia enabled religious discourse to describe experiences that were as real as sensory perception but (as we have noted) more intense, extraordinary, and unified than any ordinary experience. Augustine carefully separated the senses in perception, memory, and ordinary language, but he described their fusion in the apprehension of truth, the love of God, and the Son of God. All these things were obviously beyond sense. But symbolic synesthesia offered a vocabulary for fashioning a discourse through sensory metaphors that might in some measure embody experiences that were beyond sense. Augustine found exemplary models for symbolic synesthesia in the religious experiences of Moses and Paul. Both experienced some non-sense reality that could only be described in the synesthetic terms of the fusion of the senses.

In the remarkable twelfth book of his *De Genesi ad litteram*, Augustine discussed the mystical experiences of Moses and Paul in communion with the divine. Here Augustine distinguished among three kinds of vision: (1) *per oculos*, the corporeal vision of the eyes that could behold the physical bodies of the heavens and the earth; (2) *per spiritum hominis*, the spiritual vision of the imagination that could behold the images of corporeal bodies when they were not immediately present to sense; and, finally, (3) *per contuitum mentis*, the intellectual vision that could immediately behold universal essences such as wisdom or justice, and could also behold transcendental realities of the soul or God not by means of images but directly. Corporeal vision was directed toward *corpora*, or visible bodies. Spiritual vision was directed toward *enigmas*, or images. And intellectual vision was directed toward *species*, variously translated as "essence" or "sight." Augustine's distinction between *enigmas* and *species* was important. *Enigmas* were images that appeared in such spiritual visions as those of Ezekiel (Ez 37:1), Isaiah (Is 6:2), Peter (Acts 10:11), and John in the Book of Revelation. Those visionary experiences all involved some appearance of the images of corporeal objects. They were flights of imagination that were nevertheless limited to the appearance of visual images to the spiritual sight of the visionary. In that respect, spiritual visions were not like the intellectual visions of Moses and Paul. As the archetypes of that highest level of intellectual vision, the experiences of Moses and Paul involved a type of seeing that beheld the divine voice, speech, or words. Intellectual vision did not involve enigmatic images, but saw directly the *species*, the essence or sight of a higher reality. But the intellectual visions of Moses and Paul were visions of words that were beyond sight or sound. Intellectual vision, therefore, was synesthetic: Moses achieved that intellectual vision in his colloquy with God when they spoke face to face, or, literally, "mouth to mouth" (Nm 12:8), while Paul achieved that vision in his ecstatic ascent to the third heaven where he heard ineffable words that human beings were not permitted to speak (2 Cor 12:4). Both visions, therefore, were mysterious types of visionary hearing.

Augustine explained that in those intellectual visions God was not disclosed by images but by a direct intuitive vision of reality. God was not known by *enigma* but by *species*. "In that species whereby He is God," Augustine maintained, "He speaks beyond all words more secretly and immediately by an ineffable speech" (XII.27.55). In that vision, God speaks. The speech of God is not heard, but seen. In the intellectual vision beheld by Moses, Augustine observed, God spoke, not in "dark speeches," but "mouth to mouth." In his intellectual vision, Paul heard words beyond words that were seen rather than heard. Paul ascended through the first heaven of corporeal vision where he saw all that existed above the waters and the earth; he proceeded through the second heaven where he saw spiritual visions under the figures of corporeal images; but in the third heaven seeing coalesced with hearing as Paul saw ineffable words not given to human beings to speak. Carried by ecstatic rapture to the third heaven, where eternal essences were apprehended by a mind separated and cleansed from the carnal senses, Paul nevertheless was "able ineffably to see and to hear" (XII.34.67). Intellectual vision, therefore, represented the convergence, interpenetration, and transfer of sensory modes that we have been calling synesthesia. Ineffable, perhaps, but still capable of being symbolized in terms of a discourse that fused seeing with hearing in the radical perceptual discourse of symbolic synesthesia.

Through attention to perceptual symbolism, we have gained a greater appreciation of the ways in which Augustine's symbolic vocabulary— in phrases such as "eye of the soul" and "ear of the heart" and even in his most fundamental Christological symbols of word and light— were informed by a very specific and carefully articulated understanding of the senses and how they worked. We have seen how the visual and aural modes, particularly as Augustine explicated them in his *De trinitate*, generated a dramatically different range of symbolic associations, tending toward continuity in the visual mode and discontinuity in the aural or verbal mode. Furthermore, we have gained a greater sense of how those associations formed visual and verbal symbolic models that related perception, mind, and God in different ways. Finally, we have once again encountered the curious fusion of the senses in symbolic synesthesia. In Augustine's discourse, synesthesia assumed two forms: First, a type of synesthesia appeared in the convergence of metaphors drawn from all the senses, or the interior senses, to represent a unified apprehension of sacred truth. And, second, the more radical synesthetic transfer across sensory modes appeared in the human heart— where hearing is seeing, seeing is hearing—as well as in the inner word of the human mind, in the being of the Son of God, and in the intellectual visionary experiences of those two scriptural exemplars of the encounter between humans and God, Moses and Paul. In all these instances, Augustine symbolized the tension between continuity and discontinuity in the relation between human beings and the sacred by means of a carefully and consistently articulated discourse of perception that distinguished the senses, but fused them in the metaphors of symbolic synesthesia.

4

Myth

In his *Essay on Man*, Ernst Cassirer reflected on the symbolic significance of Augustine's literary self-examination in the autobiographical narrative of the *Confessions*. That narrative was not merely the story of Augustine's life, Cassirer decided, but "the religious drama of mankind." Cassirer noticed a certain mythic quality to the narrative that seemed to encompass a comprehensive human pattern of fall and redemption within the horizon of a single life story. Within the text of Augustine's autobiographical narrative, Cassirer discovered a deeper mythic intention. "Every line of Augustine's book," he concluded, "has not merely a historical but also a hidden symbolic meaning."[1] Augustine's narrative was structured by myth—the myth of fall and redemption, the myth of procession and return, the myth of the incarnation, and, as I will suggest, the mythic configuration of word and light that permeated Augustine's symbolic universe. Narrative structure and textual imagery in the autobiographical chapters of the *Confessions* were informed by a symmetry of verbal and visual perceptual categories. As we will see, the autobiographical narrative embodied the Christian mythic constellation of word and light and, thereby, transformed Augustine's personal life story into myth. This mythic character of Augustine's autobiographical narrative, however, only becomes apparent by paying close attention to the perceptual categories through which the narrative was organized. Again, attention to visual and verbal models can disclose unfamiliar features of even such a familiar story as Augustine's *Confessions*.

In his *Soliloquiae*, Augustine had insisted that his single intention was to know God and the soul (I.2.7). That controlling purpose was pursued in the intense introspection of the *Confessions*. Augustine searched for those living moments in his own life in which God and soul met. Augustine recorded his soul's longing, in his blindness and deafness of spirit, for some contact with God's word and God's light. Furthermore, Augustine recorded numerous instances in which he encountered the divine word and the divine light. But the verbal and the visual modes in general provided a constant reservoir of metaphoric resources for Augustine's *Confessions.*

The experience of extraordinary voices was a consistent theme in the autobiographical narrative of the *Confessions.*[2] The things of creation exclaimed, *voce magna,* that they had been created by God and beauty declared their divine origin (X.6). Evil spoke in the voice of opinion (I.11), the voice of error (IV.15), and the voice of shadows (XII.10). It spoke in human custom (I.16), in carnal relations (VIII.11), in Folly (III.6), and in Vanity (VIII.11). Truth, however, spoke in the scripture (X.31). Every word of the Old and the New Testaments was a *vox, eloquium,* or *oraculum* spoken by God. This was the Lord's style of speech (IX.5). Likewise, visionary experiences and encounters also abounded in the autobiographical narrative of the *Confessions.* Augustine described the healing of the sight of his mind (VII.8), his discovery of a light within (VII.7), and the possibility of becoming light in the Lord (VIII.10). The scriptures were not only described as the word, speech, or voice of God, but also as brilliant with God's own light (IX.4).

In the first book of the *Confessions,* Augustine underscored the importance of auditory and visual experience in his relationship with God by praying to hear and to see the divine presence. Addressing God, Augustine wrote: "Speak so that I can hear. See, Lord, the ears of my heart are in front of you. Open them and say unto my soul: I am thy salvation. At these words I shall run and I shall take hold of you. Do not hide your face from me. Let me die, lest I should die indeed; only let me see your face" (I.5). The opening of the eyes and ears of the heart was the dominant narrative theme of the *Confessions.* Augustine had "grown deaf through the clanking chains of . . . mortality" (II.2) and had suffered "the punishment of blindness over unlawful desires" (I.18). In the course of his autobiography, Augustine traced the healing of this spiritual deafness and blindness as the fundamental precondition for his conversion. The narrative path to the word and light of God led through a process of healing the eyes and ears of the soul.

Augustine deployed the perceptual imagery of the *Confessions* within a larger symbolic structure defined by the balance, symmetry, and sometimes convergence of visual and verbal models. As we will see, Augustine placed the verbal and visual in counterpoint, creating a narrative tension between them, only to include that tension at a higher level of resolution. Augustine orchestrated the narrative around a balance of seeing and hearing that replicated the visual and verbal models through which he understood God to relate to humans and humans to relate to God. Peter Brown hinted at the delicate balance of sights and sounds in Augustine's environment—and in his symbolic universe—when he suggested that, from the glory of the African sunlight to the glow of the Easter candle, Augustine was particularly sensitive to the effects of light. "Above all," Brown noted, "he was surrounded by light." But Augustine was equally sensitive to the delights of the ears, in the eloquence of speech, the singing of the psalms, and the voice of the heart—in both the fullness and the poverty of words. "Above all," Peter Brown added, "there will be many voices."[3] Above all else, Augustine was alive to the vitality of light and voice in human experience.

Even further above the sights and sounds of ordinary experience, however, Augustine was concerned with the human encounter with the sacred. According to Augustine, God encountered human beings "by means of those senses and faculties, internal and external, which you bestow on us" (I.6). In one respect, the *Confessions* was dedicated to exploring those senses—the eyes and ears of the soul—through which human beings related to God. But the *Confessions* was also dedicated to the eyes and ears of God. Augustine offered his confessions to the divine eyes and ears: "Lord to your eyes the very depths of man's conscience are exposed. . . . I do not make my confessions by means of the words and sounds of the flesh, but with the words of the soul and the crying out of my thought which your ear knows" (X.2). Eyes and ears, seeing and hearing, visual and verbal orientations, and ultimately the light and word of God are the elements that were interwoven in fashioning the autobiographical narrative of Augustine's *Confessions*. As we will notice, those elements were organized in a narrative structure that might be identified as a symmetry of word and light.

Narrative Structure

The entire autobiographical narrative of Augustine's *Confessions* was structured in terms of a symmetrical balance between visual and verbal categories. Augustine organized his life story as a symmetry of verbal and visual orientations that ultimately led to his Christian conversion. Augustine's program for the *Confessions* seemed to call for an outline of the ways in which his verbal and visual experience—in the occupations and preoccupations of his life—related to the divine word and light. Augustine organized his life story as a transition from unsatisfactory verbal and visual experiences in the earlier stages of his life that had to give way before he could enter into the transforming experience of the word and light of God.

To define this structure simply: The narrative alternated between the exclusively verbal orientation of rhetoric and the exclusively visual orientation of Manicheism that both dominated Augustine's life before his conversion. As he described it in the *Confessions*, Augustine's experience of rhetoric, the arts of eloquence in which he was trained and in which he trained others, represented an exclusively verbal orientation. By learning to speak, a child passed into the "stormy intercourse" of human life (I.8). By mastering the rhetorical arts of eloquence, Augustine was convinced that he was pursuing a path that would lead to wealth and success in the world. Through rhetoric, Augustine became a master of the spoken word. How did this verbal orientation in the schools of rhetoric relate to the word of God? At the same time, however, Augustine was involved with the Manicheans, an involvement that he maintained for at least nine years, and in which he was preoccupied with an exclusively visual orientation toward the imagination. Augustine recalled that the Manicheans imagined that they were particles of light broken off from the divine light. In his *Confessions*, Augustine claimed that the Manicheans were preoccupied with speculative knowledge about the luminous celestial bodies and with bright phantasms of imaginary heavens. During the course of his involvement with the Manichean movement, as Augustine recalled those years in the *Confessions*, he was a student of those luminous fantasies. How did this visual orientation in the schools of the Manicheans relate to the light of God?

The key to the structure of Augustine's autobiographical narrative, I would suggest, is the symmetry of verbal and visual experience represented by rhetoric and Manicheism. At the beginning of Book Four, Augustine described his life as a course that moved between these two poles. On the one hand, he sought wealth and prestige through the vain pursuit of eloquence. On the other, he devoted himself to the secret service of the Manichean elect and to the observances of the Manichean faith. These two poles defined the public and private dimensions of Augustine's life. Augustine described his situation: "My public life was that of a teacher of what are called 'the liberal arts.' In private I went under cover of a false kind of religion" (IV.1).

The exclusively verbal character of rhetoric and the exclusively visual character of Manicheism, at least as they featured in Augustine's narrative, can be clearly set in relief by tracing the thematic trajectory of "pride" through the *Confessions*.[4] That root of all sin was a common moral theme throughout Augustine's work. He began his *Confessions* by acknowledging the sin of pride, "Thou resistest the proud," just as he later began his *City of God* with "God resistest the proud and giveth grace to the humble" (Jas 4:6; 1 Pt 5:5). The transition from *superbia* to *humilitas* was certainly the dominant moral impetus in Augustine's conversion and confessions. Augustine declared that he longed for "an eternal life promised us through the humility of our Lord stooping to our pride" (I.11). For Augustine, pride was a condition of alienation that separated the soul from the supreme humility embodied in the incarnation and crucifixion of Christ. Pride was self-love that separated the soul from the love of God, a pervasive perversion of the will that prevented its conversion.

By examining carefully Augustine's descriptions of his verbal experience in the schools of rhetoric and his visual experience in the cells of the Manicheans we find both characterized by the sin of pride. Rhetoric was a "pride of the word," which alienated Augustine from the word of God; Manicheism was a "pride of the light," which separated him from the light of God. Therefore, the structure of Augustine's autobiographical narrative established an opposition between the verbal and visual poles of his experience and then traced his movement from pride to humility precisely in terms of those verbal and visual options. In his conversion, Augustine renounced rhetoric to enter into the "humility of your Word" (VIII.2). In the same way, he defied the arrogance of the Manicheans in order to surrender to "the true Light that enlighteneth every man that cometh into the world" (VIII.10). The autobiographical narrative of Augustine's *Confessions*, therefore, was structured by a symmetrical opposition between a "pride of the word" and a "pride of the light." Those structural oppositions, however, were resolved by a conversion in which Augustine entered into the humility of the divine word and light. In this respect, the entire narrative was permeated—in narrative imagery, structure, and movement—by the central Augustinian mythic constellation of the word and light of God.

Perversion of Word and Light

As one of the few viable means of upward social mobility available to an aspiring young man of Augustine's abilities in the later Roman Empire, rhetoric provided a vehicle for the expression of vaulting ambition.[5] Whether in the vocation of teaching, in legal practice, or in government service, a career in rhetoric promised a degree of notoriety

and wealth that might otherwise be unattainable. Augustine received
an education in rhetoric, as he recalled, in order that he might "excel
in the kind of literary and rhetorical learning which would provide . . . a
reputation among men and deceitful riches" (I.9). This ambition for
wealth and fame through the pursuit of rhetoric, to which his parents
directed him and his teachers exhorted him, represented for Augustine
a self-centered alienation from the word of God in the vanity of merely
human words. The communication of desires and the techniques of
persuasion, which Augustine represented as the aims of rhetoric, were
not only vain; they alienated the soul from the divine word as well.
Augustine maintained that his education was a pointless attempt to
satisfy the insatiable desires for "that wealth which is poverty and the
glory which is shame" (I.12), by mastering "the art of eloquence, which
is so essential for gaining your own ends and for expressing your own
opinions" (I.16). In this solipsistic pride in the attainment of rhetorical
skill, Augustine stated, "I was swept away into vanities and I went
out of your presence, my God" (I.18).

Augustine certainly could refer to precedents in Greek and Latin
antiquity for this mistrust of the pursuit of eloquence for its own sake.
The philosophical traditions of both Plato and Aristotle — in the attacks
against the sophists in Plato's *Phaedrus,* and the careful subservience
of rhetoric to philosophy in Aristotle's *De rhetorica* — suggested an
important tension in classical rhetorical theory between "truth" and
"verbal expression." In more popular terms, the dramatist Aristophanes
and the satirist Lucian gave artistic expressions to this popular apprehension regarding the dangers of rhetoric.[6] The fear of unbridled verbal
expression appeared in early Christian thought on education and the
role of classical culture in the formation of Christian learning. To cite
one example at random: Gregory Nazianzus summarized a pervasive
Christian distrust of rhetoric by praising a uniquely Christian education
"which disregards rhetorical ornaments and glory."[7] This connection
between rhetoric and vain self-glorification was consistent with Augustine's symbolism of the rhetorical "pride of the word" in his *Confessions.*

In the first book of the *Confessions* Augustine described his rhetorical
training in the school of pride, amplifying upon the verbal context in
which he later understood that he had been alienated from God. Augustine symbolized the exclusive preoccupation with the verbal dimension of human experience in the schools of rhetoric as a "darkness
of affection" and a "blindness." The preoccupation with words resulted
in the loss of the visual presence of God. As Augustine recalled, the
rhetoricians told their tales of lust in the most impeccable style. In this

verbal ornamentation of illicit desire, for which "they were praised . . . by others and would take pride in it themselves," a darkness of affection separated the masters of words from God: "For to be in the darkness of affection," Augustine noted, "is to be far from [God]" (I.18). The alienation from God in rhetoric was not a spatial distance that could be traversed by foot or on the wing, but a spiritual alienation of affection, a separation of the human heart from the heart of God.

We should expect this alienation of the heart to have been translated by Augustine into sensory terms. That is precisely what Augustine did when he identified this condition in the schools of rhetoric as a moral blindness. Recalling his preoccupation with words, his ambition for learning to make a good speech, and his desire to become a persuasive orator capable of swaying an audience, Augustine exclaimed: "Such is the blindness of men, that blindness should become an actual source of pride" (III.3). Augustine's employment of the textual imagery of "blindness" to characterize rhetoric recurred later when he described his own students at Carthage: "The very blindness with which they act is their punishment" (V.6). In worldly ambition, desire, lust, and arrogance, the "pride of the word" created a distance of affection from God that Augustine symbolized as a spiritual blindness. Augustine described the final years of his education in recalling that "by now I was a senior student in the school of rhetoric, and very pleased with myself and proud and swelling with arrogance" (III.3). From Augustine's perspective, this "pride of the word" was a spiritual blindness, a darkness of the heart, a darkness of affection that had to be illuminated by the presence of God.

While recollecting his "pride of the word," Augustine did not neglect the symbolic dynamics of the visual mode, or the symbolism of light, in constructing the narrative of his life before conversion. Augustine placed his verbal experience in the schools of rhetoric in counterpoint throughout the autobiographical narrative of his *Confessions* to the corresponding visual experience represented by the obsessive preoccupation with visual imagination that he found in the religion of the Manicheans.[8] From his first contact with the movement, Augustine represented the Manichean worldview as an exclusively visual orientation. They were concerned with two aspects of visual experience: looking at the corporeal bodies of the physical world and seeing the spiritual bodies of the visual imagination.

Under Manichean influence, Augustine recalled, "my eyesight could reach no further than bodies and the sight of my mind no further than fantasy" (III.7). The Manicheans involved themselves in elaborate speculations regarding the physical creation, particularly the contemplation

of the celestial spheres, "heavenly and shining" (III.6). Following their
lead, Augustine became absorbed in these astrological speculations. Far
more insidious from Augustine's later standpoint, these speculations
based on the evidence of physical sight led to extraordinary delusions
of the spiritual sight. In a convincing way, the Manicheans presented
to Augustine their "glittering fantasies" of the imagination. As Augustine later insisted, even the worship of the physical creation would
have been preferable to this delusional exercise of the visual imagination. Augustine stated: "It would be better to love the actual sun,
which is real to our sight at least, than those false fantasies which
make use of the sight to deceive the mind" (III.6). Therefore, the
symbolic role played by the Manicheans in the *Confessions* was to
represent precisely this deceptive visual experience that corresponded
to the deceptive verbal experience in the schools of rhetoric. Augustine
counterpoised their alienating "pride of the light" to the rhetorician's
"pride of the word."

Whereas the rhetoricians were effectively characterized by their
blindness and their darkness of affection, the Manicheans, in their
exclusive obsession with vision and the visual imagination, were characterized by dumbness. The Manicheans were "dumb talkers (dumb
because they never uttered your Word)" (VII.2). As the rhetoricians
were alienated from the word of God in the pride of their verbal
experience, the Manicheans were alienated from the light of God in
the pride of their visual fantasies. Manicheans imagined God as "un-
measured light" or a "vast luminous body." They saw themselves as
"a sort of piece broken off from this body" (IV.6). From Augustine's
later vantage point, the supreme "pride of the light" consisted in this
assumption that the soul was light—in and of itself, without any need
of divine illumination—identical to the essence of God. This was the
"pride of the light": "How could anything be more proud than to
assert, as I did in my incredible folly, that I was by nature what you
are" (IV.15).

Manicheans and other such purveyors of philosophical *gnosis* imagined themselves to be "high up and shining with the stars." In their
"pride of the light," they "will boast of their knowledge and will be
praised for it, thus turning away from you in their evil pride and losing
the light that comes to them from you" (V.3). From Augustine's later
perspective, this was the most dangerous visual fantasy of all—the
presumption that the soul was light in itself and did not need to be
enlightened by God. This pride of the visual imagination effectively
alienated the soul from any authentic contact with the divine light.
According to Augustine, the Manicheans failed to understand that

human beings "are not ourselves the light which enlighteneth every man, but we are enlightened by you" (IX.4). By assuming that they were light in themselves and therefore of coequal essence with God, the Manicheans were alienated from the eternal light that Augustine was later convinced illumined the soul, so that, "having been sometime darkness, we may be light in Thee" (IX.4).

Augustine's notion that darkness could be transformed into light by divine illumination was certainly foreign to Manichean cosmology, which posited light and darkness as independent, antithetical powers at war with each other over the human soul. The soul was by nature a portion of light, having no essential connection with the realm of darkness in which it struggled for release in order to return to its luminous source. How could the soul become light when it was already light? In his autobiographical narrative, Augustine represented this definition of the soul as light as an exclusive development of the symbolic continuities inherent in a visual model. In their "pride of the light," Manicheans claimed that their souls were particles of light, identical in nature to the luminous body of God. Augustine objected to the Manichean claims by directly pointing to their exclusively visual orientation. In their fantasies of light, the Manicheans "do not know the way, which is your Word" (V.3). This exclusively visual orientation was inadequate and needed somehow to be transformed through the influence of the divine word. As the verbal orientation of rhetoric led to a blindness that required the light, the visual orientation of Manicheism resulted in a dumbness and deafness that needed to be corrected by the divine word.

As a result of the exclusively visual orientation he developed among the Manicheans, Augustine was "unable to form an idea of any kind of substance other than what my eyes are accustomed to see" (VIII.1). Augustine agonized over his inability to escape the limits of the visual imagination. He tried to beat away the corporeal images, forms, and fantasies that, he later observed, swarmed around the "eye of my mind." Under the influence of the Manichean visual orientation, however, Augustine was unsuccessful in transcending the imagination of corporeal forms. Feeling that the forms of the visual imagination pressed upon his sight and clouded it, Augustine recalled that he "was still forced to think of [God] as a corporeal substance occupying space" (VII.1). In this visual orientation, whatever did not have the qualities of substantial form, extended in space, could not be imagined to exist. The visual imagination required the same kinds of spatial conditions that applied in ordinary visual perception. In his struggle to conceive of God under these visual conditions, Augustine complained that "the images in my mind were like the shapes I was used to seeing with my eyes" (VII.1). Again, the visual model tended toward symbolic continuities—the continuity between sight and visual imagination, the continuity between corporeal and fantasy forms, and ultimately the luminous continuity between the soul and a God imagined as a vast body of light. In the exclusively visual orientation of the Manicheans, it did not occur to Augustine that "the very act of the mind by which I formed these images was something of a different nature altogether" (VII.1).

Augustine recalled that "these corporeal images stood in my way and prevented me from returning to [God]" (VII.7). In his "pride of the light"—a visually oriented pride that Augustine ironically described as causing his cheeks to be so swollen up that he could not see out of his eyes—Augustine noted that God "had not yet enlightened my darkness" (VII.1). This "pride of the light" alienated Augustine from God: "I was separated from you by the swelling of my pride" (VII.7). Experiencing intense frustration at his inability to conceive of God except in the corporeal images of the visual imagination, Augustine condemned the Manicheans as "deceived deceivers" because "they never uttered [God's] word" (VII.32). The divine word was not an object of imaginative vision in quite the same way that light was. In Augustine's verbal symbolic model, word was a dynamic activity: speaking, creating, commanding, and instructing. In their exclusively visual orientation, Manicheans were alienated from any awareness of these invisible activities of the divine word.

Conversion of Word and Light

At this point it might be useful to collect some of the themes we have been tracing through the autobiographical narrative of the *Confessions*. First, Augustine structured the narrative by organizing his life story into a balanced counterpoint between verbal and visual orientations. As we will see, that tension between the verbal and the visual moved toward narrative resolution in Augustine's account of his conversion. He represented the event of his conversion not only as a resolution of pride in the humility of Christ, but more specifically as a resolution of the "pride of the word" and the "pride of the light" in the humility of the word and light of God.

In the construction of his autobiographical narrative, Augustine not only held the verbal and visual orientations in careful balance, but he also developed the consistent symbolic entailments that were associated with each model. The second point to recall, therefore, is Augustine's consistent association of the verbal model with discontinuity and the visual model with continuity. The verbal orientation involved a number of basic discontinuities: The difference between rhetoric and philosophy, eloquence and wisdom, *signa* and *res,* or *modo loquor* and *quod loquebatur* were all ways of posing the basic discontinuity between words and truth. As he had earlier argued in his *De magistro,* Augustine in his *Confessions* denied every possible logical connection between verbal signs and truth (V.6). In the verbal orientation, words were fundamentally discontinuous with truth, incapable of presenting reality directly to the eye of the mind. As masters of the word, rhetoricians were implicated in this fundamental discontinuity in relation to truth, reality, and God. In order to counteract their exclusively verbal orientation, Augustine insisted that their blindness could only be healed by the divine light.

By contrast, Augustine consistently associated the visual orientation with continuity. Visual perception and visionary imagination involved presence, immediacy, and connection that Augustine suggested were carried to dangerous extremes in the exclusively visual orientation of the Manicheans. Preoccupied with the symbolic implications of vision, Manicheans imagined that they were sparks of light in continuity and even identification with the divine light. An exclusively visual orientation, therefore, led to imagining a relationship between human and divine based on identity. What the Manicheans required, Augustine insisted, was the symbolism of difference implicit in the divine word.

To put the structural opposition simply: Rhetoricians could not see the light, Manicheans could not speak or hear the divine word. These fundamental incapacities resulted from their exclusively verbal or visual orientations. In his public and private life, Augustine himself was torn between these two poles of perceptual orientation. As a result, Augustine described himself as spiritually deaf, dumb, and blind. In order to enter into a specifically, and paradoxically, Christian relationship with God, Augustine simultaneously had to affirm continuity and discontinuity. Symbolically, this paradoxical affirmation required a convergence of the verbal and visual domains. If the word symbolized discontinuity and the light continuity, Augustine's experience of a God who was both word and light had to embrace both. As we have noted, the discursive strategy of symbolic synesthesia provided one way of simultaneously affirming discontinuity and continuity in descriptions of a divine voice that illumines.

Augustine described how he found a provisional, preliminary encounter with the divine word and light in the books of the Platonists. Recalling that his readings in Neoplatonism represented a significant stage on his path toward conversion, Augustine noted that for the first time he was able to conceive of God as both word and light. In the synesthetic imagery of a divine word that illumines the soul, Augustine found a crucial antidote for the "pride of the light" under which he had suffered as a Manichean. Augustine learned that the soul was not light in and of itself but depended upon illumination from the transcendent word of God. Under the influence of Neoplatonism, Augustine declared: "The soul of man, though it bears witness to the light, yet itself is not that light; but the Word, God Himself, is that true light that lighteth every man that cometh into the world" (VII.9). As we have seen on many occasions, the human soul has tended to be symbolized as continuous with God in the visual symbolic model. In the exclusively visual orientation of the Manicheans, the deployment of light-imagery gave the impression that the soul was essentially identical to God. In the symbolism of the word, however, the soul was obviously different from God. In Augustine's verbal model of speech and hearing, the soul was consistently implicated in a discontinuous relationship with God. The books of the Platonists suggested for Augustine the possibility of a symbolic formula that combined the visual continuity of the divine light with the verbal discontinuity of a transcendent word of God.

Augustine recounted how he benefited from the merger of word and light in the books of the Platonists. First, Augustine overcame the tyranny of visual, corporeal, and spatially extended forms in his attempts to conceive God that had plagued his religious experience as a Manichean. "I woke up in you," he reminded God, "and saw you infinite in a different way, and that sight was not from the eyes of the flesh" (VII.14). Second, Augustine's Manichean inclination to identify the soul with the essence of God based on an exclusively visual orientation was tempered by a new awareness of the soul's dependence on the transcendent word of God. Augustine realized that "whoever sees should not so glory as if he had not received—received indeed, not only what he sees but also the power to see it" (VII.20). That power to see was received from the divine word. Both of these advances, Augustine implied, resulted from the merger of verbal and visual models he found in the books of the Platonists. The synesthetic convergence of divine word and light allowed him to see differently, to see in ways that were unlike the sight of the flesh and in ways that were empowered from a transcendent divine source. Visual continuity merged with verbal relations of discontinuity, difference, and transcendence in his discovery of the word and light of God in the books of the Platonists.[9]

Augustine's experiences of Neoplatonic, mystical ascent in the seventh book of the *Confessions* demonstrated this new convergence of visual and verbal models. For example, Augustine recounted that he was elevated in a continuous visionary ascent toward the divine light that raised him up so he could see, but at the same time he found himself "far distant from [God], in a region of total unlikeness, as if I were hearing [God's] voice from on high" (VII.10). The ascending vector of vision met the descending vector of distance, unlikeness, and transcendence associated with the voice of God.[10] Although he clearly benefited from this new symbolic configuration of light and voice, Augustine nevertheless associated the books of the Platonists with the sin of pride. The texts had been given to him by an unnamed individual whom Augustine simply described as "an extraordinarily conceited person" (VII.9). Throughout his discussion of these texts, Augustine associated them with pride. "Humility," he noted, "was not a subject which those books would ever have taught me" (VII.20). In the books of the Platonists, Augustine found the eternal word and light of God. What he failed to find, however, was the humility of the word and light that he subsequently found in the incarnation of Christ. The Platonic texts did not introduce him to the supreme Christian example of both humility and (as we should note for our interests) of symbolic synesthesia: the divine word made visible in the human world. Although he was initiated into the symbolic convergence of an eternal word and light by the books of the Platonists, Augustine recalled that he "did not find then that the Word was made flesh and dwelt among us" (VII.9).

At this juncture in his narrative, Augustine described a time in which he was profoundly dissatisfied with the verbal and visual orientations that had defined the boundaries of his public and private life. Inspired by the books of the Platonists, he desired to experience more fully the word and light of God. Moving toward his conversion, Augustine's spiritual senses of hearing and seeing became more intimately engaged by the reality of Christ. Augustine recorded two exemplary stories that were told to him just prior to his conversion. These stories were carefully woven into the narrative as preludes to conversion. They presented significant precedents for Augustine's own act of turning toward God. The stories had the same impact on Augustine that he must have intended his own life story in the *Confessions* to have on his readers — inspiring a major life-change by illustrating commitment to the humility of Christ. More than that, however, these two stories were woven into Augustine's own story as narrative correctives to the "pride of the word" and the "pride of the light" that had blocked him from entering into the humility of word and light represented by Christ. To simplify:

The story of the rhetorician Victorinus decisively countered the "pride of the word," while the story of the monk Antony effectively countered the "pride of the light." Both stories served as narrative preludes to Augustine's own story of his conversion.

The story of Victorinus told by Simplicianus was almost entirely framed in imagery drawn from the verbal orientation. Essentially, Victorinus was presented as a famous rhetor who renounced the "pride of the word" and retired from the profession of rhetoric in order to enter into the humility of the Christian community. Simplicianus related the story of Victorinus, as Augustine recalled, "in order to lead me toward the humility of Christ" (VIII.2). Not only was Victorinus a prominent master of eloquence, but, as translator of the Platonic books, Victorinus appreciated that in those philosophical texts "God and his Word are everywhere implied" (VIII.2). Although Victorinus read Christian literature in private and thought of himself as a Christian, Simplicianus insisted that it took the social statement of full membership in the church for Victorinus to surrender to the "humility of the Word" (VIII.2). Indeed, Victorinus demonstrated that humility by making a public profession of his Christian faith. Victorinus had been an accomplished master of words as a teacher of rhetoric, "speaking his own words in front of crowds of people who could scarcely be described as sane" (VIII.2). Entering into Christian humility, however, Victorinus faced the "meek flock" of a congregation "to pronounce [God's] Word" (VIII.2).

The conversion of Victorinus, therefore, served as an exemplary representation of a transition from the "pride of the word" to the "humility of the word." Victorinus demonstrated that the verbal orientation could be entirely transformed. Although Victorinus retired from the practice of rhetoric under the force of Emperor Julian's legislation preventing Christians from teaching the liberal arts, he welcomed this withdrawal from the profession of rhetoric, "preferring to give up his talking-shop rather than your Word, by which you make even the tongues of infants eloquent" (VIII.5). In coming to the divine word, Victorinus also received the divine light. He was "enlightened by that light which those who receive, receive power from Thee to become Thy sons" (VIII.4). In renouncing the "pride of the word," Victorinus not only came into communication with the word of God but he also broke through the exclusively verbal orientation of rhetoric to enter into communion with the divine light. Augustine recalled that he was so profoundly inspired by this story of Victorinus that he was "on fire to be like him" (VIII.5).

While Victorinus exemplified a change in verbal practice, Antony stood as an example of a significant change in visual orientation. Augustine framed the story of Antony, recalling its impact when related to him by Ponticianus, almost entirely in the visual mode. As Ponticianus told the story of the ascetic rigors of Antony, the spiritual hero in the fruitful wilderness of the desert, Augustine had a visual experience of intense introspection, as if God, Augustine recalled, "were turning me around so that I could see myself" (VIII.7). As the story of Antony proceeded, Augustine felt as if God were presenting the display of his sin before his eyes. "You set me in front of my own face," Augustine reminded God, "so that I could see how foul a sight I was" (VIII.7). Augustine looked, saw, and was horrified by the sight of his sinfulness. He explained that the story of Antony had redirected the eyes of his mind, forced him to look at his own face, confront the magnitude of his sin, and find its appearance repulsive.

When the story of Antony concluded, Augustine left the company of his friends and withdrew to the garden connected to their lodgings. He recalled that his visual appearance expressed his agitation of spirit better than the words he used when departing from his companions. Precisely at that point in the narrative, Augustine recalled the Manicheans and their "pride of the light." Although he had not been involved with them for some time, Augustine noted that his new visual orientation decisively refuted their arrogant presumption that they were light of the same essence as God. Augustine explained that the Manicheans had fallen into a greater darkness because, in their pride, they "want to be light, not in the Lord, but in themselves" (VIII.10). In the visual reorientation inspired by the story of Antony, Augustine now recognized that he was not light in and of himself but required illumination from God.

The stories of Victorinus and Antony, therefore, had the narrative impact in the *Confessions* of turning Augustine away from the "pride of the word" and the "pride of the light." They succeeded in exemplifying new verbal and visual orientations that were of decisive importance in Augustine's own conversion to the word and light of Christ. Augustine's description of that conversion embodied the verbal and visual orientations represented by the stories of Victorinus and Antony. Augustine described his spiritual crisis in both visual and verbal terms. He related that "now from my hidden depths my searching thought had dragged up and set before the sight of my heart the whole mass of my misery" (VIII.12). This intense visual introspection was expressed in words, not in the learned forms of rhetorical eloquence, but in the spontaneous outpouring of the voice of his heart. Augustine recalled that his friend, Alypius, "could feel the weight of my tears in the sound of my voice." Augustine related that he left his friend "so that I might pour out all these tears and speak the words that came with them" (VIII.12). In recalling his spiritual crisis, Augustine described it as an agony of the sight and voice of his heart, a spiritual anguish at his perceived separation from the word and light of God.

In the narrative of the *Confessions*, Augustine's agony was resolved by a mysterious experience of voice and light. In keeping with the symmetry of visual and verbal orientations throughout his autobiography, Augustine brought the narrative to a climax by representing his conversion event in the garden of Milan as a strange coincidence of hearing a mysterious voice and receiving divine illumination. Augustine's account of his conversion began with that mysterious voice: He recalled that he heard the voice of a young child repeating the words, "Take it and read." Augustine left the identity of the speaker and the location from which these words were spoken ambiguous. For our purposes, we can simply note that in the midst of his spiritual crisis, as Augustine recalled, "suddenly a voice reached my ears" and when it instructed him to read, Augustine concluded that he had to "interpret this as a divine command" (VIII.12). Whatever the source of this mysterious voice, therefore, Augustine received it as if it were the voice of God commanding him to take the scriptures and read. Taking his copy of the Pauline letters, Augustine moved from the verbal command to its visual consequences as he "read in silence the passage upon which [his] eyes first fell" (VIII.12). The first passage that appeared to his eyes directed him to the humility of word and light in Christ: "Put ye on the Lord Jesus Christ (Rom 23:13-14). Suddenly, Augustine recounted, he experienced a dramatic transformation that he described in visual terms, "as though my heart was filled with a light of confidence and all the shadows of my doubts were swept away" (VIII.12). Commanded by the divine voice, Augustine's heart was infused with light. As the climax of his autobiographical narrative, Augustine's conversion event fused hearing and seeing in a dramatic experience of the divine voice and light. Putting on the humility of Christ, Augustine symbolized his conversion as a synesthetic convergence of word and light.[11]

In the *Confessions*, Augustine suggested that God encountered human beings "by means of those senses and faculties, internal and external, which you bestow on us" (I.6). Augustine's conversion was symbolized as a correction, culmination, and convergence of the verbal and visual orientations that had been outlined throughout the course of his autobiographical narrative. The senses of sight and hearing—both internal and external—were the crucial locations for relations between human and divine. By converting his verbal and visual orientations to the humility of Christ, Augustine entered into the central symbolic configuration of word and light in Christian myth.

In the ninth and final book of the strictly autobiographical part of his *Confessions*, Augustine reflected one last time upon the verbal orientation of rhetoric and the visual orientation of Manicheism that had provided the basic structural opposition in his narrative. Augustine recalled that he retired from his teaching position in Milan, renouncing his own "talking-shop," to confirm his departure from the "pride of the word" that had characterized the exclusively verbal orientation of rhetoric. Augustine declared to God: "You rescued my tongue as you had rescued my heart" (IX.4). Augustine intended to devote his verbal expression in writing and teaching to the service of God, even if during the period of the Cassiciacum dialogues written after his conversion he still gave some evidence of the residual influences of the rhetorical "school of pride" (IX.4). As for the Manicheans, Augustine recounted that he found ample evidence for the refutation of their "pride of the light" in his readings of Christian sacred texts. In his new orientation toward the internal senses of sight and hearing, Augustine referred to the Manicheans as "deaf corpses" who had not heard the divine word. Augustine had heard and seen, but the Manichean continued to raise his "barking voice against these writings which are so honey sweet of heaven and brilliant with [God's] own light" (IX.4). Augustine's conversion, therefore, was specifically formulated to symbolize a transformation of verbal and visual orientations in which the eyes and ears of the soul were healed to behold the word and light of God. Rhetoric and Manicheism effectively served as foils in Augustine's autobiographical narrative as perverted verbal and visual orientations that stood in opposition to Augustine's Christian experience of the divine voice and light.

5

Ritual

After all our attention to symbolic synesthesia in his discourse, we should not be surprised to find that Augustine defined the ritual practices of the Christian sacraments as "visible words." Like discourse, ritual practice provided opportunities for the senses to converge and interpenetrate. Baptism, eucharist, and the other sacraments obviously involved natural symbols that engaged the senses. Washing, eating, drinking, and so on, in the context of ritual space and ritual time, sacralized the senses in action. In general, ritual is immediate, concrete, and even visceral practice that is only secondarily available to abstract, conceptual thought. Particularly as it developed through the first five centuries, Christian ritual involved an interaction and convergence of the senses in both action and thought.

The ceremony of baptism, for example, involved all the modes of the human sensorium. Baptism in the West began with the opening in which the bishop touched the candidate's ears and nostrils, while reciting, "Be opened" (Mk 7:34). In his *De sacramentis*, Ambrose explained that these actions symbolized the opening of the ears to understanding and the nostrils to the "good odor of Christ" (I.2). Washing the body with water and anointing it with oil and myron engaged the sense of touch. Afterwards, a drink of milk and honey appealed to the initiate's sense of taste (*Apostolic Tradition* XXIII.2-3). Finally, the sense of sight was included by the custom, recorded in *De lapsu virginis* of the Pseudo-Ambrose, of presenting the neophyte with a lighted candle to carry (V.19). However, the entire baptismal ceremony—words, scent, taste, touch, and gestures—was rendered visually in the familiar phrase of Justin Martyr when he identified baptism as illumination (*photismos*). As the ritual practice of baptism developed, therefore, it involved a

convergence of all the senses. Perhaps changes in ritual practice indicated significant historical shifts in perceptual orientation: When Protestant reformers in the sixteenth century reduced baptism to the element
of water in the name of the Trinity, rejecting the use of oil, candles,
salt, milk, honey, and spit as unnecessary accretions to the ritual, they
signaled a dramatic narrowing of the perceptual field in Christian ritual
practice by denying the rich, complex convergence of all the senses in
baptism.

Apparently, a more radical form of synesthesia appeared in the ritual
practice of the eucharist. Not only did communion involve all the senses
but the practice was often interpreted in terms of intermodal sensory
transfers. For example, Theodore, in his *Catechetical Homilies*, instructed
participants to adore the bread by applying it to their eyes before eating
it (XVI.27-28). Cyril of Jerusalem recommended that communicants
should bow in worship and touch their eyes, foreheads, and other
senses with any wine that might remain on their lips (*Mystagogic Catecheses* V.21-22). The preferred liturgical song for the eucharist, according to both the *Apostolic Constitutions* (VIII.13.16) and Cyril of
Jerusalem, *Mystagogic Catecheses* (V.20), was specified as Psalm 33:8:
"Taste and see." Rather than merely ornamental decoration, the convergence and interpenetration of the senses revealed something important about Christian ritual: Ritual was self-involving because it involved all the senses in symbolic action.[1]

Following his conversion, baptism, and entry into communion with
the Christian community, Augustine remained concerned with working
out the new implications of his lifetime occupation—education. Although he had left the "talking-shop" of rhetoric, Augustine continued
to take an interest in the theory and practice of learning. In order to
convert learning to his new Christian orientation, however, Augustine
made it into a ritual. This may seem strange, but in Augustine's early
Christian writings one of the most important ritual practices was the
practice of learning. Augustine worked out a distinctive analysis of the
learning process, often called his "doctrine of illumination," in which
he concluded that in every act of learning "Christ, the truth, teaches
within." While Augustine's learning theory has generated a considerable
conflict of interpretation, I will suggest that some clarity can be gained
by once again paying attention to the symbolic dynamics of the perceptual models in which he formulated his theory. As Augustine would
later define all Christian ritual, he defined the ritual of learning as a
practice in which "visible words" played the central role. More than
that, however, Augustine's theory suggested that learning was a ritual
activity in which the same word and light of creation entered human

experience through education. Attention to the symbolic dynamics of word and light in Augustine's understanding of creation and education discloses unexplored dimensions of the ritual of learning.

THE RITUAL OF LEARNING

Widespread disagreement exists about exactly what Augustine might have meant by his theory of learning in which Christ, the truth, teaches within. The precise interpretation of Augustine's doctrine of illumination has been the subject of centuries of debate. How is this kind of learning process that Augustine outlined, a process by which the word of God illumines the soul, to be understood? Three major schools of thought on Augustine's learning theory have dominated the debate: (1) the *ontologistic* version, which has regarded the immediate presence of the divine light, establishing continuity between the human mind and the mind of God, as primary in the process of learning; (2) the *ideogenetic* version, which has regarded the activity of the word of God, mysteriously producing ideas in the human mind, as primary in the learning process; and (3) a position that might be called the *normative* version, which has argued that the metaphor of illumination in Augustine's learning theory referred to the way in which the divine light provided an ultimate standard of certainty by which knowledge could be evaluated, rather than describing an inner, psychological process through which learning occurs.[2] This *normative* approach—which has been subscribed to by such Augustinian scholars as Gilson, Jolivet, Bourke, Howie, Copleston, and TeSelle—has been very popular, largely because it provides a convenient way to accommodate both Augustinian and Thomist approaches to knowledge.[3] It seems to me, however, to be inadequate for at least two reasons.

First, since there is no Aristotelian agent intellect in Augustine's thought, the *normative* interpretation leaves a vacuum in his account of knowledge. If illumination is not responsible for the content of ideas, which is, according to Gilson and others, better explained by the activity of the agent intellect, then what is, in fact, responsible for their content. This position denies the possibility that ideas are seen in the mind of God, as the *ontologists* would have it, or mysteriously generated by the word of God, as the *ideogenetic* theory would hold; but the *normative* position develops no alternative explanation consistent with Augustine's own philosophical positions.

Second, the *normative* version ignores what might be called the mythic basis of Augustine's learning theory, the assumption by Augustine that the primordial word and light of creation were active in

the actual, dynamic process of learning, not merely representing ultimate standards of certitude. In reexamining Augustine's learning theory,
I would like to develop insights drawn from the crosscultural history
of religions to suggest that Augustine understood learning as a ritual
activity that enacted the Christian myth of creation. By taking seriously
Augustine's claim that the same word and light of God were present
in creation and education, we find in his theory an understanding of
learning as a ritual act, symbolically recapitulating the primordial cosmogonic myth — the dynamic creative activity of word and light —
within the life of the learner. In this way, it may be possible to work
out an interpretation of Augustine's learning theory that is more sensitive to the nuances of its mythic formulation and its ritual dynamics.

For a fully satisfactory interpretation of Augustine's learning theory
it is necessary to return to the symbolic foundations upon which it was
fashioned. What were the symbolic dynamics of the learning process?
How did Augustine understand the word and light of God to operate
in every act of learning?[4] In the eleventh book of his *Confessions*,
Augustine introduced the theme of learning into a discussion of the
creation of the world. The universe was created through the agency
of the divine word: "Thou spakest and they were made," and "in Thy
Word Thou madest them." This word was "the beginning." But that
beginning continued to speak to human beings as a teacher. That divine
word, Augustine noted, was "our teacher who speaks to us." Here,
Augustine referred to the theory, already developed in his *De magistro*,
that the word of God — the *interior magister* — was responsible for the
process of learning. In his *Confessions*, Augustine declared this divine
word or voice as the inner teacher: "And who is our teacher except
the steadfast truth? For even when we learn something by means of
a changing creature it is to this steadfast truth that we are led, and
then we truly learn while we stand and hear Him, and rejoice greatly
because of the Bridegroom's voice" (XI.8). It was this inner teacher,
the voice of the word of God, which activated the learning process.
For Augustine, therefore, the word of creation was the same word that
was active as an inner teacher in the process of learning. Augustine
found this connection between the divine word in creation and education captured succinctly in the verse: "He is the Beginning and speaking unto us" (XI.8).

Continuing his meditation on creation and education in Book Eleven
of his *Confessions*, Augustine proceeded to identify the beginning with
wisdom. As in the tradition represented by Proverbs 8 and Sirach 24,
Augustine attributed a creative power to divine wisdom.[5] He stated
that wisdom was "the beginning" in which God made heaven and

earth. "It was in this beginning, God, that you made heaven and earth speaking wonderfully, creating wonderfully in your Word, your Son, your power, your wisdom, your truth" (XI.9). This verbal process of God's primordial creative speaking, however, was experienced by Augustine in a dramatic visual epiphany of divine light. Augustine described a light that shone through him, terrifying and inflaming him, and concluded: "It is Wisdom, Wisdom herself that shines through me." The wisdom that spoke in creation, therefore, could enter directly into human experiences as this "Wisdom of God, light of minds" (XI.11).

Clearly, Augustine described divine wisdom in the symbolic synesthesia of an illuminating voice, a divine word that spoke light. In addition, however, the symbolic dynamics underlying Augustine's learning theory were disclosed as a correspondence between the word and light in creation and the word and light of wisdom that teaches the soul from within. Every act of learning, therefore, recapitulated the primordial creation in that convergence of word and light. There has been an almost universal tendency in Augustinian scholarship to understand Augustine's doctrine of illumination solely as an abstract epistemological theory. The temptation has been to explain Augustine's learning theory conveniently in terms of Platonic conceptual categories (or Aristotelian categories, in the case of the Thomists) as if the doctrine of illumination were nothing more than such an abstract theory of knowledge. First and foremost, however, Augustine's learning theory was a religious statement based on a correspondence between the intrinsic process of human learning and the primordial creative event. Augustine's theory of learning reflected a dynamic internalization of the same word and light, the same extraordinary verbal and visual configuration that operated in the original creation of the world.

Myths of creation, of course, have achieved a definite power and prestige within the history of religions. Cosmogonic myths often have defined symbolic patterns that can be imitated in various kinds of human activity. The symbolic power of the creation myth may also extend to other significant myths of origin within a religious tradition. Human activity, and particularly ritual activity, may participate directly in the power of these primordial, creative events through practices of repetition. Ritual recapitulation of cosmogonic myth was a familiar and perhaps central theme in historian of religions Mircea Eliade's understanding of myth and ritual. Eliade consistently maintained that "the cosmogony becomes the exemplary model for 'creation' of every kind," and he adduced numerous examples from the history of religions to illustrate a process of repetition, reenactment, or symbolic return of the primordium in ritual action.⁶ From this perspective, creation myths performed a formative function in religious traditions by providing a paradigmatic pattern for the organization of other areas of human life and operated as a sacred time to which human beings could return — in the ritual transformation of their time, space, and experience — through the ritual reenactment of events of the cosmogony.

Certainly, objections to Eliade's theory of religion could be and have been raised.⁷ The principle of repetition, however, does seem to be a viable dimension of many types of ritual activity. Reenactment of myth has been an important element in Christian ritual. Categories and insights that have been drawn from the crosscultural history of religions may prove useful in the analysis of Christian ritual. As Jonathan Z. Smith noted: "Elements such as the Old Testament and New Testament as myth, the whole range of Jewish and Christian rituals and initiations, the liturgical year, etc., would profit from a careful examination in the light of analogous structures in the History of Religions."⁸ In Christian ritual, the sacraments of baptism and eucharist involve obvious reenactments of mythic prototypes that appear in mythic narratives of the life of Christ. Ritual participation with the sacramental symbols of water, bread, and wine symbolically transmitted power that was at least to some extent derived from the power present in the controlling myth.

For Augustine, however, Christ was involved in every sacrament. All Christian ritual provided access to the central figure of the Christian myth, the incarnate Christ, by means of a specific symbolic correspondence. Just as Christ in the incarnation became the "Word made visible," the sacraments were understood by Augustine to be "visible words." In his commentary on the Gospel of John, Augustine explained that "the word is added to the element, and there results the sacrament, as if itself also a kind of visible word" (80.3). The power and presence of Christ in the ritual enactments of the Christian sacraments was symbolized by Augustine in the discourse of symbolic synesthesia. The visible words of the sacraments coalesced verbal and visual coordinates of experience in ritual. Clearly, this synesthetic convergence corresponded to the symbolic pattern of Christ's incarnation. In both incarnation and sacraments, Augustine held that the power of the invisible word was visibly present and accessible to human beings.

The symbolic resonance of Augustine's understanding of the sacraments, however, did not stop there. His representation of the sacraments as "visible words" was in line with the discourse of symbolic synesthesia that ran throughout the mythic narrative of the Christian tradition. To note this point once again: The most crucial manifestations of the sacred in the tradition were embodied in the synesthetic convergence and interpenetration of seeing and hearing. The theophanies of Christian myth—creation, revelation, incarnation, and Pentecost— were all symbolized as dramatic instances of visual-verbal synesthesia. By understanding the sacraments as "visible words," Augustine placed Christian ritual in line with these other significant eruptions of the sacred into the world. In other words, Augustine's symbolic understanding of the sacraments, as visible words, corresponded to the general tendency within the tradition to symbolize significant sacred events as the convergence of auditory and visual categories.

How did learning fit into all of this? The two most compelling influences on Augustine's learning theory have often been identified as Plato and Cicero. It has been said that Augustine's doctrine of illumination was intended to take the place of Plato's theory of reminiscence as a way of explaining the process of learning.[9] Plato introduced his notion of *anamnesis* in his *Meno* as an attempt to account for learning as a function of memory. In effect, Plato maintained that human beings could not learn anything that they did not already know. In preembodied existences, souls had immediate access to the realm of eternal ideas. In the body, however, a veil of forgetfulness interceded between the soul and the knowledge that was proper to it. Learning pierced that veil and recalled to the soul the forms of knowledge with which it had formerly been in direct contact. The result was a dynamic activity that broke the bonds of human temporality. In the context of a general myth of eternal return, learning, as recollection, allowed the soul to return to a timeless state of awareness that it had occupied before assuming a body. Therefore, Plato understood learning as a transformation of human consciousness from time to eternity in its reconnection with original, eternal ideal forms of reality.

In the case of Cicero, Augustine had a more practical agenda for education. Cicero outlined a program for the formation of effective statesmen and responsible citizens. Yet Cicero had a similar concern for the value of learning as a means of transforming the human experience of time. According to Cicero, the purpose of education was to free the student from the tyranny of the present.[10] Study in the liberal arts—the distinctively Roman combination of philosophy and literature that was to have such a decisive influence on the development of Christian education—provided a means of transcending the temporal limitations of ordinary experience and a way of connecting the student with a living tradition and a continuous sense of identification with the Roman *res publica*. The ultimate end of learning, however, was not merely to prepare citizens to share in the rights and respon-

sibilities of the commonwealth. In its ability to transcend the finite
limitations of temporal experience, learning was a signal of transcendence, an important factor, like the study of music and the study of
divine things, in attuning the soul to the eternal music of the spheres.
For both Plato and Cicero, therefore, learning transformed the learner's
experience of time and corresponded to a general pattern of cosmogony.

For Augustine, however, the pattern of the cosmogony was defined
neither by the Platonic myth of eternal return nor by the hierarchical
order of the celestial spheres, but by a singular convergence of word
and light at the beginning. Just as the Platonic doctrine of *anamnesis*
internalized the cosmic pattern of eternal return, and Ciceronian education was ultimately synchronized with the pattern of the celestial
hierarchy, Augustine's learning theory corresponded to his understanding of creation. This correspondence was not merely formal, which
might be the case if Augustine understood learning as simply an im-
itation of the pattern of the cosmogony. On the contrary, Augustine
explicitly insisted that the same divine activity was present in the
creative act and the process of learning. The eternal word and light of
creation entered human experience in the activity of learning.

Therefore, to arrive at an adequate understanding of Augustine's
learning theory it is necessary to begin where he began—with the
beginning—by analyzing Augustine's symbolism of creation. How did
Augustine understand the divine word and light to have operated in
the creation of the world? Augustine attributed specific, consistent
symbolic values to word and light in his exegetical commentaries on
the creation narrative in Genesis. Only after carefully outlining the
symbolic associations that attended word and light in creation can we
appreciate a theory of learning in which Christ, the divine word and
light, teaches within, a theory of learning explicitly based on a correspondence between creation and education: *Docet nos, quia Principium
est, et loquitur nobis.*

WORD AND LIGHT IN CREATION

Augustine often noted that the creation of the world was a majestic
text in which could be read the fundamental pattern of life. In one
sermon he declared: "Creation is a great book. He set before your eyes
the things He had made. Can you ask for a louder voice than that?"[11]
Augustine devoted considerable time and energy to explicating the
book of creation. His literal and allegorical commentaries on Genesis
attempted to unpack the condensed, symbolic discourse in which Augustine felt that Moses had embodied creation's process and pattern.

On Genesis Augustine wrote an early incomplete work, *De Genesi opus imperfectum*, against the Manicheans (388-89); the magnificent *De Genesi ad litteram* (393-94), which was more consistently allegorical than literal in its exegesis; the evocative commentary on Genesis that comprised the last three books of the *Confessions* (401); a long and detailed commentary on Genesis (402); and a commentary on Genesis that appeared in Books Eleven and Twelve of *De civitate Dei* (417). Although minor variations in emphasis and nuance may be found in these several commentaries on the creation narrative, sufficient consistency remains to develop a sense of how Augustine understood the word and light of God as motive and formative forces in the beginning. The symbolic associations of word and light in creation can be outlined with special attention to the first five chapters of Augustine's *De Genesi ad litteram*. There Augustine carefully worked out the symbolic significance of the divine word and light in creation.[12]

Augustine began with the beginning. How were we to understand the opening phrase: *"In principio?"* Augustine wondered whether it was to be understood as the beginning of time in which all things had been made, or as the word of God through which all things had been made (I.2). The first solution would have defined the *principium* as the chronological beginning of creation. The second solution, however, would have defined the *principium* as creation's logical beginning, the preeminence of the divine word in the logical order of creation, in keeping with the opening of the Gospel of John: *In principio erat Verbum*. Augustine accepted both definitions of the beginning. In the beginning, God made heaven and earth, both at the chronological beginning of time and through the creative agency of the divine word.

After Augustine had established a sense of beginning, his next problem was to decide exactly what was intended by *coelum et terra*. According to Augustine, heaven and earth defined the two major subdivisions of the primordial creation. The *coelum* was essentially the spiritual creation, the *coelum coeli* of the *Confessions* (XII.13) that from the beginning was formed, perfect, and beautiful (I.3). The *coelum* was an intellectual creation in eternal contemplation of its creator. The *terra*, however, was an unformed corporeal substance. It had been created in the beginning through the creative agency of the word, but it lacked the perfection of order or form. It was this *informis materia* that Augustine understood by the phrase: *terra invisibilis et incomposita erat*. The original "earth" of creation was a kind of primary matter, unformed, yet capable of receiving form.

The crucial descriptive characteristic of this unformed matter was its lack of light. In *De Genesi opus imperfectum*, Augustine referred to this unformed matter as deprived of light: The unformed matter of creation was in a state of chaos "because it was not light" (12). Without light, unformed matter was "an unformed and lightless abyss" (14). A direct correlation between light and form was made explicit in *De Genesi ad litteram*. Essentially, to be formed was to be illumined. The only way in which this unformed matter of creation might receive its proper form was to turn, or be converted, to the light of its creator. "Only in this way," Augustine insisted, "is it able to be formed, so that it might not be an abyss; and to be illumined, so that it might not be shadows" (I.3). The spiritual creation, *coelum*, already had form because it was turned to "the unchanging and incorporeal light, which is God" (I.3). Corporeal matter in the beginning, the original *terra*, was unformed because it had not yet received light.[13]

The turning of the unformed matter toward its creator was inspired by the call of the divine word, which said, "Let there be light." Augustine was intrigued by the nature of this voice and the manner of its speaking in creation (II.4-5). Were the words "Let there be light" spoken temporally or in the eternal divine word? How is it possible to conceive of a voice unless it proceeds temporally and moves through some created medium? Augustine asked if this primordial creative voice was spoken corporeally, as he imagined the voice that announced Jesus as the Son of God to have been spoken (Mt 3:17); and he asked if this creative voice moved through the medium of the spiritual creation or the primary matter that both had been produced in the beginning. By what language, Augustine asked, were these words spoken before the proliferation of tongues at Babel? Who existed at that time to hear and understand those words? Augustine quickly dismissed these conjectures by asserting that the words *Fiat lux* were not spoken by means of sound or conveyed through a medium. As he said in *De Genesi opus imperfectum*, "We ought to accept that God said, 'Let there be light,' not by means of a voice given birth by the lungs, nor by means of tongue and teeth" (19). Rather, the words were spoken by the *Verbum Dei* through whom all things were made (Jn 1:3). Human words were utterly different than divine. The words spoken by humans were temporal, but the word of God was eternal. It was the eternal word of God that in the beginning and, as Augustine maintained, in eternity, uttered the words "Let there be light" (II.6).

Now that he had established the symbolism of the word as the eternal agency through which creation was spoken, Augustine turned his attention to the symbolism of light. He asserted that this light that was spoken into being by the eternal word was continuous with the primary creation that had been previously referred to under the figure of *coelum* and which was complete in its formed, ordered, and perfect state. The voice of God, *Deus dixit*, described the process by which God called back, or converted, primary matter to be illumined and, thereby, formed (III.7). The *informis materia* was called by the divine word to turn toward its creator and receive the light.

At this point, Augustine introduced the figure of wisdom into his commentary on the creation narrative. In the beginning, when the unformed matter was made, it was not the place to say *Deus dixit*, because that which was imperfect did not imitate the perfection of the word by which God eternally spoke all things, not by the sound of voice, nor by thought composed in sounds, but by the eternal light of wisdom. In creation, God spoke the eternal light of wisdom (IV.9). The voice of God was that light. Therefore, Augustine distinguished between two stages in creation: In the beginning, God made the unformed matter. In the second stage, however, God spoke the light of wisdom by which that primary matter was formed. In Augustine's reading of the creation narrative in Genesis, *Deus fecit* referred to the generation of the primary matter which, as we noted, was brought into being at the beginning of time and through the creative agency of the eternal word of God. But *Deus dixit* referred to the process by which God spoke forth light and gave form to creation. Creation was given order through this convergence of word and light: Creation was "formed by being converted to the unchanging light of wisdom, the Word of God" (V.10).

The picture of creation emerging from Augustine's commentary on Genesis is one in which the symbols of word and light, the auditory and visual textual imagery, seem to flow into each other and blend into a single event. There seems to be an almost interchangeable quality to the symbols of word and light. But our brief review of the first five chapters of *De Genesi ad litteram* has disclosed basic characteristics that Augustine associated with word and light in creation. It is possible at this point to isolate the basic associations that have emerged: First, the word of creation was radically different than human words. The creative word was so different that it could not be conceived in terms of sound or even in terms of thoughts composed of sounds. Second, this word represented the principle of agency. The original creation was called into being through the agency of the divine word in the beginning. Third, the light of creation was continuous with creation. The visual imagery of illumination in which the primary matter was formed represented a continuity between the light of wisdom, the light born of God, and the creation, the light made by God (*De Genesi opus imperfectum* 20). Although they may have been different in degree, the uncreated and created lights were definitely in continuity in the creative process in which God said, "Let there be light." Fourth, the light represented the principle of form. The original unformed matter was defined as a condition without light, while to be formed (*formari*) was to be illumined (*illuminari*).

Fifth, word and light fused in a dynamic symbolic synesthesia at the creation of the world. The cosmos came into existence when God spoke by means of the light of wisdom. In this synesthetic convergence, the agency of the word fused with the formative influence of the light to realize the potential of creation. Word and light, therefore, had different symbolic associations in creation, but those differences coalesced in the imagery of symbolic synesthesia to represent a unified creative process in which creation was simultaneously evoked and illumined, activated and formed, by the divine word and light.

In Augustine's exegetical analysis of creation, therefore, consistent symbolic associations attended word and light: Word was difference. Light was identity. The creative word was agency, and the creative light was form. These associations were of crucial importance to Augustine's understanding of the Christian cosmogonic myth. Word and light represented two distinct logical moments in the cosmogonic process. Augustine went to great lengths to distinguish a first stage that called matter into being from a second stage that illumined that primordial matter with form. Nevertheless, Augustine maintained that those two moments occurred at the same time. Matter and form came into being simultaneously, "so that form should follow matter with no space of time" (*Confessions* XIII.13). God made matter out of nothing and gave form to that formless matter in a single, simultaneous creative event: The illumination was one with the invocation. The divine word spoke light to simultaneously activate and form creation. Although word and light were symbolically distinct, Augustine insisted that they were fused in God's creative act. Implicit in the simultaneity of matter and form was the fusion of the divine speaking and illuminating that converged in the creation of the world. Logically and symbolically distinct, word and light nevertheless merged in the synesthetic event of creation in which God spoke the light of wisdom and gave form to the primary potential of creation. For Augustine, this was the synesthetic event— fusing word and light, difference and identity, agency and form—that defined the beginning in which all things were made.

Augustine elaborated upon this type of symbolic synesthesia of the verbal and visual modes in the thirteenth book of the *Confessions*. Discussing the lights of the firmament, Augustine indicated that even the heavens demonstrated a mysterious interpenetration of light and sound: "It is as if God said: Let there be light in the firmament of heaven; there came suddenly a sound from heaven, as if it had been the rising of a mighty wind, and there appeared cloven tongues like as of fire and it set upon each of them. And there were made lights in the firmament of heaven, having the word of life" (XIII.19). Even the heavenly firmament was based on a coalescence of visual and auditory categories that had set the original pattern for the creation of the cosmos. Augustine noted that the visual and verbal synesthesia of the heavens was internalized in the lives of Christian saints. The saints embodied the divine word and light. They were "lights in the firmament, your saints holding the word of life and shining in sublime authority raised up by spiritual gifts" (XIII.34). The same dynamic convergence of word and light that brought the original creation into being also manifested in the heavenly firmament and the holy lives of the saints. Perhaps the same symbolic synesthesia of word and light was also found in the process of human learning. Augustine held that the word of the beginning was still speaking to human beings in every act of learning; he held that the light of human minds that enabled them to learn was the same divine light operating in the creation of the world. If the same word and light were present in creation and education, perhaps the symbolic associations that attended them in creation also operated in human learning. A sensitivity to those symbolic associations allows us to uncover a new appreciation for Augustine's learning theory by understanding his doctrine of illumination in terms of the symbolism of word and light in which it was formulated.

Word and Light in Education

At the end of his career, Augustine recalled in his *Retractationes* that he had been writing a book on creation against the Manicheans at the same time that he was working on a book on education, the *De magistro* (388-89). Beginning with his earliest writings, therefore, Augustine connected these two major themes, creation and education. Augustine found a particular kind of sense in working on the issues involved in a proper understanding of creation and education at the same time. It is also significant that in writing those two books Augustine was responding to the two dominant influences on his pre-Christian life: The excesses of the visual imagination represented by the Manicheans and the science of verbal expression developed in the schools of rhetoric. Augustine's theory of learning represented a kind of ritual resolution of those visual and verbal concerns.

The *De magistro* was a dialogue between Augustine and his son,

Adeodatus, that claimed to be an authentic record of a conversation between father and son, arriving, through a somewhat circuitous journey, at the conclusion, which Augustine recalled in his *Retractationes,* that "there is no other teacher than God who teaches man knowledge" (I.12). Augustine distinguished between the outer teacher—the *exterior magister*—who attempted in vain to present realities with words and the inner teacher—the *interior magister*—who, in the words of George Howie, "is the Word of God, which in the moment of illumination 'shows' the immaterial realities, i.e., the eternal truths to the learner who is seeking to understand them."[14] Specifically, the word of God, by whom all things were made, was active in the process of human learning. Augustine's understanding of creation, therefore, necessarily informed his theory of learning. The extent of this correspondence, however, can only be disclosed by examining the symbolic formulation of his learning theory, with special attention to its verbal and visual components.[15]

The dialogue of Augustine's *De magistro* began with this question: "What do you think we purpose to do when we speak?" (I.1). This question set the stage for an extended exploration of the precise nature of verbal expression and experience, outlining both the potential and the limitations of human signification. By sign, *signum,* Augustine understood everything by which anything might be signified. Sign was a general classification, therefore, that encompassed two main subdivisions: words that referred to the sense of hearing and gestures that referred to the sense of sight (IV.8). This distinction between verbal and visual signs was important for Augustine's development of the symbolism of the learning process. By *verbum* Augustine did not understand all signs, "but only those which are uttered by the articulate voice" (VII.20). When Augustine inquired into the function of articulate sounds, he initially proposed that human beings spoke for the purpose of teaching (I.1). But how did words teach? If a teacher spoke a word to students, either they knew what the word meant or they did not. If the students knew what it meant, then they did not learn anything, because the teacher had merely reminded them of something they already knew. On the other hand, if the students did not know what the word meant, they also did not learn anything because no effective communication could possibly have taken place. Augustine concluded: "By means of words, therefore, we learn nothing but words, in fact, only the sound and noise of words" (XI.36).

In the sound or noise of human words, hearers were either reminded of some knowledge already known or they merely experienced the senseless sound of words striking their ears. In either case, nothing was learned by words. Verbal expression, and auditory experience in general, was held in very low estimation in the *De magistro*. Augustine noted a curious inadequacy in verbal expression. No inherent connection existed between words and reality, words and meaning, or even between words and the mind that thought to utter them (XIII.41). In his analysis of creation, Augustine had emphasized the radical difference between the divine word and human words. When the soul examined words, Augustine suggested, it found them to be utterly different than the word of God. The soul found human words to be far below God's word, below reality, and even below its own nature as a soul. As Augustine worked out the discontinuity between words and reality, this low estimation of words was decisive for his theory of learning. Augustine noticed an intractable problem with words. On the one hand, he noted, "we use them for the purpose of teaching" (IX.26). On the other hand, however, "we do not learn anything by means of signs called words" (X.34).

Augustine did attribute a legitimate function to these signs called words that was related to his association of the verbal model in general with agency, impact, and process. Augustine derived the etymology of *verbum* from *verberare*, "to strike" (V.12). This etymology not only suggested the way in which words struck the ear in the process of hearing—the common explanation of hearing, as we have noted, in ancient theories of perception—but also indicated the role of words in activating the learning process by providing an impulse that was required to motivate learners to learn things that they did not already know (XI.36). Therefore, Augustine identified the proper function of words in the learning process as a particular kind of agency that directed the learner's attention toward realities, even though words lacked the capacity to present those realities as objective contents of knowledge (VIII.21). As in Augustine's analysis of creation, words initiated action. In learning, the word was incapable of presenting realities to the mind, but it was able to perform a necessary function in providing the shock, impulse, or motive force that directed the mind toward a knowledge of realities whenever words struck the ear.

As opposed to the empty (yet activating) noise of words, Augustine represented the manifestation of reality to the mind in terms of the visual model. Augustine declared: "Does not God, and does not nature exhibit and manifest directly to the gaze of all, this sun and the light that bathes all things present" (X.32). God and nature did what words could not do: They made reality present "to the gaze of all." Therefore, knowledge was accessible to the learner, not through words, but through seeing the thing itself. For Augustine, vision provided the symbolic

pattern for all direct knowledge. "I shall learn the thing I did not know,"
Augustine explained, "not by means of the words spoken, but by seeing
it" (X.35). Augustine observed an objective manifestation of reality, a
continuity between knower and known, that was present in the visual
model. This visual continuity in knowledge was certainly consistent
with the continuities that Augustine had traced in the symbolism of
light in his analysis of creation. As the light of divine wisdom had
impressed its forms upon the world, Augustine held that the contents
of knowledge were immediately present to vision in the process of
learning.

Up to this point in his argument, Augustine had only considered
the process of learning in terms of the "sense of the body" (XII.39).
In other words, Augustine had only discussed what the Platonists called
the "sensible" level of knowledge and what, from his biblical perspective, he referred to as the "carnal" level of knowledge. Shifting
the frame of reference, Augustine began his analysis of how learners
learned those realities that could be gained only by the "sense of the
mind" in the intelligible or spiritual realm. On this higher level, Augustine discovered that the same pattern of verbal and visual coordinates in learning obtained. Those things perceived by the mind, Augustine suggested, "we behold in that interior light of truth which
effects enlightenment and happiness in the so-called inner man" (XII.40).
In the intelligible realm, learning occurred through a visual process of
illumination. As in the senses of the body, realities that were learned
were not revealed by means of words. Rather, the contents of knowledge were manifested to the vision of the mind. When learners learned
anything, it was not due to the efforts of a teacher, but rather to their
own abilities to see the forms of reality that were made manifest to
them by God revealing them within their inner selves (XII.40).

The things of the senses were not taught by hearing, but by seeing.
Likewise, the things of the mind, the intelligible forms of human understanding, were not taught by means of words, but were learned
through direct contemplation. "At the same time," Augustine explained,
"if the one who hears me likewise sees these things with an inner and
undivided eye, he knows the matter by which I speak by his own
contemplation, not by means of my words" (XII.40). In the process of
learning, on both the sensible and intelligible levels, words were fundamentally inadequate. Nevertheless, Augustine continued to recognize
a certain value in the verbal dimension of the learning process as an
impulse that sets the whole process in motion. When learners learned
through the senses of the body, learning was given an impetus and
direction through the impact of words striking the ears. But when

learners learned through the sense of the mind, this active role was performed by the agency of the word of God. "Concerning all those matters which we understand," Augustine concluded, "we take counsel not of the speaker who makes the outward sound, but of truth which presides inwardly over the mind itself, perhaps admonished by words to take this counsel" (XI.38). Although words might exhort the learner to turn within, the actual process of learning depended upon an inward consultation with the objective manifestation of truth within the soul. It has been pointed out that Augustine did not literally refer to the "Word of God" in this passage.[16] But Augustine's reference to taking counsel with the truth within should indicate the verbal symbolism implied in this consultation with the internal teacher. The learner listened to the *interior magister.* Or, in synesthetic terms, the learner listened and saw, the truth spoke within and illumined. Consultation with the internal teacher did not reveal words, but "visible words" that manifested the contents of knowledge in every act of learning.

The parallels between learning and creation should help to suggest how Augustine might have imagined this process to work: First, in both areas a radical difference between human words and the divine word was recognized. Augustine consistently maintained that "man's words are external and serve only to give reminders," but "Christ teaches within the mind" (XIV.45). Although the learner turned to this inner "Word of God" to be instructed regarding the realities of the understanding, the divine word remained supremely transcendent. Augustine suggested this quality of transcendence in his symbolism of word by maintaining, somewhat enigmatically, that the divine word in learning appeared to be within the learner but was actually in heaven. Basing this assertion on the biblical statement that "there is one in heaven who is the teacher of us all" (Mt 23:9), Augustine went on to say that "what 'in heaven' means He Himself will teach us, who has also counseled us through the instrumentality of human beings— by means of signs, and externally—to turn to Him internally and be instructed" (XIV.46). Second, the next thing that must be noticed about the symbolism of the word is that the word was the agency through which learning occurred. The divine word was active in the process of learning, using external signs—"when he spoke externally he reminded us that He dwells within us"—and participating in the internal dynamics of every act of understanding (XIV.46). The word of God actively directed the learner toward realities, not by referring the eyes of the body to the forms of the world, but by referring the eyes of the mind to the forms of the spirit.

Like the forms of the world, these intellectual forms of the spirit were symbolized in terms of vision and light. Third, therefore, as in creation, the symbolism of light involved a certain degree of continuity between God and the world. In Augustine's understanding of learning, however, this continuity was even more pronounced. A definite continuity existed between the human mind and the divine light in Augustine's symbolism of the learning process. In the *Confessions*, Augustine equated the wisdom of God, the *lumen sapientiae*, with the "light of minds" (XI.11). Learning occurred in the direct, immediate presence of that light; "that light," as he noted in *De Genesi ad litteram*, whereby the soul is enlightened so that it beholds all things the object of the intellect. For that light is God Himself" (XII.31.59). It is this visual continuity between the human mind and God that has caused the most controversy over the centuries in the interpretation of Augustine's learning theory. For the most part, this controversy has resulted from confusion regarding the symbolic implications of light in creation and education. Fourth, as in creation, the symbolism of light in the process of learning was associated with form. Obviously, the intellectual apprehension of intelligible forms played a major role in Platonic theories of knowledge. In keeping with this Platonic influence, Augustine understood one aspect of learning as a direct intuition of intelligible forms. Those forms, which in Plato's thought often seemed to reside in some eternal realm of ideas, were transferred by Middle Platonists, at least from Philo on, into the mind of God.[17] The forms of intelligible reality were situated in the divine *nous*. Seeing the forms would seem to imply a direct visual access to the mind of God. Many interpreters of Augustine's learning theory have had definite reservations about recognizing any possibility that humans could have such direct access to God's mind. While an *ontologistic* reading of Augustine's theory drew the conclusion that a direct vision into the mind of God was precisely what Augustine meant, both the *ideogenetic* and the *normative* readings insisted on the transcendence of God. God might have been the transcendent generator of ideas or the ultimate standard for the certainty of ideas, but neither the *ideogenetic* nor the *normative* interpretations of Augustine's learning theory could accept the consequences of visual access to ideas once Middle Platonists and Neoplatonists had placed those ideas in the mind of God.

We miss the symbolic basis of Augustine's learning theory, however, if we insist on interpreting it exclusively in terms of Platonic categories. Augustine understood learning as a reflection of a deeper symbolic process, based on the paradigm of creation, in which the word was agency and the light was form. The word initiated the act of learning, while the light gave it intelligible form. There was, therefore, a more fundamental exegetical basis for Augustine's understanding of learning that connected his learning theory directly with his interpretation of the myth of creation rather than with any secondary philosophical categories. The symbolic dynamics of the cosmogonic myth set up patterns of correspondence and association that were more immediately compelling in Augustine's understanding of learning than his Platonism. Learning worked just like creation, as the central symbolic dynamic of creation—the word speaking light—was internalized in the process of learning. The word was the internal agency of learning, teaching within the soul, and it spoke by illumination.

If we take seriously Augustine's insistence that the same word and light of creation were active in learning, then we might notice the same kind of symbolic associations reflected in his understanding of how the word and light functioned in both contexts. Based on the pattern of creation, therefore, it might be possible to conclude that the word, as the *interior magister,* initiated the process of learning by generating ideas in the human mind. But the divine word, as it had acted in the generation of the primary unformed matter of creation, may have generated ideas without form and without light. In other words, it might be the case that the activity of the divine word as the inner teacher should be understood as the motive force that generated ideas within the human mind *in potentia.* The activity of the word, in this sense, would be a kind of living potential for knowledge, as yet unformed and unrealized, that had to be completed by the illumination of the light. The light, then, would bring intelligible form and order to the potentiality that had been generated in the mind by the agency of the divine word. And, as in creation, these two operations would have to be regarded as separated by no space of time. Word and light would come to life simultaneously in the act of learning. The distinction between them would merely clarify the two dimensions of the learning process—the agency of the word, the formative influence of the light—which Augustine understood to occur simultaneously as Christ taught within the soul in every act of learning.

I present these conclusions tentatively, but I do think they provide important clues to an understanding of Augustine's learning theory. With this insight into Augustine's symbolism of learning, we can refer to the controversy of interpretation regarding his learning theory to observe that there was some truth in both the *ideogenetic* and *ontologistic* versions of his theory. The *ideogenetic* version was correct with respect to the word. It succeeded in isolating the transcendent and mysterious agency of the divine word in the learning process.[18] However, the *ontologistic* version was correct with respect to the light. It captured the continuity between the human mind and the light of God in every act of learning.[19] What both failed to appreciate, however, was the paradoxical way in which Augustine symbolized word and light—the transcendent and the immanent, discontinuity and continuity, agency and form—as fused in the operation of the learning process. Augustine's learning theory, I would suggest, cannot be reduced to either the verbal or the visual dimension of its symbolic formulation: Every act of learning symbolically recapitulated the primordial creation in the convergence of word and light. Learning, therefore, corresponded to the pattern of the cosmogony as an important ritual practice that repeated the primordial event of creation and transformed the life of the learner by bringing the eternal word and light of God directly into human experience. At least, that is how Augustine's learning theory appears if we place it within the consistent symbolism of word and light, within the synesthetic mythic horizon and the synesthetic sacramental universe in which Augustine symbolized the ritual of learning as an inner illumination of the divine word.

6

Tradition

At this point, we leave Augustine. We leave him at the point at which he had normalized a certain pattern for the perceptual symbolism of the visual and verbal models—the symbolism of seeing, hearing, and synesthesia in his religious discourse—particularly in his work up to and including the *Confessions*. Augustine's career continued for another thirty years after this point. While the symbolic associations of word and light persisted, his work increasingly shifted toward a preoccupation with the verbal symbolic model. Augustine's later orientation may be seen most clearly in his polemic against the Pelagians in which he developed a theology of predestination based on God's mysterious, inscrutable call of election. But the predominance of the verbal model in Augustine's later symbolic orientation may also have been related to his responsibilities as bishop in a small North African Christian community. No longer at leisure to contemplate the light, Augustine was compelled to preach the word to an intransigent congregation. In one sermon, he complained about how the demands of preaching had drawn him away from the practice of silent contemplation: "Nothing can be better, nothing more sweet for me than to gaze upon the Divine treasure without noise and hustle: this is what is sweet and good. To have to preach, to inveigh, to admonish, to edify, to feel responsible for every one of you—this is a great burden, a heavy weight upon me, a hard labor."[1] In this practical context, the verbal model came to dominate Augustine's later work.

In taking leave of Augustine, I would like to turn our attention to a brief investigation of one aspect of the Augustinian tradition—the subsequent history of visual and verbal models. To narrow the discussion, I would like to examine two Augustinian learning theories,

theories developed by Bonaventure and Melanchthon, in order to discover how they might have been related to an Augustinian tradition
of the symbolism of word and light. By using learning theory as an
index, we may be able to learn something about the subsequent appropriations and deployments of perceptual models in the Augustinian
tradition.

The Augustinian Tradition

Any definition of a continuous, consistent Augustinian tradition is
problematic. A descriptive definition would conveniently include anyone who claimed to be an Augustinian. But can the tradition be specified
with any more precision than that? In an otherwise impossible analysis
of discourse, Michel Foucault suggested that a tradition cannot be
defined as a continuous transmission, but as a series of discontinuous
appropriations and deployments of discursive formations. A tradition
is not unified by a common set of objects to which interest or attention
is directed, nor by a common style, nor by a common, coherent, and
logically consistent body of concepts, nor even by a persistent recurrence of common themes.[2] Indeed, it is not possible satisfactorily to
define an Augustinian tradition in terms of a coherence of objects,
styles, concepts, or themes. Nevertheless, it is still possible to refer to
an Augustinian tradition in two senses: First, an Augustinian tradition
may be defined in the descriptive sense in which being an Augustinian
merely represented an intentional alliance. Second, however, an Augustinian tradition may be defined in an operational sense in which
subsequent self-proclaimed Augustinians have appropriated symbolic
forms and discursive practices from Augustine—forms and practices
that had assumed a particular pattern in Augustine's work—and have
deployed them in new configurations.

The arrangement of symbolic elements in Augustine's work provided
a set of objects, styles, concepts, and themes that have been appropriated at each moment in the tradition to be transformed and recom-
bined in new arrangements. Rather than a series of footnotes to Augustine, these acts of appropriation have rewritten the original
Augustinian text by taking original elements out of context, inevitably
and unavoidably out of context, in order to deploy them in new symbolic configurations. In this sense, the history of a tradition is a chronicle
of the kaleidoscopic permutations of original elements, changing the
patterns of combination, and shifting the center of gravity to adapt to
new and different ecological situations of thought and action. On this
point, the insight of Foucault may be instructive: "The problem is no

longer one of tradition, of tracing a line, but one of division, of limits; it is no longer one of lasting foundations, but one of transformations that serve as new foundations, the rebuilding of foundations."[3]

Therefore, an Augustinian tradition regarding the verbal and visual dimensions of the process of learning must be seen not as a stable, continuous project built on the foundation of Augustine's work, but as a series of appropriations and deployments that built new configurations of symbolic discourse in Augustine's name. Distinctions between seeing and hearing remained important. In the preface to his *Institutiones*, for example, the Augustinian monk and scholar Cassiodorus maintained that learning required a combination of the visual and verbal models that had to be carefully distinguished. According to Cassiodorus, "learning is in a certain sense two-fold in character, inasmuch as a clear description first carefully permeates the sense of sight and then, after having prepared the ears, penetrates the hearing."[4] While appropriating the distinction between hearing and seeing from Augustine, Cassiodorus clearly deployed the perceptual models involved in learning in a different configuration. For Augustine, hearing words preceded seeing realities. Cassiodorus rearranged the perceptual models so that sight preceded hearing. While such a rearrangement may have been relatively insignificant, it did demonstrate the shifting foundations that were constantly being built and rebuilt in the construction of an Augustinian tradition.

Other appropriations and redeployments of Augustinian symbols, however, clearly had more significant implications. In terms of perceptual models, the most significant appropriations were those that adopted one symbolic model to the exclusion of the other. The learning theories of two Augustinian educators, Bonaventure and Melanchthon, emerged in two very different moments and contexts in the history of the tradition to appropriate and deploy perceptual models for representing the nature, function, and value of human learning. The predominant deployment of light-imagery in Bonaventure's *De reductione artium ad theologiam* created a visual, contemplative context for learning, while the exclusive deployment of verbal-action in Melanchthon's *Responsio ad Picum* engaged his learning theory in a defense of rhetoric, the promotion of eloquence, and the pursuit of a responsible civic role for education. Beyond their implications for a theory of learning, however, these two moments of symbolic appropriation within the tradition demonstrated the ways in which the original Augustinian configuration could be transformed by later Augustinians. In the learning theories of Bonaventure and Melanchthon, the Augustinian symbolic values of word and light were rearranged in significantly new patterns. In fact, by almost exclusively appropriating one model and factoring out the other, Bonaventure's visual model and Melanchthon's verbal model revealed the implications that each model entailed when isolated from the symmetrical balance in which the verbal and visual had been held by Augustine. Bonaventure's learning theory revealed the symbolic implications of what we might call a primacy of the light, while Melanchthon's theory revealed the implications of a primacy of the word. Both learning theories were grounded in perception and conversant with the Augustinian associations that attended the senses; but each rebuilt the Augustinian foundation for a theory of learning around a different center of gravity—one around the eyes, the other around the ears—by basing their learning theories on either light or word.

Certainly, I exaggerate. But I exaggerate to set the symbolic entailments of word and light in a later Augustinian tradition in stark relief. For example, we might expect that Bonaventure's visual model would trace continuities, while Melanchthon's verbal model would require discontinuity, divisions, and differences. As we will see, this was the case. In Bonaventure's *De reductione*, the visual model immediately entailed a learning theory based on a continuous visual field. Bonaventure's primary focus was the pattern, order, or design that gave coherence to the arts and sciences of human learning. Ultimately, Bonaventure based his visually oriented learning theory on a continuity between God and the world by which he could trace all the arts and sciences of human learning back to their source in the divine light of God.

By contrast, Melanchthon oriented his learning theory around verbal action and practices. Emphasizing a perceptual model based on hearing, Melanchthon argued that the value of learning was to be found in the impact of eloquence. As sound struck the ears, the art of eloquence affected relatively passive subjects with its impact on their moral characters. In keeping with the verbal model, Melanchthon concentrated on discontinuity—the division between speaker and hearer, the division between humanists and "barbaric" scholastics, the division between public education and the private obscurities of the Renaissance academies. Ultimately, however, human learning was implicated in a discontinuity between God and the world—between the transcendent word of God and human words—that made learning an instrumental tool that might be used in the service of God, but not a medium that could establish continuity with God or a path that might lead back to the divine light of God.

As we found in Augustine, the verbal model was associated with discontinuity, the visual model with continuity. Rather than achieving

Augustine's integration of both the verbal and the visual models, however, Bonaventure and Melanchthon demonstrated the symbolic implications of a relatively exclusive appropriation of either word or light in the Augustinian tradition.

BONAVENTURE: THE PRIMACY OF THE LIGHT

The predominance of visual metaphors in Bonaventure's *De reductione artium ad theologiam* (*On Tracing the Arts back to Theology*) was immediately evident from its opening line: "Every good gift and every perfect gift is from above, coming down from the Father of lights" (Jas 1:17).[5] Clearly, Bonaventure indicated by such a beginning that he intended to place learning, the arts, and sciences within a theological framework based on the continuity of the visual model of light. As Augustine had maintained, the light of God, the source and substance of all other lights, was continuous with the light of the mind. Bonaventure established a theory of learning based precisely upon such a continuity of light. Commenting on his opening biblical citation, Bonaventure noted that "this passage both indicates the origin of every illumination, and suggests that there are many lights generously flowing from this fontal brilliance."[6] As the Augustinian principle of continuity, this light-imagery established the light of God as the *fons et origo* of every illumination, including the illuminations that formed the basis of the arts and sciences in human learning.

Visual continuity not only provided Bonaventure with a metaphysical principle for the organization of reality, but also a framework for ordering the branches of human learning. Bonaventure distinguished four basic lights that emanated from the divine light and represented it on different levels of learning. The scale of learning comprised these four lights: the inferior light of sense perception, the exterior light of the mechanical arts, the interior light of philosophical wisdom, and the superior light of divine grace through the sacred scriptures. These lights comprised gradations on a visual continuum, differing in degree but not in kind from the light of God that was their ultimate source. In his visual model, therefore, Bonaventure traced human learning on a continuous trajectory back to the divine light.

First, Bonaventure identified the "Inferior Light" that "provides illumination for the perception of natural forms" as the level of sensory perception.[7] In his *De magistro* Augustine had formulated his theory of illumination to explain how human beings learned about intelligible realities, rather than how they acquired sensory information. Bonaventure expanded the entire analysis of illumination to include sensory perception as one of the lights of learning. As one level of divine illumination, the Inferior Light formed the basis for all sensory perception in Bonaventure's account. The Inferior Light was the organizing principle of space. Since perception operated in space, Bonaventure concluded that the light that organized space was the necessary condition for the operation of all the senses. Bonaventure reduced not only seeing, but also hearing, smelling, tasting, and touching, to the Inferior Light that emanated from the Father of Lights. Bonaventure wrote: "Luminosity or light, acting as the principle of distinction of bodily objects, either exists in its own perfection and purity, and is then perceived by sight; or is mixed with air, and is then perceived by hearing; or with vapor, and is then perceived as odor; or with fluid, and then gives rise to taste; or with the solidity of earth, and then provides touch."[8] Two conclusions are obvious from Bonaventure's account of sensory perception: Sight was the most perfect and pure sense, because it perceived the luminosity of the Inferior Light in its unmixed state; and light was the common denominator in all sensory perception, because the mode of perception depended upon the manner in which light was mixed with the different elements that engaged the various senses.

In the Inferior Light, therefore, all the senses were variations on sight, perceiving the light in different ways, but nevertheless sensitive to the luminosity that made perception possible. On the level of perception, the sensitive soul was of the same nature as the light. "The sensitive soul," Bonaventure noted, "possesses the nature of light, and thus remains alert in the nature whose character it is to be clear and penetrable."[9] The visual model, therefore, established continuities and correspondences in Bonaventure's analysis of sensory perception: All was light, all was sight, and the sensitive soul shared the same luminous nature as the Inferior Light. Because that light of perception emanated from the divine light, it was inferior only on a scale of continuous gradation, not because it was different than the Light of God. In all these ways, Bonaventure deployed a symbolic visual model of continuity in his analysis of sensory perception.

The other lights also participated in this visual model of continuity. The "Exterior Light" of the mechanical arts, which according to Bonaventure, "sheds its radiance upon shapes in artifacts," was responsible for human creativity within the seven arts of weaving, fabrication, farming, hunting, navigation, medicine, and drama. All of these arts could be traced back to the divine light.[10] The "Interior Light" of philosophical knowledge, which "provides illumination for the search of intellectual truths," represented the original scope of Augustine's doctrine of illumination. Through this light, Bonaventure held that intelligible reality was illumined to be seen by human understanding.[11] Finally, the "Superior Light" of divine grace and the holy scriptures "provides illumination for the search of salutary truths."[12] Bonaventure's definition of scripture as light represented the culmination and fulfillment of all the various lights of human perception, arts, and learning. His definition of scripture may also present an important point of comparison with Melanchthon, the difference between scripture as light and scripture as word. For Bonaventure, the scripture was a "Superior Light," because "it leads to higher things by manifesting what is above the mind; and also because it derives, not from man's own findings, but from the Father of lights, by inspiration."[13] The scriptures were derived not by verbal inspiration, but by luminous inspiration from the Father of lights. The scriptures, therefore, were the high point of a continuous hierarchy of lights that formed the continuum from saving grace, through wisdom, learning, and the arts, down to the foundation of human knowledge in sensory perception. The entire scheme formed a luminous continuum in Bonaventure's theory of learning.

Scripture, however, not only represented the summit of a visual continuum, but it also provided the basic pattern by which Bonaventure traced all the arts back to theology. Through a visual pattern of correspondence, Bonaventure tried to show that human arts and learning duplicated the pattern of scripture. The pattern of the "Superior Light" of scripture had three aspects or levels that constituted its basic design. Above and beyond the letter of the scriptural text, Bonaventure outlined the three spiritual senses of scripture that had played such an important role in medieval biblical exegesis as the three levels of this "Superior Light": "the Allegorical, by which we are taught what to believe concerning the divinity and humanity of Christ; the Tropological, by which we are taught how to live; and the Anagogical, by which we are taught how to cleave to God."[14]

For Bonaventure, these three levels of biblical exegesis represented the essentially luminous content of scripture as three aspects: (1) the eternal generation and incarnation of Christ, (2) the norm of life, and (3) the union of the soul with God—three aspects that all scripture illuminated. Bonaventure's actual *reductio*, tracing human arts, sciences, and learning back to the divine light, was an attempt to show that each branch of learning corresponded to these three aspects. Systematically proceeding through each art, science, or discipline of learning, Bonaventure tried to demonstrate that each followed a pattern of operation that duplicated the incarnation of Christ, the norm of life, and the union with God. In this way, he hoped to show that "the whole body of our knowledge, therefore, must rest in the knowledge of sacred scripture, most of all in its anagogical sense by which any light is retraced to God from which it had come forth."[15] Bonaventure's retracing of human learning to the divine light, therefore, not only defined the Father of lights as the source of all learning, but also established the union with God as learning's implicit and ultimate goal in every one of its arts, sciences, or disciplines. The anagogical union with God represented the supreme continuity between the arts of learning and theology, a connection that revealed their common source and ultimate end in the divine light.

We can illustrate Bonaventure's procedure in tracing the arts back to the divine light by examining one example, the reduction of rhetoric. This example not only indicates how Bonaventure proceeded to trace all the arts and sciences of human learning back to God, but also how he accommodated an obviously verbal science into a visual scheme of light. According to Bonaventure, rhetoric was the "Light of Discursive Philosophy." As every other art, rhetoric was one of the luminous gifts descending from the Father of lights that could be traced and followed back to its source in the light of God. In addition, however, Bonaventure's analysis of rhetoric indicates how he assimilated the art of speaking, and the entire range of verbal-action, into his predominantly visual framework of illumination. To illustrate, Bonaventure distinguished three aspects in rhetorical science: (1) the speaker, (2) the spoken word, and (3) the hearer. With regard to the speaker, Bonaventure suggested that an analogy was established between the science of rhetoric and the incarnation of Christ. Just as Christ was made visible in the flesh, the speaker's mental concept became known by assuming an external form. We might recall here that Bonaventure identified that external form of sound as a mixture of light and air. In the science of rhetoric, speakers made their mental concepts perceptible by clothing them in sound, yet, at the same time, mental concepts remained in the minds of the speakers. In his visual orientation, Bonaventure found a continuity between the speaker's thought and word that was not found by Athanasius or Augustine. The speaker in rhetoric was analogous to the incarnation, Bonaventure explained, because the divine word "put on the form of flesh . . . and yet remained in the bosom of the Father."[16] Likewise, since the speaker's thoughts were clothed in sound, yet remained in the mind of the speaker, the role of the speaker in the science of rhetoric demonstrated an analogy with the incarnation.

Second, Bonaventure drew the analogy between the spoken word in the science of rhetoric and the second aspect of the "Superior Light" of scripture, the moral norm of life. Rhetorical standards of style duplicated that level of sacred scripture that was devoted to setting out the moral standards for a good human life. The norms of rhetoric—which Bonaventure identified as fittingness, truth, and style—disclosed that aspect of rhetorical science that revealed its origin in the tropological level of the light of scripture. In this way, Bonaventure traced rhetorical norms of eloquence back to the normative dimension of that "Superior Light."

Finally, Bonaventure concluded his analysis of rhetoric by referring to its goal, the effect of speech upon hearers. Here Bonaventure's preoccupation with light-imagery was decisive in his definition of the ultimate goal of rhetoric as the illumination of hearers. In this respect, the goal of the science of rhetoric duplicated the third level of the "Superior Light" of scripture in the anagogical union with God. Bonaventure noted that rhetoric's three goals were to express, to teach, and to persuade. Expression occurred through the medium of a species, teaching through a convincing light, and persuasion through a compelling power. Citing the authority of Augustine, Bonaventure traced these three goals of rhetoric back to the illumination of the divine light. In rhetoric, the genuine teacher must "impress the species, infuse the light, and implant it within the heart of the listener."[17] The compelling power of the science of rhetoric, therefore, resulted from the teacher impressing, infusing, and implanting the light within the listener's heart. Bonaventure made the analogy between the goal of rhetoric and the union with God explicit: "As nothing is known perfectly except through species, light, and power united to the soul, so also the soul, to be formed to the knowledge of God through His inner conversation, must necessarily be united to Him."[18] The end of rhetoric, therefore, duplicated the soul's union with God.

In discussing rhetoric, the "light of discursive philosophy," Bonaventure came close to the original Augustinian symbolism of word and light in education. Bonaventure traced the goal of rhetoric back to a union with God who "is the brightness of His glory and the image of his substance . . . upholding all by the word of his power" (Heb 1:3).[19] Largely distilled from Augustine's own writings, Bonaventure's discussion of the light of rhetoric came close to establishing a synesthetic convergence of visual illumination and verbal power in his analysis of the process of learning. Rather than maintaining the Augustinian tension between visual continuity and verbal discontinuity, however, Bonaventure dissolved the symbolic tension between word and light into an exclusively visual model. The result was Bonaventure's assertion that the science of rhetoric ultimately duplicated the anagogical union with God. The goal of rhetoric, which Bonaventure identified as impressing, infusing, and implanting a certain intellectual light in the soul, was an anagogical figure for the union with God achieved in mystical contemplation.

The predominant and pervasive light-imagery in Bonaventure's *De reductione* established a luminous continuum and structural pattern for all the arts, sciences, and disciplines of human learning. In this context, we are left with the impression that Bonaventure subsumed rhetoric, along with all the other arts, into an exclusively visual model. To appreciate that visual model, we must remember Bonaventure's contemplative orientation and the visual symbolism which that orientation implied. For example, Bonaventure's *Itinerarium mentis ad Deum* provided a kind of contemplative's guidebook that outlined stages of "looking" at each level of a continuum on the soul's ascent to union with God. Through these stages of ascent, the soul journeyed from the world, through the mind, and ultimately to God. Each level involved a change in being that was symbolized as a different mode of seeing. The ultimate stage of union with God established a supreme visual continuity in the conjunction between seer and seen. Human and divine image, human and divine vision, human and divine being became one in that contemplative transformation of seeing.[20]

This contemplative vision was not only a mystical path toward union with God, but an aesthetic orientation toward continuities and correspondences in the world. As a result of this visual orientation, as Erwin Panofsky noted, "the whole material universe becomes a big 'light' composed of countless small ones as of so many lanterns . . . every perceptible thing, man-made or natural becomes a symbol of that which is not perceptible, a stepping stone on the road to Heaven."[21] In symbolizing the patterns of continuity and correspondence beyond sense, Bonaventure relied on a symbolic model derived from the sensory perception of sight. Although the visual model achieved its highest fulfillment in the unitive vision of God, Bonaventure demonstrated how the visual model could organize all of the various branches of human learning into a luminous pattern that originated and led back to the original divine light. In Bonaventure's visual model, "God Himself lies hidden within everything either perceived or known."[22] In learning, God was hidden, but also revealed in the exclusively visual model of Bonaventure's *De reductione* as light.

MELANCHTHON: THE PRIMACY OF THE WORD

That the Protestant Reformation of the sixteenth century was also a revolution of the word has been noticed on several different levels.

A symbolic transformation occurred in the reorientation of Christian belief and practice around verbal symbols—the "Word of God," the text of the Bible, and the verbal-action of preaching the Gospel. As F. W. Dillistone noted, "now the all-important symbolic objects were the pulpit and the Bible resting upon the pulpit or upon a separate lectern."[23] The Protestant emphasis on awakening faith through the hearing of the word, *fides ex auditu*, signaled a dramatic reorientation of the center of gravity in the Christian symbolic universe from the imagery of light to the agency of the word. This reorientation around the word has been variously interpreted: It may have been related to the emergence of the "Gutenberg galaxy" in which the printed word influenced not only the distribution but also the content of the Protestant message; it may have been related to changing patterns of economic activity in which verbal and contractual agreements assumed new importance; it may have been related to the democratization of religious mysteries in the Reformation in which every speaker and hearer could participate as priests without being tied to the centralized authority of the visible Church. In any event, Protestants appropriated and deployed the verbal model as the predominant and practically exclusive model for symbolizing the relations between human beings and the sacred.

This new symbolic orientation toward hearing was anticipated by the German mystic Meister Eckhardt when he claimed that "the power of hearing is better than that of seeing, for one learns more wisdom by listening than by looking." In this formula, Eckhardt reversed the preference for sight over hearing that we found in the religious discourse of Philo, Augustine, and Bonaventure. Certainly, Eckhardt maintained the conventional associations that had attended seeing and hearing as perceptual systems. He understood vision to be initiated by the sensory organ of the eye that extended out its visual ray to contact visible objects. He understood hearing to be initiated by some external agent that struck the air and produced an impact on the relatively passive perceiving subject. However, Meister Eckhardt argued that ears were better suited than eyes for the relation between human beings and God. The visual ray, he suggested, "gives out more, even in the very act of looking." But hearing brought in more (it was more receptive) and, therefore, it was the appropriate sensory mode to receive the impact of the divine word that acted upon relatively passive human beings. "And therefore," Eckhardt concluded, "we shall all be blessed more in eternal life by our power to hear than our power to see. For the power to hear the eternal word is within one and the power to see will leave one."[24]

In this curious reversal, Meister Eckhardt may have departed from the conventional Augustinian preference for eyes over ears, but he anticipated the perceptual reorientation that permeated Martin Luther's insistence that salvation could only be attained through a faith that was awakened by the independent agency of the "Word of God," mediated through the text of scripture and the sermon of the preacher, that had a decisive impact on the ears of those who faithfully listened. Not only did Luther insist that faith came through hearing, but he even went so far as to deny any value at all to the visual model by maintaining that "a right faith goes right on with its eyes closed; it clings to God's Word; it follows that Word; it believes that Word."[25] Obviously, therefore, a shift in perceptual orientation toward an exclusively verbal model was a significant part of the religious project of the Protestant Reformation.

What did this verbal reorientation signify? The verbal model, implying a relationship between a separate external agent that acted with compelling force upon a passive subject, seemed to provide a symbolic center around which many of the most distinctive Protestant commitments revolved. First, scripture was rendered exclusively in the verbal model. Not the "Superior Light" described by Bonaventure, scripture was an exclusively verbal proclamation of the "Word of God." In keeping with the pattern of discontinuity built into the verbal model, this verbal model of scripture insisted on its radical transcendence above and beyond human reason. No luminous trail traced a continuous path from the arts, sciences, and disciplines of human learning back to the scriptural light; rather the word of scripture stood high above all forms of human knowledge and learning as their transcendent judge.

Second, the verbal model was also built into Protestant theories of justification. Luther's notions often referred to as "forensic justification" and "passive righteousness" seem to have been suited to the verbal model. Justification depended upon the authority of a verbal proclamation by which God declared sinners to be righteous, even though by absolute standards of righteousness they remained unavoidably sinners. Again, discontinuity was built into the verbal model, in this case, the unbridgeable discontinuity between God's righteousness and human sin. In Luther's verbal model, that gap could only be bridged on the authority of God's verbal declaration.

Third, the verbal model that placed the "Word of God" high above the human word seemed to result in a general pattern of discontinuity between divine and human realms. Luther's doctrine of the "separation of kingdoms" may have given human beings greater latitude to govern the political order, but it achieved that latitude by establishing a discontinuity between the social and spiritual realms. Divine love would never govern the human world; and "in the spiritual realm the Word of God alone rules, not human power."[26] Although certainly informed by other motives, one motive force in this separation of kingdoms was the tendency toward establishing the discontinuous relationship between human beings and the sacred that was inherent in the verbal symbolic model.

Exclusively appropriating the implications of Augustine's verbal model, Protestant reformers nevertheless understood themselves as authentic Augustinians. We might note that they tended to appropriate the writings of the later Augustine—the Augustine who worked out a verbal model for predestination, rather than the Augustine who worked out a visual and verbal model for illumination—but the reformers clearly perceived themselves to be developing a theology that was faithful to Augustine. Luther's devotion to Augustine was evident in 1517, when he declared that "our theology and that of St. Augustine are going ahead, and they reign in our university, and it is the Lord's doing."[27] As a close associate of Luther, Philip Melanchthon formulated the first systematic Protestant theology, the *Loci communes*. For his contributions to education, Melanchthon became known as the "Praeceptor Germaniae." In 1529, Luther declared that his own translation of the Bible and Melanchthon's *Loci* were the only texts necessary for theology. When he compared his work with Melanchthon's, Luther revealed his orientation toward the verbal model by concentrating on their different rhetorical styles. Luther wrote:

> I prefer the books of Master Philipus to my own. I am rough, boisterous, stormy and altogether war-like. I am born to fight against innumerable monsters and devils. I must remove stumps and stones, cut away thistles and thorns and clear the wild forest; but Master Philipus comes along softly and gently, sowing and watering with joy, according to the gifts God has abundantly bestowed upon him.[28]

Melanchthon did not agree that the Bible and his *Loci* were the only sources necessary for theology. He added Augustine to that list. At one point, Melanchthon condemned the theological faculty of the University of Paris, because "there is no one on the whole Sorbonne faculty who has come in contact with Augustine."[29] Like Luther, Melanchthon had come into contact with Augustine. But both exclusively appropriated the verbal model from Augustine's symbolic discourse and deployed that model in the development of a Protestant theology. As a master of rhetorical eloquence, however, Melanchthon extended that verbal model toward the end of his career to offer a Protestant theoretical defense of learning based on his understanding of rhetoric. Melanchthon not only worked out a learning theory based exclusively on a verbal model, but also demonstrated some of the symbolic implications of an exclusive appropriation of the verbal model in the Augustinian tradition.

Melanchthon's defense of rhetoric was delivered in his *Responsio ad Picum* (1558). This work itself was a rhetorical exercise because it was addressed as an open letter to the Renaissance humanist Pico della Mirandola who had been dead for over fifty years. Melanchthon may have had a personal interest in addressing Pico: The German humanist Reuchlin was both a student of Pico and a teacher of Melanchthon. The reformer, therefore, was part of a living tradition that reached back to the schools of Renaissance humanism, particularly the school of Florentine Platonism with which Pico was associated. But Melanchthon's primary interest seemed to be to argue against the philosophical, contemplative orientation of the Florentine academy by defending the theory and practice of verbal eloquence associated with rhetoric.

In a famous series of letters with Ermolao Barbaro reflecting the debate over the relative importance of philosophy and rhetoric in Florence at the end of the fifteenth century, Pico had argued that philosophy and rhetoric were incompatible. Rhetoric merely dealt in words, verbal ornaments, that were intended to persuade, but inevitably deceived. On the other hand, Pico insisted, philosophy provided a wordless contemplation in which the truth could be seen, known, and demonstrated. Philosophy, therefore, was a visually oriented contemplative discipline that provided direct access to truth; the verbal eloquence of rhetoric, however, was at best ornamentation, but at worst deception that distorted the philosopher's clear vision of truth. Like Bonaventure, Pico ultimately traced all the branches of human knowledge and learning back to God in a visual pattern of continuities and correspondences that were most clearly worked out in his *Oration on the Dignity of Man.* In keeping with his exclusively visual model, Pico denied any value to the verbal eloquence of rhetoric in his theory of human learning. Over fifty years later, Melanchthon countered this visual orientation with his *Responsio ad Picum.*

Curiously, Melanchthon framed his defense of rhetoric not by attacking Pico, but by attacking medieval scholastics who had based their theologies on philosophical contemplation. He opposed those scholastics, particularly Thomas and Scotus, who he labeled "barbarians." Setting aside any explicitly theological differences, Melanchthon attacked these scholastic barbarians on account of their lack of eloquence.

In militant terms that Luther had claimed as his own, Melanchthon declared: "I am always waging a truceless war with the foes of the right sort of studies . . . having repulsed the barbarians, we should shortly redeem the Roman cause and return the arts to their glory."[30] The scholastic barbarians betrayed the Roman cause of Latin rhetoric through their lack of eloquence. Their technical terminology, monstrous expressions, and inexplicable fancies, Melanchthon insisted, had oppressed theology. On account of their deficiencies in eloquence, Melanchthon was convinced that the Greek saying "It's all one ash-heep" accurately summed up the scholastics.[31]

Pico had defended the scholastics: Because they recognized that philosophy had no need of rhetoric, the scholastics attained knowledge beyond words through contemplation. But Melanchthon rejected wordless contemplation for a rhetoric of words in action. In his *Responsio*, Melanchthon's theological orientation toward the authority and agency of the divine word was related to his humanistic concern with the eloquence, authority, and action of human words in rhetoric. Therefore, Melanchthon assigned the highest priority to his defense of eloquence: "For what subject can possibly be richer than that of the dignity and utility of eloquence? How many errors in religion and the other arts have come from this one source: that of neglected and irregular training in the art of Rhetoric?"[32] In responding to Pico, Melanchthon argued that proper training in rhetoric would provide a practical means for rectifying both religion and education.

Melanchthon proceeded to defend rhetoric on three grounds: He insisted that rhetoric was indispensable in communication, in education, and in service to the public good. First, rhetoric was necessary for effective communication. Melanchthon denied Pico's claim that rhetoric and philosophy were incompatible by resorting to Cicero's ideal of a balance between wisdom and eloquence. "There is no use for wisdom," Melanchthon insisted, "unless we can communicate to others the things we have with wisdom deliberated and thought upon."[33] Through rhetoric, truth became capable of expression. Eloquence, therefore, was not merely artificial ornamentation. "On the contrary," Melanchthon argued, "it is the faculty for proper and clear explication of mental sense and thought; in this it even serves worth and truth, so that they may be aptly and correctly expressed."[34]

However, rhetorical communication had an even more crucial function: It took truths that might be seen in private and declared them in public. Consistent with the Protestant democratization of the mysteries, Melanchthon defended rhetoric as the means by which the private became public. "We do not speak concerning secret doctrines which have to be concealed for a time," Melanchthon explained, "but of such as should be brought out in the open, i.e., things which are by all odds the most important part of Christian doctrine."[35] In contrast to the visual-contemplation of the Florentine academy, the verbal-action of Protestant eloquence proclaimed the "Word of God" in public. Melanchthon identified concealment as one of the undesirable implications of an exclusively visual model. Indeed, Pico and other Florentine Platonists had been convinced that some truths had to be concealed from the masses until their eyes were ready to behold them. Petrarch had even identified concealment as one of the responsibilities of the poet. "It is the poet's endeavor," he noted, "to adorn the reality of truth with a beautiful garment, so that it may be hidden from the doltish rabble."[36] In this visual model, the poet revealed truth, but at the same time concealed it from those who lacked the eyes to see through its garments. Unlike the visionary poet, however, Melanchthon argued that the preacher made a public proclamation of truth. To communicate effectively with the public, Melanchthon concluded, preachers of the "Word of God" needed to be skilled in the rhetorical arts of eloquence.

Second, Melanchthon claimed that rhetoric played the central role in any program of education. Without rhetoric, education could not proceed. The primary function of rhetoric was realized in teaching. The business of the rhetor, according to Melanchthon, was "to teach men about the highest affairs."[37] In education, both dialectic and rhetoric were necessary: one "shows by what sort of words things should be explained," while the other "shows the method of teaching."[38] Again, Melanchthon insisted that both wisdom and eloquence were required, but the wisdom of dialectical reason was useless unless its terms could be taught effectively through the eloquence of rhetoric. Learning resulted from the effect that eloquence had upon learners.

In Melanchthon's verbal orientation, no inner illumination was imagined to occur in the process of learning. Melanchthon was less interested in the internal dynamics of learning than he was concerned with the impact and effect, the power and authority, of the word in the educational activity of teaching and learning. Eloquence gave power and authority to education. According to Melanchthon, eloquence was the "power divinely bestowed upon the human race, so that men may be able to teach each other concerning religions, concerning the nature of celestial and other things, concerning right and justice, and concerning every duty of virtue."[39] Augustine had insisted that words did not teach; but, in a dramatic departure from Augustine's learning theory, Melanchthon insisted that eloquence was a gift from God that empowered human beings to teach and to learn precisely by means of words. In the absence of any visual model of learning as illumination, Melanchthon derived the power and authority of words from his exclusive preoccupation with the verbal model. In his learning theory, Melanchthon argued that learning resulted from the powerful impact of words upon learners that occurred in the exercises of eloquence made possible by rhetoric.

Finally, Melanchthon defended rhetoric on the basis of its utility for the public good. Rhetoric was not only pleasurable and instructive; it was also useful for maintaining the public order and administering the public affairs of society. In fact, Melanchthon argued that rhetorical eloquence was the origin of human society. Social order originated in rhetoric, and its institutions of law, religion, marriage, and so on, were maintained by rhetoric. According to Melanchthon, rhetorical eloquence made society possible: "When men were still dispersed and nomadic they were gathered together by eloquence, and by it states were founded; by it rights, religions, legitimate marriage, and the other bonds of human society were constituted. In fact, it is by eloquence that these things are maintained in commonwealths."[40] In this way, Melanchthon was able to trace all human civilization back to the originating and sustaining power of eloquence.

When Melanchthon traced these institutions back to their origin, however, it is significant that he did not follow the example of Bonaventure in tracing them upward to a continuous emanation from the Father of lights. Not space, but time provided the conditions for Melanchthon's verbal model. In keeping with that model, Melanchthon traced these institutions back in time, back along a historical trajectory to an originating eloquence. In this verbal model, the source of human arts, sciences, and institutions was not light, but the eloquent power of words. According to Melanchthon, that verbal power was the beginning of society and it continued to act in the maintenance of public life. The orator, therefore, was the public figure who exercised this practical power in human society. "We indeed call the man an orator," Melanchthon stated, "who teaches men accurately, clearly, and with a certain dignity concerning good and necessary things."[41] Combining wisdom with eloquence, the orator taught those things that were useful for public life. As the exemplar for the active life of civic responsibility, the orator represented verbal action opposed to the visual contemplative orientation represented by Pico. Public utility, Melanchthon concluded, was the genuine measure of the philosopher: "I call a philosopher one who, when he has learned and knows things good and useful for mankind, takes a theory (*doctrina*) out of academic obscurity and makes it practically useful in public affairs."[42]

Communication, education, and usefulness in the public arena, therefore, were the grounds upon which Melanchthon defended rhetoric. All of these defenses, however, were derived from Melanchthon's exclusive preoccupation with working out the implications of a verbal orientation, his exclusive appropriation of the verbal model for symbolizing not only human learning, but ultimately the relations between human beings and the sacred. In the end, Melanchthon did not define learning as a visual contemplation of the divine light that permeated all the arts and sciences and illuminated the mind. Rather, Melanchthon defined learning as the verbal action of eloquence that produced practical effects in society for the public good. In keeping with the tendency toward discontinuity in the verbal model, Melanchthon maintained that the public good of human society was qualitatively different than the highest good that could only be attained through the "Word of God." Nevertheless, the temporal, practical, and active associations of the verbal model insured that Melanchthon's learning theory had to be very different than Bonaventure's theory of human learning based on the visual model. Although they were both Augustinians by self-definition, Bonaventure and Melanchthon demonstrated the dramatically different symbolic implications entailed in an exclusive appropriation of either the visual or verbal model. Although learning theory has merely served as an index to the appropriation and deployment of perceptual models, a comparison of the theoretical orientations of Bonaventure and Melanchthon at the very least has suggested how an Augustinian tradition has been built and rebuilt on the shifting symbolic foundations of word and light.

Conclusion

It may be useful to recall one last time the outlines of the conceptual map we have used to explore the perceptual symbolism of word and light in religious discourse. First, we have entertained the notion that symbolic discourse is grounded in perception. The symbolic discourse of seeing, hearing, and synesthesia is predetermined by physiology, determined by culturally constructed associations, and overdetermined by the surplus of signification and the resistance of the living body to symbolic reduction. Within this dialectic in the symbolic discourse of the body, perceptual metaphors are generated by the body, articulated in discourse, but always forced back again to their physiological ground in the lived experience of the body. Nevertheless, while they linger in the patterns and processes of symbolic discourse, perceptual metaphors provide rich, vital resources for signification in religious thought and action. If nothing else, this book has suggested the potential that lies in attention to perceptual metaphors for making even familiar religious discourse look and sound different. While these explorations have been preliminary and suggestive, I think that attention to perceptual models promises to open up the eyes and ears of religious discourse in new ways by returning discourse to the living, signifying, and signified body that produces and consumes it.

Second, seeing and hearing have generated perceptual models with consistent associations: From ancient Greek science of the senses to the phenomenology of perception, seeing and hearing have been distinguished as separate perceptual systems that relate human beings in different ways to their world. In the deployment of perceptual models in religious discourse, we have seen how Philo, Arius, Athanasius, Augustine, Bonaventure, and Melanchthon all were engaged in working out the symbolic implications of the visual and verbal models. Not only concerned with analyzing relations between self and world, these religious thinkers deployed perceptual models of light and word to symbolize the continuous and discontinuous relations they perceived among self, world, and the sacred. As we have noted, perceptual models symbolized certain structural oppositions: Continuity and discontinuity, space and time, copresence and succession, simultaneity and sequence, presence and distance, immediacy and referentiality, contemplation and action, and so on, were all consistently associated with the visual and verbal models respectively. In keeping with the dialectic of physiological symbols, these oppositions (and their resolutions) had as much to do with the demands of discourse as they did with the body. Yet perceptual models signified structural oppositions that allowed religious discourse to embody conceptual relations that were beyond the body by means of physiological symbols of sensory perception.

Third, and finally, symbolic synesthesia has surfaced frequently in these explorations of perceptual symbols. In religious discourse, synesthesia symbolized both an antistructural breakthrough—as we have noted, a breakthrough in language that signaled a more intense, extraordinary, and unified experience of the sacred—as well as a coincidence of opposites that fused the structural oppositions built into the visual and verbal models. Attention to perceptual models has allowed us to reconstruct an Augustinian symbolic universe, in particular, in a new and perhaps strange way. The most important manifestations of the sacred in Christian myth, the synesthetic theophanies, were recapitulated in Augustine's discourse about the sacred, in the synesthetic terms in which he presented sacred truth, the love of God, the Son of God, the heavenly firmament, the lives of the saints, and the human heart that met and matched the word and light of God. In synesthetic terms, Augustine recalled his own conversion, described the sacraments as "visible words," and analyzed the ritual of learning as an inner illumination of the divine word. Using learning theory as an index, we have seen some of the symbolic consequences entailed by an appropriation of either the visual or the verbal model for symbolizing relations among human beings, education, and the sacred. Although the learning theories of Bonaventure and Melanchthon were still developed within an Augustinian tradition, they represented significant departures from the religious discourse and sensibility that Augustine had based on the convergence and interpenetration of word and light. In that respect, the almost exclusive appropriation of either the visual or verbal model signaled the beginning of the end of a unified Augustinian symbolic universe of word and light. They were forerunners of a post-Augustinian world.

LOST HORIZON

In the end, therefore, we not only take leave of Augustine, but we leave the Augustinian tradition that had ceased to provide a coherent symbolic horizon in European thought by the end of the sixteenth century. This is not to say that no one read Augustine, thought about him, or claimed his authority for various intellectual or religious projects. It is only to acknowledge that after the sixteenth century no one moved within the distinctively synesthetic horizon of an Augustinian symbolic universe of word and light. Even Bonaventure and Melanchthon—although they exclusively appropriated either the visual or the verbal model—still moved within an Augustinian universe in which divine word and light provided the structural possibilities for symbolizing relations between self and world or human beings and the sacred. We have used learning as an index to these symbolic linkages among humans, world, and the sacred in the Augustinian tradition. Increasingly divorced from its Augustinian context, human learning became an autonomous activity with no reference to the perceptual models that had ultimately related learning—in all its arts, sciences, and disciplines—to the sacred. No longer moving within a synesthetic world of word and light, eyes and ears were on their own to work out some autonomous meaning for the activity of learning.

Significantly, the transition from the Augustinian world to what might be called a modern world involved a divorce of the senses from their synesthetic unity in the symbolism of word and light. In his monumental study of the human sciences, *The Order of Things*, Michel Foucault suggested the importance of perceptual orientations in that transition. According to Foucault's reconstruction, the medieval period was characterized by a general epistemic field in which the visible and the expressible were endlessly interwoven through discourse. Words and things were joined by bonds of similitude, the heard and the seen interpenetrated in what I have been calling a synesthetic symbolic universe. A synesthesia of the verbal and visual set a consistent pattern for the arts, the sciences, and ultimately the perceived relations between human beings and the sacred that coordinated human understanding of the arts and sciences in the Augustinian tradition. At the end of the sixteenth century, however, the arts and sciences were divorced from that medieval symbolic order of word and light. Identifying this transition as a radical historical disjuncture, Foucault noted that at the end of the sixteenth century "things and words were to be separated from one another." As a result, "the eye was thenceforth destined to see and only to see, the ear to hear and only to hear."[1] At that point, the Augustinian tradition — as a unified symbolic horizon of word and light, verbal and visual, hearing and seeing, ears and eyes, words and things— lost its grip on the western imagination. Eyes and ears defined independent fields of discourse, knowledge, and power divorced from their sacred convergence and interpenetration in any symbolic synesthesia.

Many commentators have noticed that during the seventeenth and eighteenth centuries the eye came to dominate the epistemic field of western European thought. Walter Ong, for example, identified that period as "a shift toward the visual throughout the whole cognitive field."[2] The eye dominated discourse, knowledge, and power in the arts and sciences of human learning. In this new perceptual posture, the eye constituted the sole criterion of validity. As Foucault noted, knowledge became "a visibility freed from all other sensory burdens"; discourse became the "description of the visible"; and power was invested in a knowledge and discourse in which "hearsay is excluded; which leaves sight with an almost exclusive privilege."[3] The power of vision also defined new institutional arrangements — such as the clinic, the asylum, and the prison — that were based on practices that subjected human bodies to visual observation.[4] This tyranny of the eye over the entire epistemic field determined the conditions of possibility for what might count as legitimate and meaningful statements in the arts and sciences of human learning. In this visual orientation, spatial continuity organized legitimate discourse and knowledge about reality. Examples of this visual orientation could be multiplied: The taxonomy organized knowledge in a spatial field so that Linnaeus "distinguishes the parts of natural bodies with his eyes"; Buffon claims that "our general ideas are relative to a continuous scale of objects"; and Bonnet maintains that "there are no leaps in nature; everything is graduated."[5] Separated from the discontinuity, difference, reference, succession, temporal sequences, and so on, associated with the verbal model, this epistemic model of visual continuity achieved a certain autonomy in the human sciences. Legitimate knowledge could be presented in a visual model of continuous taxonomic relations in which time and discontinuity disappeared. Vision organized discourse, knowledge, and power in human learning by establishing its autonomous regime of continuity.

This visual pattern of intelligibility, however, was displaced at the beginning of the nineteenth century by a new epistemic orientation in the human sciences that made room for categories of understanding derived from the verbal or auditory model. A new interest in time, sequence, and history in the organization of discourse and knowledge disclosed the emergence of the auditory, verbal model as a new source of power in the human sciences. Regularities of temporal succession replaced regularities of spatial copresence in the organization of legitimate knowledge about reality. As Foucault noted, this preoccupation with temporal succession was part of an epistemic field "in which visibility no longer plays a role."[6] The shift from a visual to a verbal orientation was perhaps most evident in nineteenth-century theories of language that were almost exclusively preoccupied with its auditory components, the fundamental elements of syllables, phonemes, sounds, and their transformations. Language was defined in terms of the sounds that composed it. No longer was the study of language conditioned by a visual concern for the signifying relations involved in the representation of one element of the visible universe by another. The dominant nineteenth-century science of language was not the analysis of visual representation, but "an analysis of sounds, of their relations, and of their possible transformations into one another."[7] In other words, a new orientation toward the perceptual resources of hearing resulted in a linguistic science in which "languages are defined, at least in their general typology, according to the way in which they link together the properly verbal elements that compose them."[8]

In the nineteenth century, therefore, the perceptual resources of the eye were to a significant extent displaced by the resources of the ear in forming the conditions of possibility for legitimate discourse and knowledge in western thought. At least that is how Foucault analyzed the epistemic field that dominated nineteenth-century human and natural sciences in Europe and America. The entire field of knowledge and discourse was organized by the verbal model. In keeping with the verbal model, nineteenth-century sciences were primarily interested in arranging distinct and discontinuous elements into temporal, developmental, or historical sequences. "From the nineteenth century," Foucault recalled, "history was to deploy in a temporal series, the analogies that connect distinct organic structures to one another."[9] In the search for origins, the attempt to establish historical transformations, and the entire, pervasive evolutionary project of the nineteenth century, the dominant epistemic field of the human and natural sciences was conditioned by the temporal associations of the verbal model. In that temporal orientation, legitimate knowledge was not concerned, as Foucault noted, with "the constitution of a continuous table of species, [but] with the description of discontinuous groups."[10] Visual continuities were replaced by the temporal arrangement of discontinuous elements in the dominant epistemic field of discourse and knowledge during the

nineteenth century. In this sense, legitimate learning proceeded along
a path determined by the ear rather than the eye—the temporal succession of the history rather that the spatial copresence of the taxonomy—
in its organization of a human understanding of reality.

(an unw. ?
condn)

If we accept Foucault's reconstruction, a history of perceptual orientations suggests that a medieval, Augustinian synesthetic horizon
was shattered, leaving only the pendulum-swing alterations between
a visual pole preoccupied with a spatial order in which continuous
taxonomies could be established and a verbal pole concerned with
arranging discontinuous elements in temporal sequences of origin,
transformation, development, evolution, and progress. Seeing and hearing, therefore, became two antithetical, autonomous options for organizing knowledge, no longer two coordinates of a unified perceptual
sensibility. In this modern sensibility, a division of labor governed the
several senses. The verbal became increasingly alienated from the visual
in the world of discourse that might be called the modern world.
Horkheimer and Adorno noted this division of sensibility in a modern,
rationalized scientific world: "For science the word is a sign: as sound,
image, and word proper it is distributed among the different arts, and
is not permitted to reconstitute itself by their addition, by synesthesia."[11]
This rationalization of the senses prevented any synesthetic convergence or interpenetration of perceptual modes in the arts, sciences, or
disciplines of human learning. Such a synesthetic, unified sensibility
also disappeared from symbolic discourse about the sacred. As a result,
the modern religious world might be described as a world in which
the synesthetic fusion of word and light no longer held as a symbolic
center of gravity. When eyes only see and ears only hear no possibility
is left for the symbolic discourse of word and light, a discourse central
to the Augustinian tradition, that once coordinated seeing and hearing—in perception, in learning, and in the relations between human
beings and the sacred—as two distinct modes of a unified sensibility.

What are we to make of all this? What does it mean to outline such
a generalized history of western thought as a shifting transposition of
perceptual orientations? Do we see it or hear it this way? Do we smell,
taste, or touch its lingering influence in our present intellectual world?
Or are we sensitized to it by recognizing a lost horizon in which
perceptual-intellectual systems were unified, a synesthetic horizon in
which the visible and expressible were interwoven in a more integrated
symbolic discourse that related human beings to their world and to
whatever they perceived as sacred in that world? One of the many
tasks of the history of religions, I would suggest, is an imaginative
recovery of the potency of perception in religious discourse and practice.

?

In conclusion, therefore, I would like to make some proposals for considering the wider salience of seeing, hearing, and synesthesia in the history of religions.

SEEING AND HEARING

Attention to the play of perceptual metaphors in symbolic discourse has revealed some unexpected features of the western religious imagination. For one thing, generalizations about western religions, particularly, as religions of the sacred book, need to be modified. In a perceptive discussion of Hindu imagination, Diana Eck repeated a common generalization about western religious traditions: They have been oriented around a verbal model based on the sacred word. She noted that "Western traditions, especially the religious traditions of the 'Book'— Judaism, Christianity, and Islam—have trusted more the Word than the Image as a mediator of the divine truth."[12] By implication, this generalization has often been taken to mean that western religious traditions have somehow preferred the hearing of the word to the sight of the eye. After exploring the symbolic universes of important figures in the western religious traditions of Judaism and Christianity, however, I think we must be extremely wary about this generalization. At least in the case of Philo, Athanasius, Augustine, and Bonaventure, as we have seen, the verbal model of words, speech, and hearing was clearly subordinated to the visual model of sight. By contrast, however, a verbal model was preferred by Arius, Eckhardt, Luther, and Melanchthon. I think these differences in perceptual orientation within what might generally be called western religious discourse calls for at least three conclusions.

First, generalizations about the role of seeing and hearing for something that might be labeled "religion in general" are useless. In this regard, the work of Walter Ong might serve as a cautionary example. In his celebrations of the oral-aural dynamics of religion, Ong has advanced generalized assertions about sight and sound that tend to suggest his own commitment to an auditory model of reality. According to Ong, words convey "meaning more powerfully and accurately than sight."[13] Arguably, he might be right, but such a conclusion was not drawn by Philo, Athanasius, or Augustine, for example, and therefore cannot be extended as a descriptive generalization about the perceptual orientation of religion in general, or, for that matter, of western religions. According to many significant representatives of western religious traditions, sight accessed reality far more directly and accurately than speech and hearing. In the generation of religious discourse, therefore, a visual model of continuity between seer and seen established the basic conditions for accuracy in perception, thought, and even the relations between human beings and the sacred.

Disclosing his own auditory orientation, Walter Ong has actually reversed the symbolic associations that have attended sight and hearing in western thought. Going back to ancient Greek science, western religious imaginations have tended, as we have seen, to associate sight with continuity, presence, and the immediate, presentational disclosure of information; hearing, however, as we recall, has been associated with discontinuity, absence, and a referential, mediated disclosure of information. In reversing the historical terms by which sight and sound have been contrasted, Ong has asserted that, "Because of its association with sound, acoustic space implies presence far more than does visual space."[14] More recently, he has maintained that, "Sight isolates, sound incorporates. Whereas sight situates the observer outside what he views, at a distance, sound pours into the hearer."[15] Obviously, these conclusions about sight and sound are at variance with the ways in which they were imagined by most of the western religious thinkers we have examined in this book.

Although one of his intentions has been to counteract the domination of visual print and electronic media in the modern world, Walter Ong has also drawn sweeping conclusions about religion in general. "Religion has to do somehow with the invisible," Ong has stated, "and when the earlier oral-aural world, with its concentration on voice and sound, finally yields to the more markedly visual world incipient to script and print, one may be tempted to argue, religion finally must go."[16] Not wanting religion to go, Walter Ong has tried to recover what he has regarded as religion's oral-aural vitality. Therefore, he has claimed that an imageless, auditory, verbal model is more suited to the invisible reality of religion. In criticizing Ong on this point, C. Mackenzie Brown has noted that his assertions about the psychodynamics of sight and sound are out of place in a Hindu context, where *darsan*—seeing and being seen by the deity—has been at the center of Hindu worship. Having rejected the relevance of Ong's generalizations about sight and sound for India and, therefore, for any notion of religion in general, Brown nevertheless granted that Ong's generalizations might be relevant to western religious traditions. Since "Ong clearly bases much of his analysis of sight and sound on the Christian-Hebraic tradition," Brown concluded that his "views may have a certain plausibility in a Western context."[17] The question of plausibility for a western context, however, brings me to my next point.

Second, to address this problem more directly, generalizations about seeing and hearing in western religious traditions are extremely problematic. I think that the selected case studies of seeing and hearing in this book have called into question Walter Ong's conclusions. However, without denying the plausibility of Ong's assertions about hearing and seeing in *any* western religious context, I would only caution that his generalizations could not possibly apply to *all* western contexts, let alone some entire, totalized western context. In brief, western religious traditions of seeing and hearing have not comprised a unified perceptual field. Obviously, the shifting perceptual orientations we have tracked — from Philo, Arius, and Athanasius, through Augustine, to Bonaventure and Melanchthon — have indicated that no generalization about the perceptual orientation of a western religious context could possibly be adequate. Analysis of seeing, hearing, and religious discourse requires a meticulously detailed investigation of multiple symbolic universes. Unstable, fluid, and contested, those universes of perception and discourse resist any secure generalization.

Nevertheless, it may be possible to chart trends in the shifts, movements, and conflicts of perceptual orientations. Attention to seeing and hearing in medieval Jewish thought, for example, suggests at least two reasons why a western religious tradition might be resistant to generalizations about its perceptual orientation. First, to draw a stark contrast, some see and hear, but some do not, insisting on thinking in conceptual abstractions instead. Since any exegetical tradition is comprised of a repertoire of strategies for engaging a text, I would like briefly to contrast these two: One that is sensitized, the other that is desensitized to perceptual content. Let me point to an illustration that focuses this contrast on the interpretation of a biblical passage we have already considered: "All the people saw the voice(s)" (Ex 20:15). We recall what Philo made of this passage. Similarly, Rabbi Akiva was sensitive to the perceptual dynamics of seeing the voice on Sinai. According to Akiva, "They saw and heard that which was visible. They saw the fiery word coming out of the mouth of the Almighty as it was struck upon the tablets." By contrast, Judah the Prince gave an intellectualist, abstract, perceptually desensitized reading of the same passage. He said, "This is to proclaim the excellence of the Israelites, for when they all stood before Mount Sinai to receive the Torah they interpreted the divine word as soon as they heard it."[18] One a mystical perception of a luminous voice, the other a conceptual realization of abstracted ideas, these two options continued to find defenders throughout the tradition.

Even those sensitized to the dynamics of seeing and hearing, however, have come into conflict over perceptual orientation. A second reason, therefore, for being skeptical about broad generalizations regarding the perceptual orientation of western religious traditions is the fact that seeing and hearing have often been implicated in symbolic conflicts within religious traditions. Elliot Wolfson has documented the disagreements within medieval Jewish mysticism over whether sight or hearing was the dominant perceptual model. This tension between the senses, however, was embodied in the dual perceptual orientation of the mystical tradition itself, "generated by the emphasis on the visionary component of mystical experience on the one hand, and the adherence to the oral nature of kabbalah, on the other, the latter being transmitted primarily through hearing and not sight."[19] Positioning themselves within this tension, some mystics argued for hearing, while others argued for sight as the most appropriate perceptual model for symbolizing the relation between human beings and the sacred. In that tension, as in the conflict between word and light at Nicaea, perceptual orientations were strategies for working out symbolic claims within and upon a common tradition of religious discourse. At the very least, however, those contests over sight and hearing undermine any generalizations about Judaism, or, by extension, other western religions, as having a distinctive perceptual orientation toward hearing.

Third, and finally, generalizations about the perceptual orientations of so-called eastern religions are also, equally problematic. To cite only one illustration: Bernard Faure has analyzed conflicts between Ch'an Buddhism and indigenous, local, popular religion in China as, in part, a conflict over perceptual orientations. In visual metaphors, exponents of Ch'an symbolized space as homogeneous, based on an insight into a Buddhist reality that was everywhere, nowhere, utopian in the truest sense of the word. Popular religion, however, tended to perceive space as heterogeneous, anchoring the sacred in specific, localized sacred places in the environment. These conflicting spatial orientations, however, may have been related to a conflict between visual and auditory orientations. Faure noted that "it may be argued that the dichotomy between the visual metaphors of Ch'an and of popular religion is in fact the projection onto the plane of the dominant discourse of Ch'an of a more fundamental dichotomy between visual and auditory metaphors." Noting that visual imagery is associated with continuity, spatial simultaneity, and a presentational disclosure of information, while auditory imagery refers to discontinuity, temporal sequence, and a referential disclosure of information, Faure suggested that "these epistemological dichotomies underlie the opposition between Ch'an and popular religion."[20] Obviously, this opposition undermines any generalization that might be made about the visual orientation of Chinese or other so-called eastern religions. More specifically, however, Faure's analysis calls attention to the situational, relational, and meticulously detailed perceptual orientations that can be implicated in religious conflicts within a particular geographical region, historical moment, or religious environment. Certainly, analysis of perceptual symbolism requires attention to precisely those kinds of local conflicts.

SYNESTHESIA

Not only implicated in conflicting perceptual orientations, however, seeing and hearing have often been deployed in the symbolic strategy of resolution that we have called symbolic synesthesia. As an important symbolic resource, synesthesia bears both a wider and a more detailed investigation in the history of religions. I have argued that, at least in one respect, synesthesia represents an antistructural symbolic resource in religious discourse and practice. Concrete, involving, and even visceral like sense perception, synesthesia nevertheless represents an antistructural breakthrough from sense to non-sense. Synesthesia is a perceptual strategy particularly suited to marginality or liminality in religious discourse and practice. Violating the ordinary order of the senses, synesthesia often represents a liminal breakthrough in language and thought at those points, perhaps, at which ordinary language and thought break down. In the Christian tradition, synesthesia has appeared particularly in the discourses of mysticism and the practices of ritual, but, as I have emphasized a number of times, the entire mythos of the Christian tradition is structured by crucial breakthroughs of the sacred into the world—theophanies of word and light—that have taken precisely the form of symbolic synesthesia. Clearly, those synesthetic theophanies require further investigation in the Christian tradition. In conclusion, however, I would like to make some brief remarks about the wider application of the analysis of symbolic synesthesia for the history of religions.

As I have noted, symbolic synesthesia generates symbols that are concrete like sense perception, but more immediate, charged, and compelling. In this respect, symbolic synesthesia represents a perceptual resource in religious discourse that embodies qualities of intensified energy. By virtue of this highly charged quality, synesthesia might be deployed as a symbol of power or authority in religious discourse. Perhaps the primary synesthetic symbol of compelling power is thunder and lightning, obviously a recurring motif in the history of religions. As Mircea Eliade noted, "Thunder is a weapon of the sky god in all mythologies, and any spot he struck with lightning becomes sacred (*enelysion* to the Greeks, *fulguritum* to the Romans)."[21] Examples could be almost endlessly multiplied. In thunder and lightning, religious discourse found a synesthetic motif for a highly charged fusion of sight and sound. The synesthetic motif of thunder and lightning recurs frequently in religious discourse as a symbol of compelling power and authority. Not only sky gods, but also powerful, authoritative religious persons may be enveloped in synesthetic imagery of thunder and lightning. For example, the Buddha's entry into *parinirvana* at his death was symbolized as a synesthetic event of thunder and lightning: "Fearsome thunderbolts crashed down on the earth. . . . And the world when the Prince of Seers had passed beyond, became like a mountain whose peak has been shattered by a thunderbolt."[22]

As we have seen, the Hebrew Bible symbolized the authority of the law as a synesthetic event, not only an event in which the people saw the voice, but also in which "thunder began to be heard and lightning to flash" (Ex 19:16). It has often been noted that thunder and lightning represented a significant symbol of divine power in the biblical tradition, as in the Book of Job, "his light is upon the ends of the earth. After it a noise shall roar: he shall thunder with the voice of his majesty" (Jb 37:4). Attention to the synesthesia of thunder and lightning, however, might even suggest a possible clarification of a textual problem in biblical scholarship, Paul's conflicting accounts of his meeting with Christ on the road to Damascus in the Book of Acts. According to the narrative, "as he journeyed he approached Damascus, and suddenly a light from heaven flashed about him. And he fell to the ground and heard a voice saying to him, 'Saul, Saul, why do you persecute me?' " (Acts 9:3-4). Like thunder and lightning, this light and voice was a synesthetic theophany. The authenticity and authority of Paul's experience was certified by the claim that he both saw and heard that synesthetic manifestation of the sacred. In recalling that event, however, the Book of Acts involved Paul in a curious contradiction: In one account Paul recalls that "the men who were traveling with me stood speechless, hearing the voice but seeing no one" (Acts 9:7); while a second account observes that "those who were with me saw the light but did not hear the voice of the one who was speaking to me" (Acts 22:9). Obviously, these accounts are contradictory. Whether they heard but did not see, or saw but did not hear, however, the point of these conflicting accounts seems to be that those who were with Paul did not do both. In symbolizing Paul's authentic, authoritative encounter with Christ, therefore, the compelling quality of that experience was represented as a synesthesia of light and voice, immediate and powerful as a thunderbolt, certifying Paul's authority on the basis of what he had both "seen and heard" (Acts 22:14).

In providing a symbolic vocabulary for transcendence, symbolic synesthesia is a resource in religious discourse for moving in and through sense to non-sense, signaling some transcendent, extraordinary, or supernatural frame of reference that rises above or goes beyond the world of ordinary sensory perception. Within Hindu tradition, for example, symbolic synesthesia has been an important, recurring signal of transcendence. The Vedas personified word or speech—*Vac*—as a transcendent, creative, and communicating force, but represented that transcendent power in specifically synesthetic terms. One text had *Vac* declare: "Through me alone all eat the food that feeds them, each sees, breathes, hears the word outspoken."[23] This synesthetic, transcendent quality of speech in the Vedas, however, was replicated in the synesthetic claim that the words and sounds of the revealed, orally transmitted Vedic texts had been *seen* by the sages. Synesthetic symbols of transcendence multiplied throughout the Hindu tradition: The universal transcendence represented by Brahman in the *Upaniṣads* was symbolized as a convergence of all the senses, "that which is the hearing of the ear, the thought of the mind, the voice of speech, as also the breathing of the breath, and the sight of the mind," or "as food, as breath, as hearing, as mind, as speech." This synesthetic convergence of all the senses, however, signaled a transcendent reality that was beyond sense, that which was "soundless, touchless, formless, imperishable, likewise tasteless, constant, odorless," and "without eye, without ear, without voice."[24] As a synesthetic bridge between sense and a transcendent non-sensory reality, the mystic syllable *Om* was symbolized as "the light of lights."[25] "One should worship," the *Chandogya Upaniṣad* instructed, "that light which is seen and heard."[26] These examples merely hint at the rich, extraordinary synesthetic resources that have been deployed in the Hindu tradition to symbolize a transcendence beyond ordinary sensory perception by means of the perceptual fusion and transfer of symbolic synesthesia.

Transcendence has also frequently been symbolized in synesthetic terms in religious discourse about death and afterlife. In the *Tibetan Book of the Dead* (*Bardo Thödol*), for example, the transition of death was symbolized as an entry into the light and sound of Buddha nature. As the body dissolved into its elements, the transiting consciousness encountered a radiant sound: "From the midst of that radiance, the natural Sound of Reality, reverberating like a thousand thunders simultaneously sounding will come."[27] To cite only one other example: The Zoroastrian tradition symbolized an afterlife paradise as the "perfect House of Song" that emanated a fragrant perfume and "the Endless Light where all is bliss."[28] In these sensory symbols of transition and transcendence, synesthesia provided a vocabulary for signaling realities beyond the ordinary world of the living.

Finally, symbolic synesthesia has frequently appeared in religious discourse and practice to signal a more unified, complete, total, and all-encompassing experience. Certainly, as we have seen, symbolic synesthesia has been deployed in accounts of mystical experience, reproducing in its perceptual unity a union between mystic and the sacred. Mystical techniques, meditations, and other rituals, however, have often used synesthesia: A Hindu practice combined tones and visualizations—tones, incidentally, that were specifically associated with colors—with "water for bathing, cloth, sacred thread, ornaments, scents, flowers, incense, lamps, and edibles," in a multisensory, synesthetic meditation technique; a Taoist practice required an inward attention in which the meditator saw "a light circulating inside his body, and heard a rumbling of thunder at the top of his head"; a Sufi practice used music to evoke vision, because, as Al-Ghazzali noted, "God has decreed that by music vision is so intimately evoked that it is rather an image than an illustration of the spiritual experience it induces."[29] Examples could be multiplied. All suggest that symbolic synesthesia has been used not only in religious discourse but also in specific religious practices that have combined, fused, or transferred seeing, hearing, and other sensory modes to create some unified, alternative state of consciousness.

With respect to religious practice, synesthesia might prove to be a crucial ingredient in ritual. Obviously, ritual is a multimedia event, a performance that combines speech, vision, gesture, and often other sensory modes, in a unified pattern of action. Anthropologist Stanley Tambiah once observed that "the tantalizing question of how and with what effects different media are frequently combined in ritual [is] a question that has received little systematic attention."[30] Paying attention to this question of the multimedia, multisensory character of ritual, however, anthropologist Edmund Leach argued that ritual employs different sensory channels simultaneously, but participants "pick up all these messages at the same time and condense them into a single experience which we describe as 'attending' a wedding, or 'attending' a funeral."[31] In that condensation, therefore, ritual enacts a symbolic synesthesia of multiple perceptual modes in a single event. Not merely a unified, multimedia sensory experience, however, ritual performance may unify the senses in the interest of acting out the unity of a community, a culture, or a body of cultural knowledge. This synesthetic character of ritual performance has recently been noted by historian of religions Lawrence Sullivan:

The point is that performance displays the *symbolic expression* of synesthesia as it is imagined in a culture. In so doing, it renders perceptible a symbolism of the unity of the senses. The symbolic experience of the unity of the senses enables a culture to entertain itself with the idea of the unity of meaning. Cultural knowledge is obtained piecemeal from the separate senses of individual bodies in action. But it is performance that provides a culture the occasion to reflect on the unity of that body of cultural knowledge.[32]

In religious discourse, symbolic synesthesia can signal a unified perceptual field. Likewise, in religious practice and performance, that unity of the senses might act out a unified, comprehensive, total, and all-embracing cultural or social order. Attention to sensory modes, perceptual media, and synesthesia in ritual, therefore, represents a potentially fruitful area for further investigation in the history of religions.

New Horizons

Recent investigations of ritual as synesthetic performance have occurred within what might be called a new horizon of interpretation in which discourse has also been regarded as a performative practice. Further investigations into seeing, hearing, and religious discourse, therefore, will certainly require a sensitivity to the multiple, multiplying perspectives and voices at play in that plural practice. Having abandoned totalizing generalizations about seeing and hearing, analysis may be freed to explore the ways in which seeing, hearing, and synesthesia have been deployed as symbolic strategies in religious discourse. In this respect, perceptual symbols, like other types of symbolic practice, may be explored as performative strategies for negotiating or navigating in a meaningful world.

By symbolic negotiation I refer to the symbolic, strategic practice of working out what it might mean to be a human person. Although the word, "negotiation," has usually referred to the process of working out agreements in business or politics, religion, like business and politics, is a negotiated reality. In one respect, religious negotiations over what it means to be a human person tend to be worked out by negotiating relations with persons classified as superhuman and subhuman. For example, Augustine negotiated a normalized human identity through perceptual symbolism. He characterized the human in terms of a rational ability to distinguish among the five senses. In his symbolic, strategic, perceptual negotiations, however, Augustine claimed that the different senses were not distinguished by either the subhuman or the superhuman. Below human rationality, animals were unaware that they did not hear with their eyes or see with their ears. Above human rationality, for the superhuman person of Christ, seeing was hearing and hearing was seeing. In those symbolic relations, therefore, the deployment of perceptual symbolism was one among many symbolic practices for negotiating a human position between the superhuman Christ and the subhuman animals. It is precisely through such symbolic strategies that a religious worldview is constructed, not as a thing, but as a process of symbolic negotiation, an ongoing, symbolic experiment in being human.

More significantly, perhaps, symbolic negotiations are at stake in any conflict of symbols. At Nicaea, perceptual symbols were deployed in a contest over the legitimate ownership of a religious world. In the history of religions, many similar conflicts have occurred. In fact, a religious tradition might not be a continuous transmission of content, but a moving arena of conflict over legitimate ownership of the sacred. Perceptual symbolism has been deployed in those conflicts whenever privileged, exclusive claims to truth have been advanced on behalf of a visual or a verbal model. As I have argued elsewhere, a religious tradition might be defined as a process of stealing back and forth sacred symbols.[33] Maneuvering in the field of sacred symbols, strategic claims for the primacy of sight or the primacy of hearing have often been attempts to establish an authentic, privileged ownership of the sacred by those who see under the primacy of light or those who hear under the primacy of the word. In the Christian tradition, part of the vitality of its sacred symbols has resided precisely in the fact that they involve both hearing and sight. The same could be noted for other traditions as well. Any appropriation of one or the other of these two sensory modes, therefore, is a strategy for negotiating a hierarchical, privileged ownership of the whole tradition.

Although religious defenders of a visual or verbal symbolic model have often come into conflict, they have nevertheless tended to agree on symbolic terms and conditions that have negotiated the dismissal of the senses of smell, taste, and touch. In this respect, academic discussions of the relations between literacy and orality in the history of religions have been somewhat misdirected. Although often imagined to be contrasted by sight and sound, both literary and oral traditions can involve visual and verbal models. Often unspoken and invisible, however, both literate and oral textual traditions have tended to reject smell, taste, and touch as authentic modes of perception, or thought, or relation with the sacred. Not necessarily returning to R. R. Marett's aphorism, that religion, in its most basic form, is danced out rather than thought out, a new horizon of interpretation may open up in the recovery of embodied aspects of practical signification in the history of religions. In this respect, the analysis of discourse as a type of practice indicates that a particularly tactile orientation has finally entered into an engagement with symbolic universes that have been dominated by the defenders of sight or sound. Furthermore, attention to tactile, kinesthetic symbolism might be able to relate the seeing and hearing body, the body that has informed the religious discourse we have examined in this book, with other kinds of embodiment—the moving body, the gendered body, the sexual body, or the body in pain—that have tended to be ignored by proponents of both the visual and verbal models.

Embodiment, therefore, entails not only location but also movement through a world. In negotiating a meaningful world, perceptual symbolism has been deployed as a strategy of symbolic navigation, as a way of mapping out and moving through a particular kind of human place. Perceptual symbolism has been deployed in symbolic navigation, providing orientation in a world of space and time. In ways that we have noted, seeing and hearing have been implicated in spatial and temporal orientations in a meaningful world. Perceptual symbolism has been deployed in mapping regions of space and time, extension and duration, continuity and discontinuity, simultaneity and sequence, presence and absence, and so on, all the symbolic oppositions that might be drawn into mapping a structured world.[34]

In the midst of all these structural oppositions, however, symbolic synesthesia has signaled an antistructural breakthrough, so that, in terms of symbolic navigation, synesthesia has had the potential for being profoundly disorienting. Symbolic synesthesia—the radiant sound, the resonant radiance—violates the basic structures of perception, thought, and ordinary language. In this sense, symbolic synesthesia may be an instance of what Julia Kristeva has identified as unrepresentability—"that which, through language, is part of no particular language."[35] Kristeva pointed to horror as her primary example of unrepresentability, but synesthetic manifestations of the sacred in religious discourse could probably work just as well in violating, disorienting, and breaking through the ordered structures of any particular language or world. Although it violates ordinary language, symbolic synesthesia happens through language, frequently occurring in religious symbols, myths, and rituals, as an unrepresentable, yet meaningful and powerful perceptual resource for religion. Ironically, perhaps, the disorienting breakthrough of unrepresentability signaled by symbolic synesthesia has often become a central, crucial reference point for orientation in religious worlds. Not seeing or hearing, but symbolic synesthesia has defined the most disorienting orientations of the symbols of word and light.

Notes

Preface

1. P. Joseph Cahill, *Mended Speech: The Crisis of Religious Studies and Theology* (New York: Crossroad Publishing Co., 1982): 35. Cahill's catalog of visual and auditory characteristics seems to have been heavily influenced by Walter Ong, *The Presence of the Word: Some Prolegomena for Cultural and Religious History* (Minneapolis: University of Minnesota Press, 1967). See also Walter Ong, "World as View and World as Event," *American Anthropologist* 71 (1969): 634-47. For a general bibliography on the phenomenology of perception, see John W. M. Verhaar, *Some Relations between Perception, Speech, and Thought: A Contribution toward the Phenomenology of Speech* (Assen, Netherlands: Van Gorcum, 1963).

2. Mike Samuels and Nancy Samuels, *Seeing with the Mind's Eye* (Berkeley: Random House, 1975): 103.

3. Clemens E. Benda, "Language, Consciousness and Problems of Existential Analysis," *American Journal of Psychotherapy* 14 (1960): 262. Cited in Harold Stahmer, *"Speak that I May See Thee": The Religious Significance of Language* (New York: Macmillan, 1968): 5; and Amos N. Wilder, *Early Christian Rhetoric: The Language of the Gospel* (Cambridge: Harvard University Press, 1971): 11.

4. Stephen Ullmann, *Principles of Semantics*, 2d ed. (Glasgow: University Publications, 1957): 283.

5. Martin Jay, "The Rise of Hermeneutics and the Crisis of Ocularcentricism," *Poetics Today* 9 (1980): 323.

6. Don Ihde, "Studies in the Phenomenology of Sound: God and Sound," *International Philosophical Quarterly* 10 (1970): 247-48. See also Don Ihde, *Sense and Significance* (Pittsburgh: Duquesne University Press, 1973), and *Listening and Voice: A Phenomenology of Sound* (Athens: Ohio University Press, 1976).

7. Heinrich Graetz, *The Structure of Jewish History*, trans. Ismar Schorsh (New York: Jewish Theological Seminary of America, 1975): 68. Among others,

Amos Wilder has echoed this assumption by observing that "the religion of Israel is very much a matter of hearing" in *Early Christian Rhetoric,* 11.

8. Thorlief Borman, *Hebrew Thought Compared with Greek* (London: SCM Press, 1954): 206-7.

Chapter 1

1. Maurice Merleau-Ponty, *The Primacy of Perception* (Evanston, Ill: Northwestern University, 1964): 3. Merleau-Ponty's most important works on perception were his *Phénoménologie de la perception* (Paris: Gallimard, 1945), and *Sens et non-sens* (Paris: Les Éditions Nagel, 1948).

2. Leucippus, *Fragment,* A.29-30; Hermann Diels and Walther Kranz, eds., *Die Fragmente der Vorsokratiker,* 6th ed., vol. 2 (Berlin: Weidmann, 1952); Trans. G. S. Kirk and J. E. Raven, *The Presocratic Philosophers* (Cambridge: Cambridge University Press, 1957): 421-22.

3. Ibid., 422.

4. Discussing Alcmaeon, Theophrastus recorded that this notion that the eye contained fire "is, indeed, manifest, for a flash takes place within it when it receives a stroke." *De sensu* 26; Trans. John Isaac Beare, *Greek Theories of Elementary Cognition* (London: The Clarendon Press, 1906): 11.

5. Plutarch, *Epistolae,* IV.14; Hermann Diels, *Doxographi graeci,* 3d ed. (Berlin: W. de Gruyter, 1958): 405; Trans. Beare, *Greek Theories of Elementary Cognition,* 12.

6. Empedocles, *Fragment,* B.84; Diels and Kranz, *Die Fragmente der Vorsokratiker,* I:341-42; Trans. W. K. C. Guthrie, *A History of Greek Philosophy* (Cambridge: Cambridge University Press, 1965): II:235.

7. *Timaeus,* 45b-46d.

8. Francis M. Cornford, *Plato's Cosmology: The Timaeus of Plato* (Indianapolis: Bobbs-Merrill, 1937): 153.

9. *De anima,* 2.7.418b14-16; *De sensu,* 2.438a26-438b2. Although Aristotle denied the visual ray, in some instances he seemed to assent to this theory, for example, in the *De generatione animalium,* and he assumed the emission of visual rays throughout the *Meteorologica.* On this point, see David C. Lindberg, *Theories of Vision from al-Kindi to Kepler* (Chicago: University of Chicago Press, 1976): 217, n.39.

10. *De anima,* 2.7.419a14-15.

11. *De sensu,* 2.447a2-4; Trans. Beare, *Greek Theories of Elementary Cognition,* 12.

12. Samuel Sambursky, *Physics of the Stoics* (New York: Macmillan, 1959): 28.

13. Diogenes Laertius, *Vitae philosophorum,* 7.157; Trans. R. D. Hicks (Cambridge: Harvard University Press, 1959): II:261.

14. Plutarch, *Epistolae,* IV.19.3; Diels and Kranz, *Die Fragmente der Vorsokratiker,* 389; Trans. Beare, *Greek Theories of Elementary Cognition,* 102.

15. Plutarch, *Epistolae,* IV.16; Diels, *Doxographi graeci,* 406a-b16; Trans. Beare, *Greek Theories of Elementary Cognition,* 95.

16. For Anaxagoras, see Diels and Kranz, *Die Fragmente der Vorsokratiker,* I:325. Trans. Beare, *Greek Theories of Elementary Cognition,* 104; For Diogenes of Apollonia, see Diels and Kranz, *Die Fragmente der Vorsokratiker,* I:345. Trans. Beare, *Greek Theories of Elementary Cognition,* 105; For Diogenes Laertius, see Hicks, trans. *Vitae philosophorum,* (7.158): II:261.

17. *Timaeus,* 67a.

18. *De anima,* 2.8.446a20ff; *De sensu,* VI.446b5-26.

19. Hans Jonas, *The Phenomenon of Life: Toward a Philosophical Biology* (New York: Harper and Row, 1966): 144. See also Jonas, "The Nobility of Sight," *The Philosophy of the Body,* ed., Stuart F. Spicker (Chicago: Quadrangle Press, 1970): 312-33. Note that Jonas's identification of vision with simultaneity and audition with sequence contradicts the opposite position argued by Walter Ong, *The Presence of the Word: Some Prolegomena for Cultural and Religious History* (Minneapolis: University of Minnesota Press, 1967): 128. I follow Jonas in this case: Since space structures vision, it makes simultaneous presence possible; since time structures hearing, it is necessarily related to an apprehension of sequence.

20. Jonas, *The Phenomenon of Life,* 144.

21. Maurice Merleau-Ponty, *The Phenomenology of Perception,* trans. Colin Smith (New York: Humanities Press, 1962): 193.

22. Jonas, *The Phenomenon of Life,* 138.

23. Ibid., 137. C. D. Broad noted this distinction between presentational and referential disclosures of information when he distinguished between sight and hearing: Hearing is referential. We can say a sound "comes from" a clock. The sound refers back to its cause. But sight is not referential. We do not say that the greenness "comes from" the leaf. In sight, the disclosure of information is presentational. Broad, *Kant: An Introduction* (Cambridge: Cambridge University Press, 1978): 28.

24. Merleau-Ponty, *The Phenomenology of Perception,* 193.

25. Jonas, *Phenomenon of Life,* 139.

26. Northrop Frye, *Anatomy of Criticism* (Princeton: Princeton University Press, 1957): 77.

27. Ibid.

28. Cited in Jacques Derrida, *Of Grammatology,* trans. Gayatri Chakravorty Spivak (Baltimore: Johns Hopkins Press, 1974): 233.

29. Ibid., 234.

30. Ibid.

31. Walter J. Ong, "A Dialectic of Aural and Objective Correlatives," *Essays in Criticism: A Quarterly Journal of Literary Criticism* 8 (1958); rprt. in Hazard Adams, ed., *Critical Theory Since Plato* (New York: Harcourt, Brace, Jovanovich, 1971): 1159.

32. Erwin Strauss, *The Primary World of Senses: A Vindication of Sensory Experience,* trans. Jacob Needleman (New York: Free Press of Glencoe, 1963): 204.

33. Heinz Werner, "L'unité des sens," *Journal de Psychologie Normale et Pathologique* 31 (1934): 190-205; cited in Lawrence E. Marks, *The Unity of the*

Senses: Interrelations among the Modalities (New York: Academic Press, 1978): 184.

34. Marks, *The Unity of the Senses*, ix-x. Research on synesthesia might be divided into four areas of interest: (1) medical, clinical, and psychological case studies; (2) theoretical works on the meaning and significance of synesthesia in perception; (3) theoretical works on the meaning and significance of synesthesia in language; and (4) theoretical works on the meaning and significance of synesthesia in aesthetics, music, and literature. First, representative examples of the literature on cases studies of synesthesia include: Isador H. Coriat, "A Case of Synesthesia," *Journal of Abnormal Psychology* 8 (1913): 12-27; M. A. Collins, "A Case of Synesthesia," *Journal of General Psychology* 2 (1929): 12-27; and a case documented by a synesthete, Leon Ginsberg, in *The American Journal of Psychology* 34 (1923): 582-89, explained that during a period of psychological stress in 1918 he became aware of color-sensations, *photisms*, associated with every other sense. Second, theoretical works on synesthesia in percepton include: Otto Ortmann, "Theories of Synesthesia in the Light of a Case of Color-Hearing," *Human Biology* 5 (1933): 155-211; Theodore Karwoski, "Synesthesia," *British Journal of Psychology* 25 (1934): 29-41; L. Simpson and P. McKeller, "Types of Synesthesia," *Journal of Mental Science* 101 (1955): 144-47; Charles E. Osgood, "The Cross-Cultural Generality of Visual-Verbal Synesthetic Tendencies," *Behavioral Science* 5 (1960): 146-69. Third, theoretical works on synesthesia and language include: William O. Krohn, "Pseudo-chromesthesia, or the Association of Colors with Words, Letters, and Sound," *American Journal of Psychology* 5 (1892): 20-41; Gladys A. Reichard, Roman Jakobson, and Elizabeth Werth, "Synesthesia and Language," *Word* 5 (1949): 266-89; and Stephen Ullmann, *The Principles of Semantics* 2d ed. (Glasgow: University Publications, 1957): 266-89. Fourth, theoretical works on synesthesia and the arts include: Theodore Karwoski, et al., "Studies in Synesthetic Thinking, II: The Role of Form in Visual Responses to Music," *Journal of General Psychology* 26 (1942): 199-22; E. L. Mudge, "The Common Synesthesia of Music," *Journal of Applied Psychology* 4 (1920): 342-45; and P. E. Vernon, "Synesthesia in Music," *Psyche* 10 (1930): 22-40. The topic of literary synesthesia was most extensively discussed in a series of articles by Albert Wellek: "Beiträge zum Synästhesie-Problem," *Archive für die gesamte Psychologie* 76 (1930): 193-201; "Zur Geschichte und Kritik der Synästhesie-Forschung," ibid., 79 (1931): 325-84; "Das Doppelempfinden im abendländischen Altertum und im Mittelalter," ibid., 80 (1931): 226-62; "Der Sprachgeist als Doppelempfinden," *Zeitschrift für Ästhetik und allgemeine Kunstwissenschaft* 25 (1931): 226-62; "Renaissance- und Barock-synaesthesie," *Deutsche Vierteljahresschrift* 9 (1931): 534-84; and "Das Doppelempfinden im 18. Jahrhundert," ibid., 14 (1936): 75-102. Discussions of literary synesthesia may also be found in Victor Segalen, "Les synesthesias de l'ecole Symboliste," *Mercure de France* 42 (1902): 57-90; See also June E. Downey, "Literary Synesthesia," *Journal of Philosophy, Psychology, and Scientific Methods* 9 (1912): 490-98; and Glenn O'Malley, "Literary Synesthesia," *Journal of Aesthetics and Art Criticism* 15 (1957): 391-411. For a cross-cultural perspective on synesthesia in aesthetics, see Steve Odin,

"Blossom Scents Take Up the Ringing: Synaesthesia in Japanese and Western Aesthetics," *Soundings* 69 (1986): 256-81.

35. Cited in Strauss, *The Primary World of Senses*, 215.

36. Ibid., 205-6.

37. John Locke, *Essay Concerning Human Understanding*, ed. A. C. Fraser (Oxford, 1894): II:38.

38. Isaac Newton, *Opticks* (I.2.prop.6) (London, 1718): 134.

39. Louis Bertrand Castel, *Optique des couleurs* (Paris, 1740); cited and trans. in Irving Babbitt, *The New Laokoon: An Essay on the Confusion of the Arts* (New York: Houghton Mifflin, 1910): 55.

40. Erika von Siebold, "Synästhesien in der Englischen Dichtung des 19. Jahrhunderts," *Englische Studien* 53 (1919): 196-334, and "Harmony of the Senses in English, German and French Romanticism," *Publications of the Modern Language Association* 47 (1932): 577-92.

41. E. B. Tylor, *Researches in the Early History of Mankind*, ed. Paul Bohannen (Chicago: University of Chicago Press, 1964): 59.

42. Evelyn Underhill, *Mysticism* (New York: Noonday Press, 1911): 7.

43. Claude Lévi-Strauss, *Tristes Tropiques*, trans. John and Doreen Weightman (New York: Atheneum, 1974): 123.

44. Ninian Smart, *Philosophy of Religion* (New York: Random House, 1970): 42.

45. Samuel Taylor Coleridge, *Biographia Literaria*, 2 vols. (London: Pickering, 1829): II:142.

46. Samuel Taylor Coleridge, *The Poetical Works* (London: Pickering, 1829): 224.

47. Cited in Marks, *The Unity of the Senses*, 225.

48. *Séraphîta*, in Marcel Bouteron, ed. *La Comédie Humaine* (Paris: Gallimard, 1950); cited in R. C. Zaehner, *Concord and Discord* (Oxford: Clarendon Press, 1970): 411.

49. Edmund Gosse and Thomas James Wise, eds., *The Complete Works of Algernon Charles Swinburne* (London: William Heinemann; New York: Gabriel Wells, 1925): III:289; VI:191.

50. Smart, *Philosophy of Religion*, 43.

51. Neville Rogers, ed., *The Complete Poetical Works of Percy Bysshe Shelley* (Oxford: Clarendon Press, 1972-75): II:369-70.

52. William Butler Yeats, "The Symbolism of Poetry," *Essays* (London: Macmillan, 1924): 193.

53. Underhill, *Mysticism*, 7.

54. Juliana of Norwich, *Showings*, trans. Edmund Colledge and James Walsh (New York: Paulist Press, 1978): 255.

55. Violet Macdermot, *The Cult of the Seer in the Ancient Near East* (Berkeley: University of California Press, 1971): 766; Underhill, *Mysticism*, 119.

56. Macdermot, *The Cult of the Seer*, 766.

57. Ibid., 765-66.

58. James M. Robinson, ed., *The Nag Hammadi Library* (San Francisco: Harper and Row, 1977): 28.

59. Ibid., 44.

60. Ibid., 44; 196; 313. It has been noticed that "the appearance of the resurrected Christ as a light and a voice represents a common way of speaking about the resurrection appearances in Gnostic circles." Marvin Meyer, "The Letter of Peter to Phillip: Text, Translation and Commentary" (Ph.D. diss., Claremont, 1979): 181.

61. Alfred North Whitehead, *Process and Reality* (New York: Harper and Row, 1960): 258.

62. Claude Lévi-Strauss, *Totemism*, trans. Rodney Needham (New York: Penguin, 1969): 171.

Chapter 2

1. See Richard M. Zaner, *The Problem of Embodiment* (The Hague: Martinus Nijhoff, 1964); Stuart E. Spicker, *The Philosophy of the Body: Rejections of Cartesian Dualism* (Chicago: Quadrangle Books, 1970); and Hubert L. Dreyfus and Paul Rabinow, *Michel Foucault: Beyond Structuralism and Hermeneutics* (Chicago: University of Chicago Press, 1982).

2. See Robert Hertz, *Death and the Right Hand*, trans. Rodney and Claudia Needham (London: Cohen and West, 1960); Marcel Mauss, "Techniques of the Body," trans. Ben Brewster, *Economic Sociology* 2 (1973): 70-88; and John Blacking, ed., *The Anthropology of the Body* (London: Academic Press, 1978).

3. Mary Douglas, *Natural Symbols* (New York: Random House, 1973): vi. See Sheldon R. Isenberg and Dennis E. Owen, "Bodies, Natural and Contrived: The Work of Mary Douglas," *Religious Studies Review* 3 (1977): 1-16.

4. Rodney Needham, "Physiological Symbols," in *Circumstantial Deliveries* (Berkeley: University of California Press, 1981): 51.

5. Michael Jackson, "Knowledge of the Body," *Man* 18 (1983): 328.

6. Pierre Bourdieu, *Outline of a Theory of Practice*, trans. Richard Nice (Cambridge: Cambridge University Press, 1977): 120.

7. Thomas Carlyle, *Sartor Resartus*, ed. Charles Frederick Harrold (Indianapolis: Bobbs-Merrill, 1977): 73.

8. Literature on metaphors and models in religious discourse is extensive: Max Black, *Models and Metaphors* (Ithaca: Cornell University Press, 1962); Frederick Ferre, "Mapping the Logic of Models in Science and Theology," *The Christian Scholar* 46 (1963): 9-39; Ferre, "Metaphors, Models, and Religion," *Soundings* 51 (1968): 341-42; Mary Hesse, *Models and Analogies in Science* (Notre Dame: University of Notre Dame Press, 1966); Hesse, "Models and Analogies in Science," *Encyclopedia of Philosophy*, ed. Paul Edwards (New York: Macmillan, 1967): V:354-55; Ian Barbour, *Myth, Models, and Paradigms: A Comparative Study in Science and Religion* (New York: Harper and Row, 1974); Victor Turner, "Social Dramas and Ritual Metaphors," in *Dramas, Fields, and Metaphors: Symbolic Action in Human Society* (Ithaca: Cornell University Press, 1974): 23-59; and W. Richard Comstock, "Metaphor, Myth, and Model: Toward the Emergence of a New World View" (Santa Barbara, Calif.: Institute of Religious Studies, 1974).

9. The division of Philo's work (32 texts preserved in Greek, 2 in Armenian) into three genres—political, expositional (or exegetical), and allegorical—has been a commonplace in Philonic scholarship since the nineteenth century. Translations are taken from Philo Judaeus, *Philo*, 10 vols. and 2 supplementary vols. trans. F. H. Colson and G. H. Whitaker (London: William Heinemann; Cambridge: Harvard University Press, 1971). Philo's texts are cited by their standard abbreviations. Without going into the the problems with the Greek texts (or the extensive commentaries dealing with those problems), I have merely attempted to build a composite picture of Philo's consistent perceptual symbolism with reference to seeing, hearing, and synesthesia.

10. Harry A. Wolfson, *Philo: Foundations of Religious Philosophy in Judaism, Christianity, and Islam*, 2 vols. (Cambridge: Harvard University Press, 1962): II:37-38.

11. Erwin R. Goodenough, *By Light, Light: The Mystic Gospel of Hellenistic Judaism* (Amsterdam: Philo Press, 1969): 216.

12. Samuel Sandmel, *Philo's Place in Judaism: A Study of Conceptions of Abraham in Jewish Literature* (New York: KTAV Publishing House, 1971): 162-63.

13. David Winston, *The Wisdom of Solomon: A New Translation with Introduction and Commentary* (New York: Doubleday, 1979): 35.

14. See Louis Ginzberg, *The Legends of the Jews*, trans. Henrietta Szold (Philadelphia: The Jewish Publication Society of America, 1913): III:119-24.

15. John Henry Blunt, *Dictionary of Sects, Heresies, Ecclesiastical Parties, and Schools of Religious Thought* (1874; rprt. Detroit: Gale Research Co., 1974); cited in Kenneth Burke, *The Rhetoric of Religion: Studies in Logology* (Berkeley: University of California Press, 1970): 13.

16. Tertullian, *Apologia*, XXI.10-14.

17. Jaroslav Pelikan, *The Light of the World: A Basic Image in Early Christian Thought* (New York: Harper & Brothers, 1962).

18. H. de Riedmatten, trans., *Les Actes du procès de Paul de Samosate* (Fribourg en Suisse: Éditions St. Paul, 1952): 147.

19. Ibid., 158.

20. Ibid., 153.

21. Socrates, *Historia ecclesia*, I.5. On the Arian controversy, see Henry Melville Gwatkin, *The Arian Controversy* (New York: AMS Press, 1979); Michel Meskin, *Les Ariens d'Occident, 335-430* (Paris: Éditions du Seuil, 1967); Rudolf Lorenz, *Arius Judaizans? Untersuchungen zur Dogmengeschichtlichen Einordnung des Arius* (Göttingen: Vandenhoeck & Ruprecht, 1979); and Robert C. Gregg and Dennis E. Groh, *Early Arianism: A View of Salvation* (Philadelphia: Fortress Press, 1981). For a useful review of research on Arianism, see Joseph T. Lienhard, "Recent Studies in Arianism," *Religious Studies Review* 8 (1982): 330-37.

22. Socrates, *Historia ecclesia*, I.5.

23. Athanasius, *De synodis*, 15.

24. Ibid.

25. Ibid.

26. Ibid., 41-45.

27. Ibid.

28. Ibid.

29. Pelikan, *The Light of the World,* 34.

30. Ibid., 59.

31. Athanasius, *Orationes contra Arianos,* I.16.

32. Socrates, *Historia ecclesia,* I.8.

33. Ibid.

34. Ibid., I.26.

Chapter 3

1. R. A. Markus, *"Alienatio*: Philosophy and Eschatology in the Development of an Augustinian Idea," *Studia Patristica* 9 (1966): 431-50.

2. Jeanne and Pierre Courcelle, eds., *Iconographie de Saint Augustin,* 3 vols. (Paris: Études Augustiniennes, 1972): III: Plates CXV and LXX.

3. Peter Brown, *Augustine of Hippo* (Berkeley: University of California Press, 1967): 177.

4. All citations of the *Confessions* are taken from Rex Warner, trans. *The Confessions of St. Augustine* (New York: The New American Library, 1963).

5. *De trinitate,* VIII.2.3; Arthur West Haddan, trans., *The Works of Aurelius Augustine,* Vol. 7, ed. Marcus Dods (Edinburgh: T & T Clark, 1873).

6. All citations of the *De libero arbitrio* are taken from Anna S. Benjamin and L. H. Hackstaff, trans., *On Free Choice of the Will* (Indianapolis: Bobbs-Merrill, 1964).

7. All citations of the *In Ioannis Evangelium tractatus* are taken from James Innes, trans., *The Works of Aurelius Augustine,* Vol. 10, ed. Marcus Dods (Edinburgh: T & T Clark, 1874).

8. Ian Barbour, *Myth, Models, and Paradigms: A Comparative Study in Science and Religion* (New York: Harper and Row, 1974): 155.

9. See Mary Ann Ida Gannon, "The Active Theory of Sensation in St. Augustine," *New Scholasticism* 30 (1956): 154-80.

10. Origen, *Contra Celsum,* trans. Henry Chadwick (Cambridge: Cambridge University Press, 1953): 121. On the doctrine of the inner senses, see P. Rahner, "Le Debut d'une doctrine des cinq sens spirituels chez Origene," *Revue d'Ascetique et de Mystique* (1932): 113-45; Jean Danielou, *Platonisme et Theologie Mystique: Doctrine spirituelle de Saint Gregoire de Nysse* (Aubier: Éditions Montaigne, 1944): 235ff.; Harry A. Wolfson, "The Internal Senses in Latin, Arabic, and Hebrew Philosophic Texts," *Harvard Theological Review* 28 (1934): 69-133.

11. Origen, *Homelies sur l'Exode,* trans. P. Fortier (Paris: Les Éditions du Cerf, 1947): 223-24.

12. Macarius, *Fifty Spiritual Homilies of Saint Macarius, the Egyptian* (New York: Macmillan, 1921): 216.

13. Origen, *Contra Celsum,* 44.

Chapter 4

1. Ernst Cassirer, *An Essay on Man: An Introduction to a Philosophy of Human Culture* (New York: Doubleday, 1954): 76.

2. See Pierre Courcelle, "Les 'voix' dans le *Confessions* de saint Augustin," *Hermes* 80 (1952): 31-46.

3. Peter Brown, *Augustine of Hippo* (Berkeley: University of California Press, 1967): 35.

4. On pride as dominant moral theme of the *Confessions,* see William McAllen Green, *Initium omnis peccati superbia: Augustine on Pride as the First Sin* (Berkeley: University of California Press, 1949): 421. See also David John MacQueen, "*Contemptus Dei:* St. Augustine on the Disorder of Pride in Society and its Remedies," *Recherches Augustiniennes* 9 (1966): 227-93; MacQueen, "Augustine on *Superbia:* The Historical Background and Sources of Doctrine," *Melanges de Science Religieuse* 34 (1977): 193-211.

5. Works on Augustine and rhetoric include: Joseph Finaert, *Saint Augustin, Rheteur* (Paris: Les Belles Lettres, 1939); W. H. Semple, "Augustinus Rhetor: A Study from the *Confessions* of St. Augustine's Career in Education," *Journal of Ecclesiastical History* 1 (1950): 135-50; and Ernest L. Fortin, "Augustine and the Problem of Christian Rhetoric," *Augustinian Studies* 5 (1974): 85-100.

6. Wolfram Laistner, *Christianity and Pagan Culture in the Later Roman Empire* (Ithaca: Cornell University Press, 1951): 50.

7. Gregory Nazianzus, *Oration* (43.11), trans. C. G. Browne and J. E. Swallow, *Select Library of Nicene and Post-Nicene Fathers,* 2d ser., VII:398.

8. Works on Augustine and Manicheism include: Henri-Charles Puech, *Le Manichéisme, son fondateur, sa doctrine* (Paris: Civilizations du Sud, 1949); W. H. C. Frend, "The Gnostic-Manichean Tradition in Roman North Africa," *Journal of Ecclesiastical* 9 (1953): 13-26; Frend, "Manichaeism in the Struggle between Saint Augustine and Petillian of Constantine," *Augustinus Magister* (Paris: Études Augustiniennes, 1954): II:859-66; and Pierre-Jean de Ménasce, "Augustin Manichéen," *Freundesgabe für Robert Curtius,* ed. M. Rychner (Bern: Francke, 1956): 79-93.

9. Works on Augustine and Neoplatonism include: Arthur Hilary Armstrong, "Salvation, Plotinian and Christian," *The Downside Review* 75 (1957): 126-39; John J. O'Meara, "Neoplatonism in the Conversion of Saint Augustine," *Dominican Studies* 3 (1950): 331-43; O'Meara, "Augustine and Neoplatonism," *Recherches Augustiniennes* 1 (1958): 91-111; O'Meara, *The Young Augustine: The Growth of Saint Augustine's Mind up to his Conversion* (London: Longmans, Green, and Co., 1954); Robert J. O'Connell, *St. Augustine's Early Theory of Man, A.D. 386-391* (Cambridge: Harvard University Press, 1968); O'Connell, *St. Augustine's Confessions: The Odyssey of the Soul* (Cambridge: Harvard University Press, 1969); and O'Connell, *Art and Christian Intelligence in St. Augustine* (Cambridge: Harvard University Press, 1978).

10. For analysis of Augustine's Neoplatonic ascents, see Pierre Courcelle, *Recherches sur les Confessions de saint Augustin* (Paris: Éditions de Boccard, 1950): 157-67; S. Connolly, "I: The Platonism of Augustine's 'Ascent' to God.

II: St. Augustine's Ascent to God. III: The Ascent in the Philosophy of Plotinus,"
The Irish Ecclesiastical Record 78 (1952): 44-53; 80 (1953): 28-36; 81 (1954):
120-33, 260-69; and Frederick van Fleteran, "Augustine's Ascent of the Soul
in Book VII of the *Confessions:* A Reconsideration," *Augustinian Studies* 5 (1974):
29-72.

11. For discussions and analysis of Augustine's conversion, see William
Simpson, *St. Augustine's Conversion* (New York: Macmillan, 1930); Jean Marie
le Blond, *Les conversions de saint Augustin* (Paris: Éditions Montaigne, 1950);
Salvatore Beniamino Femiano, *Riflessioni critiche sulla conversione di S. Agostino*
(Napoli-Roma: Istituto Editorale del Mezzogiorno, 1951); Romano Guardini,
The Conversion of Augustine, trans. E. Briefs (Westminster, Maryland: Newman
Press, 1960). Some controversy has remained whether Augustine's description
of his conversion event—particularly the *tolle, lege* incident—was realistic or
a purely literary construction. The realistic side was defended by Fulbert Cayré,
"La conversion de saint Augustin: la 'tolle, lege' des *Confessions,*" *L'Année
théologique* 11 (1951): 144-51; 244-52; Cayré, "Pour le realisme de 'tolle, lege':
Essai de concilliation," *L'Année théologique* 11 (1951): 261-71. The literary side
was defended by Pierre Courcelle, "L'Oracle d'Apis et l'Oracle du jardin de
Milan," *Revue de l'histoire des religions* 139 (1951): 216-31; Courcelle, "Note
sur le 'tolle, lege,'" *L'Année théologique* 11 (1951): 253-60; and Courcelle,
"Source chretienne et allusions païennes de l'episode du 'tolle, lege,'" *Revue
d'histoire et de philosophie religieuses* 32 (1952): 171-200.

Chapter 5

1. See David Chidester, "The Challenge to Christian Ritual Studies," *An-
glican Theological Review* 66 (1983): 23-34.

2. The most concise synopsis of the various interpretations of Augustine's
doctrine of illumination is found in Eugene TeSelle, *Augustine, the Theologian*
(New York: Herder and Herder, 1970): 103-4. For a survey of German debates
on Augustine's learning theory, see C. E. Schuetzinger, *The German Controversy
on Saint Augustine's Illumination Theory* (New York: Pageant, 1960). The best
representative of the *ontologistic* position is Ronald Nash, *The Light of the Mind:
St. Augustine's Theory of Knowledge* (Lexington: University of Kentucky Press,
1969). For the *ideogenetic* position, see Eugene Portalie, *A Guide to the Thought
of St. Augustine,* trans. Ralph Bastian (Chicago: Regenery, 1960). The most
influential proponent of what I am calling the *normative* position is Étienne
Gilson, *The Christian Philosophy of St. Augustine,* trans. L. E. M. Lynch (New
York: Random House, 1960).

3. For an early formulation of this strategy, see Regis Jolivet, *Dieu Soleil
dans Espirits, ou la doctrine augustinienne de l'illumination* (Paris, 1934). Other
examples would include the following remarkably consistent restatements of
the normative theme: "We may follow Gilson in supposing that Augustine
was not concerned to formulate a theory designed to account for conceptual
formation; rather he was establishing a basis for testing the certainty of our
judgments," George Howie, *Educational Theory and Practice in Saint Augustine*

(New York: Teacher's College, 1969,: 129; "St. Augustine's divine illumination doctrine is not so much a theory of the origin of concepts as of the manner in which the human mind is enabled to make some judgments with certitude," Vernon J. Bourke, *A Guide to the Thought of St. Augustine* (Chicago: Regenery, 1968): xxxi; "It must be remembered that Augustine's problem is one concerning certitude, not one concerning the content of our concepts or ideas: it concerns far more the form of the certain judgment and the form of the normative idea than the actual content of the idea," Frederick Copleston, *A History of Philosophy* (Westminster, Md.: Newman, 1950): II/1:80.

4. I am using the word *learning* as a shorthand term to encompass in a dialectical relationship both *docere* (to teach) and *intellegere* (to know or understand). Learning, therefore, is a process that entails the transmission, generation, or recognition of knowledge through the interaction of teacher and student. For Augustine, learning typically was imagined to occur in the context of a *disciplina* or educational discipline.

5. On the role of wisdom in ancient Greek, Hebraic, and Middle Platonic thought, see the introduction and bibliography in David Winston, *Wisdom of Solomon: A New Translation with Introduction and Commentary* (New York: Doubleday, 1979).

6. Mircea Eliade, *Myth and Reality*, trans. Willard R. Trask (New York: Harper and Row, 1963): 21.

7. Objections have been raised both within and outside the discipline of religious studies. For example, see Ninian Smart, "Beyond Eliade: The Future of Theory in Religion," *Numen* 25 (1978): 171-83; and John A. Saliba, "*Homo Religiosus*" in Mircea Eliade: An Anthropological Evaluation (Leiden: E. J. Brill, 1976).

8. Jonathan Z. Smith, "Earth and Gods," *Journal of Religion* 49 (1969): 107; rprt. in Smith, *Map Is not Territory: Studies in the History of Religions* (Leiden: E. J. Brill, 1978): 109.

9. Copleston, *History of Philosophy*, I/1:80.

10. Some passages from Cicero that suggest this transformation of time in learning would include the following: "To be ignorant of what happened before you were born is to remain always a child. For what is man's life, unless woven into the life of our ancestors by the memory of past deeds" (*De oratore* I.34); and Cicero proclaimed the learning of history as "witness of the ages, light of truth, life of tradition, teacher of life, messenger of antiquity" (*De oratore* II.36).

11. *Sermones*, 126.6.

12. For important discussions of Augustine's understanding of creation, see Christopher O'Toole, *The Philosophy of Creation in the Writings of St. Augustine* (Washington, D.C.: Catholic University Press of America, 1944); and Gilles Pelland, *Cinq études d'Augustin sur le début de la Genèse* (Tournai: Desclée; Montreal: Bellarmin, 1972).

13. For a discussion of some of the issues involved in Augustine's understanding of *materia*, see A. H. Armstrong, "Spiritual or Intelligible Matter in

Plotinus and St. Augustine," *Augustinus Magister* (Paris: Études Augustiennes, 1954): I:227-84.

14. George Howie, *Augustine on Education* (Chicago: Regenery, 1969): 15-16.

15. The following translations from *De magistro* are taken from George G. Leckie, trans., *St. Aurelius Augustinus: Concerning the Teacher* (New York: Appleton-Century, 1938).

16. Douglas W. Johnson, "*Verbum* in the Early Augustine (386-397)," *Recherches Augustiniennes* 8 (1972): 25-53.

17. On the location of the eternal ideas in the mind of God, see James K. Feibleman, *Religious Platonism* (New York: Barnes and Noble, 1959): 109ff; Philip Merlan, *From Platonism to Neo-Platonism,* 2d ed. (The Hague: Martinus Nijhoff, 1960); and John Dillon, *The Middle Platonists* (London: Duckworth, 1977).

18. It is common to point to William of Auvergne and Gundissalinus as representatives of a medieval *ideogenetic* approach to Augustine's doctrine of illumination. This observation was made, for example, in Franz Koerner, "Das Prinzip der Innerlichkeit in Augustins Erkenntnislehre" (Ph.D. diss., Würzburg, 1953): 2. See Ernest A. Moody, "William of Auvergne and his Treatise *De anima*," *Studies in Medieval Philosophy, Science, and Logic* (Berkeley: University of California Press, 1975): 1-109. The *De immortalitate animae* of Gundissalinus is almost identical to the text of William of Auvergne.

19. A list of representatives of the *ontologistic* position would include the following: For Henry of Ghent, see R. Macken, "La theorie de l'illumination divine dans la philosophie d'Henri de Gand," *Recherches de théologie ancienne de médiévale* 39 (1972): 82-112; for Marsilio Ficino, see Paul O. Kristeller, *The Philosophy of Marsilio Ficino,* trans. Virginia Contant (Gloucester, Mass.: Peter Smith, 1964): 247; and for the extreme ontologism of Malebranche, who insisted that "we see all things in God," see Thomas M. Lennon and Paul J. Olscamp, trans., *Nicolas Malebranche: The Search after Truth* (Columbus: Ohio State University Press, 1980) and Desmond Connell, *The Vision of God: Malebranche's Scholastic Sources* (Louvain: Beatrice-Nauwelaerts, 1967).

Chapter 6

1. Cited in Peter Brown, *Augustine of Hippo* (Berkeley: University of California Press, 1967): 256.

2. Michel Foucault, *The Archaeology of Knowledge,* trans. A. M. Sheridan Smith (New York: Harper and Row, 1972): 31-39. For an introductory overview of Foucault's work and some of its possible applications to the study of religion, see David Chidester, "Michel Foucault and the Study of Religion," *Religious Studies Review* 12 (1986): 1-9.

3. Foucault, *The Archaeology of Knowledge,* 5. For a more traditional assessment of the Augustinian tradition, see Étienne Gilson, *Reason and Revelation in the Middle Ages* (New York: C. Scribner's Sons, 1948): 21: "You cannot fail to know an Augustinian when you meet one in history. . . . The faith upheld

by Augustine in the fourth century was substantially the same one as that of Saint Anselm in the eleventh century, of Saint Bonaventura in the thirteenth century, of Malebranche in the seventeenth, and of Gioberti in the nineteenth, but while their common set of beliefs exhibits this remarkable stability, the received views on the proper use of human reason were constantly changing around them. In short, all the Augustinians agree that unless we believe, we shall not understand; and all of them agree as to what we should believe, but they do not always agree as to what it is to understand."

4. Cassiodorus, *Institutiones*, II.5; Leslie Webber Jones, trans., *An Introduction to Divine and Human Readings* (New York: Octagon Books, 1966):145. On medieval learning theory and practice, see Jean Leclercq, *The Love of Learning and the Desire for God: A Study of Monastic Culture*, trans. Catharine Misrahi (New York: Fordham University Press, 1961).

5. J. Guy Bougenol, *The Works of Bonaventure* (Patterson, N.J.: St. Anthony Guild Press, 1964): III:13. The following references from the *De reductione* will be cited by page number from this edition. Another English edition with a helpful commentary is provided by Emma Therese Healy, trans., *De reductione artium ad theologiam* (New York: The Franciscan Institute, 1955). Useful general introductions to Bonaventure include: J. Guy Bougenol, *Introduction to the Works of Bonaventure*, trans. Jose de Vinck (Patterson, N.J.: St. Anthony Guild Press, 1964); Étienne Gilson, *The Philosophy of St. Bonaventure*, trans. Illtyd Trethowan and Frank J. Sheed (Patterson, N.J.: St. Anthony Guild Press, 1965); and John Francis Quinn, *The Historical Constitution of St. Bonaventure's Philosophy* (Toronto: Pontifical Institute of Medieval Studies, 1973).

6. *De reductione*, 13. On the elements and gradations of Bonaventure's hierarchical worldview, see Romano Guardini, *Systembildende Elemente in der Theologie Bonaventuras: Die Lehren vom lumen mentis, von der gradatio entium, und der influentia sensus et motus* (Leiden: E. J. Brill, 1964). On Bonaventure's theory of knowledge, see Winifried Schachten, *Intellectus verbi: Die Erkenntnis am Mitvollzug des Wortes nach Bonaventura* (München: Alber, 1973).

7. *De reductione*, 15.

8. Ibid., 16.

9. Ibid.

10. Ibid.

11. Ibid.

12. Ibid., 19.

13. Ibid.

14. Ibid. On these levels of biblical exegesis, the following overviews are still useful: Beryl Smalley, *The Study of the Bible in the Middle Ages*, 2d ed. (Oxford: Blackwell, 1952); R. M. Grant, *The Letter and the Spirit* (New York: Macmillan, 1957); R. P. C. Hanson, *Allegory and Event* (Richmond, Va.: John Knox Press, 1958); and Henri de Lubac, *Exégèse Médiévale, les quatre sens de l'écriture* (Aubier: Éditions Montaigne, 1959).

15. *De reductione*, 21.

16. Ibid., 26.

17. Ibid., 27.

18. Ibid., 26-27.

19. Ibid., 28. On Bonaventure's spiritual Christology, see Zachary Hayes, *The Hidden Center: Spirituality and Speculative Christology in St. Bonaventure* (New York: Paulist Press, 1981).

20. Jose de Vinck, trans., *The Works of Bonaventure*, I:1-58.

21. Erwin Panofsky, *Meaning in the Visual Arts* (New York: Doubleday, 1955): 128.

22. *De Reductione*, 31.

23. F. W. Dillistone, *Traditional Symbols and the Contemporary World* (London: Epworth Press, 1973): 100.

24. Raymond B. Blakney, trans., *Meister Eckhardt: A Modern Translation* (New York: Harper and Row, 1941): 107-8.

25. Martin Luther, *Works*, Vol. 19, ed. Hilton C. Oswald (St. Louis: Concordia Publishing House, 1974): 8.

26. Philip Melanchthon, *Selected Writings*, ed. Elmer Ellworth Flack and Lowell J. Satre, trans. Charles Leander Hill (Minneapolis: Augsburg Publishing House, 1962): 90.

27. Martin Luther, *The Letters of Martin Luther* (London: Macmillan, 1908): 42.

28. Phillip Schaaf, *History of the Christian Church* (Grand Rapids, Mich.: Eerdmans, 1910): VII:87.

29. Melanchthon, *Selected Writings*, 84.

30. Philip Melanchthon, *Responsio ad Picum Mirandola: Responsio Philippi Melanchthon pro Hermolao*, in Carolus Gottlieb, ed., *Corpus Reformatorum* (Halis Saxonum: C. A. Schwetschke, 1834-60; rprt. New York: Johnson Reprint Corporation, 1963): IX:687-703; also in Quirinus Breen, trans., *Christianity and Humanism* (Grand Rapids, Mich.: Eerdmans, 1968): 58. The following references to Melanchthon's *Responsio ad Picum* will be cited by page number from Breen's edition. Basic introductions to Melanchthon include: Klaus Haendler, *Wort und Glaube bei Melanchthon* (Guttersloh: G. Mohn, 1968); Karl Hartfelder, *Philipp Melanchthon als Praeceptor Germaniae* (Nieuwkoop: B. de Graaf, 1964); and Leo Stern, *Philipp Melanchthon: Humanist, Reformer, Praeceptor Germaniae* (Halle: Melanchthon-Komitees der Deutschen Demokratischen Press, 1960).

31. *Responsio ad Picum*, 59

32. Ibid., 53.

33. Ibid., 54. On the Ciceronian ideal of wisdom and eloquence during the Renaissance, see Jerold E. Siegel, *Rhetoric and Philosophy in Renaissance Humanism* (Princeton: Princeton University Press, 1968).

34. *Responsio ad Picum*, 55.

35. Ibid., 63.

36. Pier Giorgio Ricci, ed., *Prose* (Milan: Riccardo Ricciardi, 1950): I:672.

37. *Responsio ad Picum*, 57.

38. Ibid., 56.

39. Ibid.

40. Ibid. Melanchthon seems to have developed in his *Responsio* a Protestant version of Horace's utilitarian justification for the arts formulated in his

"Epistle to the Pisos," a convenient edition of which is found in James Harvey Smith and Ed Winfield Parks, eds., *The Great Critics*, 3d ed. (New York: W. W. Norton, 1961): 24.

41. *Responsio ad Picum*, 57-58.

42. Ibid., 58.

Conclusion

1. Michel Foucault, *The Order of Things*, trans. Alan Sheridan (New York: Random House, 1973): 43.

2. Walter J. Ong, *Ramus: Method and the Decay of Dialogue* (Cambridge: Harvard University Press, 1958): 281.

3. Foucault, *The Order of Things*, 132; 137; 132.

4. See Michel Foucault, *The Birth of the Clinic: An Archaeology of Medical Perception*, trans. Alan Sheridan (New York: Vantage Books, 1973); and Foucault, *Discipline and Punish: The Birth of the Prison*, trans. Alan Sheridan (New York: Pantheon, 1977).

5. Foucault, *The Order of Things*, 161; 146; 147.

6. Ibid., 218.

7. Ibid., 235.

8. Ibid., 282.

9. Ibid., 219.

10. Michel Foucault, *The Archaeology of Knowledge*, trans. Alan Sheridan (New York: Random House, 1969): 36.

11. Max Horkheimer and Theodor W. Adorno, *Dialectic of Enlightenment*, trans. John Cumming (New York: Herder and Herder, 1969): 17.

12. Diana L. Eck, *Darsan: Seeing the Divine Image in India* (Chambersburg, Penn.: Anima Books, 1981): 15.

13. Walter J. Ong, *Presence of the Word: Some Prolegomena for Cultural and Religious History* (New Haven: Yale University Press, 1967): 115.

14. Ibid., 164.

15. Walter J. Ong, *Orality and Literacy: The Technologizing of the Word* (London: Methuen, 1982): 72.

16. Ong, *Presence of the Word*, 70.

17. C. Mackenzie Brown, "Purana as Scripture: From Sound to Image of the Holy Word in the Hindu Tradition," *History of Religions* 26 (1986): 86.

18. J. Lauterbach, ed., *Mekhilta De-Rabbi Ishmael, Masekhta de-Bahodesh*, 9 (Philadelphia: Jewish Publication Society, 1933): II:266-67.

19. Elliot R. Wolfson, "The Hermeneutics of Visionary Experience: Revelation and Interpretation in the *Zohar*," *Religion* 18 (1988): 340.

20. Bernard Faure, "Space and Place in Chinese Religious Traditions," *History of Religions* 26 (1987): 345.

21. Mircea Eliade, *Patterns in Comparative Religion*, trans. Rosemary Sheed (New York: Sheed and Ward, 1958): 53. For an index of mythological motifs relating to thunder and lightning, see Stith Thompson, *Motif-Index of Folk-literature*, Vol. 1 (Bloomington: Indiana University Press, 1955-58): 198-99. For the importance of thunder and lightning in the religions of the ancient Near

East, see Helmer Ringgren, *Religions of the Ancient Near East* (Philadelphia: Westminister, 1973): 61-62, 132-36, 155-56.

22. Edward Conze, *Buddhist Scriptures* (Harmondsworth: Penguin, 1959): 63-64.

23. *Ṛg Veda*, X.125; Sarvepalli Radhakrishnan and Charles A. Moore, eds., *A Source Book on Indian Philosophy* (Princeton: Princeton University Press, 1957): 16. For other examples of Vedic synesthesia, see Jan Gonda, *Eye and Gaze in the Veda* (Amsterdam: North-Holland Publishing, 1969): 38.

24. *Kena Upaniṣad*, I.2; *Taittirya Upaniṣad*, III.1; *Katha Upaniṣad*, III.10-15; *Bṛhadaranyaka Upaniṣad*, III.viii.8; all cited from Radhakrishnan and Moore, eds., *Source Book in Indian Philosophy*, 42, 62, 47, 85.

25. *Mundaka Upaniṣad*, II.ii.4-9; Radhakrishnan and Moore, eds., *Source Book in Indian Philosophy*, 53.

26. *Chandogya Upaniṣad*, III.xiii.7-8; Mircea Eliade, *The Two and the One*, trans. James M. Cohen (New York: Harper and Row, 1965): 45.

27. W. Y. Evans-Wentz, ed., *The Tibetan Book of the Dead* (London: Oxford University Press, 1957): 104.

28. R. C. Zaehner, *The Teachings of the Magi* (London: Weidenfeld and Nicolson, 1956): 135; R. C. Zaehner, *The Dawn and Twilight of Zoroastrianism* (London: Weidenfeld and Nicolson, 1961): 291.

29. Manmatha Nath Dutt Shastri, trans., *Agni Puranam: A Prose English Translation*, Vol. 1 (Varnasi: Chowkhamba Sanskrit Series, 1967); Chung-Yuan Chang, "An Introduction to Taoist Yoga," *Review of Religion* (1956): 146-47; D. B. Macdonald, "Emotional Religion in Islam as Affected by Music and Singing," *Journal of the Royal Asian Society* (1901): 195-252, 705-48; (1902): 1-28.

30. Stanley J. Tambiah, "A Performative Approach to Ritual," *Proceedings of the British Academy* 65 (1979): 114.

31. Edmund Leach, *Culture and Communication* (London: Cambridge University Press, 1976): 25.

32. Lawrence E. Sullivan, "Sound and Senses: Toward a Hermeneutics of Performance," *History of Religions* 26 (1986): 6.

33. David Chidester, "Stealing the Sacred Symbols: Biblical Interpretation in the Peoples Temple and the Unification Church," *Religion* 18 (1988): 137-62. On the "essential negotiability" of "essentially contested concepts," see W. B. Gallie, *Philosophy and the Historical Understanding* (New York: Schocken Books, 1968): 157-91. For some applications in literary studies and anthropology, see Wayne Booth, *Critical Understanding: The Powers and Limits of Pluralism* (Chicago: University of Chicago Press, 1979): 211-15, 366; and Lawrence Rosen, *Bargaining for Reality: The Construction of Social Relations in a Muslim Community* (Chicago: University of Chicago Press, 1986): 185-86.

34. See Alfred Gell, "How to Read a Map: Remarks on the Practical Logic of Navigation," *Man* 20 (1985): 271-86.

35. Julia Kristeva, "Postmodernism?," in Harry R. Garvin, ed., *Romanticism, Modernism, Postmodernism* (Lewisburg, Penn.: Bucknell University Press, 1980): 141. See Kristeva, *Powers of Horror: An Essay on Abjection*, trans. Leon S. Roudiez (New York: Columbia University Press, 1982).

Index

Synesthesia is viable iff we assume that "senses" are isolable & autonomous. If we assume in contrast that they are related & interdependent, then all percept is synesthetic.